AGONY
IN
EDUCATION

AGONY IN EDUCATION

The Importance of Struggle in the Process of Learning

EDWARD L. KUHLMAN

Bergin & Garvey
Westport, Connecticut • London

Library of Congress Cataloging-in-Publication Data

Kuhlman, Edward.
    Agony in education : the importance of struggle in the process of
learning / Edward L. Kuhlman.
      p. cm
    Includes bibliographical references and index.
    ISBN 0–89789–374–3
    1. Education—Philosophy. 2. Learning. 3. Education, Humanistic.
4. Moral education.   I. Title.
LB14.7.K84   1994
370′.1—dc20   93–362126

British Library Cataloguing in Publication Data is available.

Library of Congress Catalog Card Number: 93–362126
ISBN: 0–89789–374–3

First published in 1994

Bergin & Garvey, 88 Post Road West, Westport, CT 06881
An imprint of Greenwood Publishing Group, Inc.

Printed in the United States of America

∞™

The paper used in this book complies with the
Permanent Paper Standard issued by the National
Information Standards Organization (Z39.48-1984).

10 9 8 7 6 5 4 3 2

Copyright Acknowledgment

The author and publisher gratefully acknowledge permission to reprint the following previously
published material:

Excerpts from *Man's Search for Meaning* by Viktor E. Frankl copyright © 1959, 1962, 1984, 1992
by Viktor E. Frankl. Reprinted by permission of Beacon Press.

For Ginger
A true Agonist

Contents

Acknowledgments

Books do not come full blown like Athena from the head of Zeus; they are birthed. And the gestation period is not uncommonly accompanied by a tension between anticipation and agony—utter agony. Anticipation begins with awareness of possibilities, however uncertain they may be at the beginning when the fragile seed is sown. But the natal day rewards the effort, however agonizing it has been. Books and life are alike in that respect. Authors are agonists of a certain breed (akin to mothers) who, for the joy before them, endure.

My thanks to other agonists who have shared in the struggle. Special thanks to my colleague and friend, Dr. Howard Landis, who listened during our many discussions to these ideas as they were germinating.

I appreciate the summer stipend provided by the Messiah College Faculty Research Program and the semester sabbatical leave provided by Messiah College which gave me the leisure to devote myself to the completion of the book.

AGONY
IN
EDUCATION

Introduction

In *Habits of the Heart*, Bellah et al. called for a "moral ecology" in which communal concerns and commitments must be balanced with the indigenous individualism to which Americans are given. In the sequel of sorts, *The Good Society*, the authors question the acquiescence to technical knowledge, a proclivity toward which this generation seems suicidally prone. Bellah and his contributors rightfully contend that "we have concentrated more on the technical effectiveness of knowledge than on its moral purpose," and we face a "crisis about the purposes and meaning of that knowledge."[1]

Ideological rootlessness and relativism have become the twin turbines generating our contemporary philosophic maelstrom, and our educational institutions have succumbed to the ravages of its seemingly inexorable dynamic. Technique has been the master mover in all of this upheaval. Enchanted with novelty and obsessed with power and control, technocrats today place too little value on the past and are imprudently eager to plow under what they consider to be anachronistic relics, valued, they think, only by reactionaries. Utility and ease are the twin virtues of technopoly, and individual effort with sole recourse to personal resources and ingenuity is viewed as a time- and energy-wasting liability. Consequently, craftsmanship, personal pride in production and performance, and noble effort and ardor have little place in the new technological order. Uniformity, collective effort, predetermined and predesigned educational and social programs, and abdication of judgment to an elite corps of experts (technoligarchy) have come to characterize conditions and dominate decisions today. One does not have to be enlisted among the Luddites to recognize the peril that unlicensed pursuit of a technological order brings with it.[2]

Doomsday scenarios may be a bit overdrawn and melodramatic, but the shocking present reality of the proliferation of unbridled technology in its myriad forms with their concomitant dangers is disturbing many. Technocrats have created a social and economic order that appears to be recklessly incapable of controlling itself or delivering on its promises; it is an order from which there is no longer any retreat. In a world that prides itself on its sophistication and success, the continuing conundrum of economic disparities, social inequalities, savage exploitation of people and planet, coupled with a crippling spiritual and psychological malaise want of a solution. Our critical faculties are committed to everything except reflection on and evaluation of purposes to which we are directed. But the persistent folly of societies that have reached a level of economic and political prominence is the complacency which soon turns to arrogance. The fashionable rhetoric which is difficult to refute is self-congratulatory and hyperbolic. Instead of an ongoing self-interrogation, the society simply "makes statements" about its success and importance—statements which ossify into brittle and bone-dry reassuring slogans and shibboleths.

Stanley Jaki, astutely, states the nature of the self-deception:

Among the various fashionable phrases which nowadays are often taken in some circles as genuine signs of scientific sophistication, references to artificial minds, or thinking machines easily hold a foremost rank. Fashions, as is well known, are obeyed, rather than criticized; followed rather than challenged. Their origins are rarely investigated nor are their claims regularly submitted to thorough scrutiny. When this is done, however, the voice of criticism, highly justified as it may be, dies out quickly in the clamor that goes with the popular triumph of every fashion. With most fashions the best policy is to wait out calmly the demise of their usually ephemeral success. Scientific fashions are a different matter. They can, as the history of science amply illustrates, get hold of the minds of several generations with no small damage to cultural values. . . . In our time the growing obsession . . . is already heavily contributing to a weakening of critical sense, to a lessening of man's appreciation of intangibles, and to growth of skepticism about human values.[3]

The questionable momentum generated by powerful new techniques catches us in its cyclonic cone, like Dorothy in the *Wizard of Oz*, and sets us down on deceptive yellow brick roads—the apotheosis of means at the expense of ends. Our present situation is not unlike Sir Richard Livingstone's description of a prior generation:

A series of splendid expeditions towards the wrong goal or towards no goal at all, led by men who have all the gifts of leadership except a sense of direction and every endowment for achieving their ends except the knowledge of ends worth achieving.[4]

In *Samson Agonistes*, Milton's blind and mocked hero, now the sport of popular culture, is brought for the amusement of the jaded populace to the feast. A pitiful shadow of his once celebrated self, sightless and without strength, he's labored in the pagans' dungeons, but now is brought into the light of day to play the fool for them. But it is he who laughs last and "brings the house down" upon them and himself. A combatant in an arena of clashing ideologies, seeing with the inner vision and reenergized with regained locks of strength, with all the vigor he can muster, he directs his attack on the technocrats of Philistia and destroys himself and them. There is no other solution to the problem, no alternative to his plight. They both must perish.

Milton's tale may provide a metaphor and serve as a caveat for our own self-blinded culture. Gleefully content with our material prosperity and giddy with hedonistic indulgence, we seek to enslave and control, and technology is our obliging agent. But we have become willfully blinded to the tragic consequences that await us while we frolic in fashionable indifference, assuming that it is we who are in control, and little realizing that the technology that we think we command is already grasping the pillars upon which our social system precariously rests. It is not a "house of cards" we have built, for that fall would produce only mild dismay. We have constructed a cultural canopy that overshadows us all and an intricate social system in which we are all inextricably interconnected. If this structure collapses, it will mean not simply dismay but sudden doom. It is one thing to be shocked from our cultural insensitivities by Delilahian scorn: "the Philistines be upon thee"; it is quite another for us, as Philistines, to find the ceiling is caving in upon us. Ancient advice is sage advice: None is so blind as he who will not see.

Decades ago, a year or two after graduation from a liberal arts undergraduate college, I enrolled in a program for public-school teaching certification (which I received along with several other certificates which credentialed me to fulfill a number of role assignments). One teaching methods course I was compelled to take was not all that uninteresting, but the instructor was a highly opinionated and fairly shallow scholar. During a discussion about a controversial book, the instructor asserted that the book was biased. I raised my hand and naively asked: "But aren't all books biased? Isn't that the reason an author undertakes the writing of a book, to express his perspective, his point of view—his bias?"

The instructor looked at me, patronizingly, and replied: "Young man, that's a bad question."

To this day, I'm not sure why he considered the question to be a bad one. I thought it was a good one. In fact, it wasn't a question at all. I was declaring my opinion. Nevertheless, this book before you is clearly biased, and what I suggested to that instructor, I state unambiguously here: That's the reason I wrote it. I have a point of view I wish to express and convictions I want to share with my professional peers and the community of scholarship. To say it is biased confesses that it is polemical and mildly disputatious. It is intended to be a contribution to a growing corpus of concern about the naive indifference to and often flagrant disregard for the uncritical acceptance of technocratic-dictated solutions to contemporary social and educational problems, and particularly, the alluring, presumably painless, solutions that require no individual effort or sacrifice.

Additionally, the book proposes recovery of the concept of agonic life and its role in education, and also offers a modest proposal for implementing a school curriculum based on agonic effort. It is not more ease that we need, but more effort. As Scott Peck reminds us, most of our personal and social maladies result from the attempt to avoid legitimate struggle and suffering.[5] I plead in these pages for their reconsideration and restoration in society and in schools.

Chapter 1

The Tyranny of Technology:
Success and Excess

The post–World War II generation in the United States and Western
Europe has been the first generation in the history of the world that has
been raised in a society of affluence and excess. The unparalleled prosperity of the decades between 1950 and 1990 brought unimagined access, for
many in this generation, to the conveniences that come with economic
prosperity. Correspondingly, the proliferation of technique has produced
a veritable cornucopia of automation, devices and gadgetry with both
positive benefits and negative consequences. Undeniably, the benefits of
technology have fostered the development of laudatory labor-saving and
life-saving devices. The previous unavoidable drudgery of dehumanizing
menial labor has been alleviated by the machinery designed by human
ingenuity. The media, notably, have come to dominate the society, and the
exponential increase in and distribution of these information outlets have
revolutionized the social system in unimagined ways. Marshall McLuhan's
"global village" has eradicated distances, and internationalism dictates
local concerns and interests. The rate of change has been staggering.
Configurations rearrange too rapidly to control, and obsolescence is
calculated in generations that seemingly spring up and mature overnight.
Whether computers, automobiles, societies, or civilizations, the concept
of "generation" no longer refers to the traditional incremental growth
process; with time-lapsed speed, technologies render inventions and innovations passé or obsolete in quick succession, and the rapacious appetite
of modern society for change and novelty (irrespective of merit) translates
into a mandate for more and different, if not better.

I have lived within the generations that have witnessed these transformations, and without maudlin nostalgia for the "good old days," nevertheless, I confess to a gnawing uncertainty about the unqualified acceptance of the new as superior to the old. I have spanned the gap (chasm?) between two distinct generations that are markedly contrasted in terms not only of time but of temperament. The pre-1960 years take on a quaint coloration of Currier-and-Ives vintage when contrasted with the post-1960s era. It seems that something culturally and ideologically fundamental to America, and the Western world (if not the world globally) shifted during the 1960s decade. The naïveté of the 1950s was shaken and perhaps dislodged by the seismic events of the 1960s. I personally feel at times that I would have more in common ideologically with a compatriot of the 1860s than with someone born in the 1960s. Perhaps it is too soon to judge the cultural transformations that have occurred in society since the 1960s, but, intuitively, I sense a profound and, personally, a disturbing reconfiguration of the American psyche and social consciousness. The disparity between the two eras tends toward distortion, and the consensual reality that had been the agreed-upon stuff of discourse has been fragmented so that congenial agreement appears less possible. Change has itself become the only consensus. Shames's description and analysis of the anomaly of the 1980s, which he contends began with the heady, cocksure optimism of the 1950s, parallel my own perceptions, and his conclusion that the 1990s have ushered in an era which will be forever unlike the last four decades appears to be valid. No generation can ever expect to duplicate the economic expansion and affluence of the years between the 1950s and the 1980s. Depletion of resources, economic scale down, and scarcity will characterize the era to come.[1]

My personal jeremiad may not reflect the prevailing mood of the times, and I am not sufficiently a seer to project conclusions or predict outcomes, but I hope, however, that my unease is not simply symptomatic of a personally carved-out worldview which fits into no discernible pattern of what really is. The malaise that is implied in the unabated references to "modern" describes in part my apprehension.[2] The controversy concerning the "modern" versus the "previous" has been a perennial one, of course, but the present inability by this generation of post-1960s people to relate to the previous (primarily because it has vanished) is disconcerting. Contemporaneity has obliterated precedent, or to use the witticism of the cynic with reference to the standard of time: Yesterday was a good year. We have compressed our time frame from millennia and centuries to months or weeks or even days, and the criterion for the test of time (if there is a test) is not longer than yesterday. Each generation has prided itself in living in the modern, most up-to-date period, and our fondness for references to our time frame (i.e., after all these are the 1990s!) has been self-congratulatory, but never too-seriously taken, rhetoric. But today, it appears that it is. This generation actually believes it is living in the "end of time," and that beyond this, there is nothing; and to live in this time, of course, is to assume that this is the best, the paragon period. An infatuation with what is current as well as a maniacal preoccupation with what will quickly and inevitably come to displace the current, becoming itself current, may soon take on the proportions of a passion. The slow ebbing of time has been displaced by the electronic buzzing, the faster-than-speed impulse.

The metaphors we use to describe our perception of time not only reflect the changes but project new ones as well. The imagery is often prophetically self-fulfilling. The "lazy river" image that time often took, the "just keeps rolling along" melodic strain created a vision of a languid, never-ending stream of diffused events which had a certain benign inevitability and provided a continuous security. The image evokes thoughts of time when streams and trickles lazily, inexorably, and perhaps divinely, were sired by eternal rains emerging from subterranean springs, or distilled from celestial clouds. Although at times generating sufficient force to cascade with full fury from precipitous falls, the stream of time was, nevertheless, a metaphor of manageability, anticipation, and unity.

Such an image today is unable to communicate the frenzied, almost frantic pace time has assumed. A less-languid image is needed, and the pulsations of lasers and speed of computers more adequately convey the frenetic pace time now takes. And a critical and perhaps lamentable consequence of all this is that precedence along with tradition and reflection have been jettisoned as needless vestiges of a much too-deliberate age. The concept of "generation" that carried with it what may now be deemed as cumbersome and ponderous has been replaced with a slimmed-down, slicked-up version that compresses a generation into a fraction of its former self.

Not only has technology generated its own mandate for rapid change, it has provided a metaphor for time that abjures anything traditional or historic. The most-conspicuous instrument of this transformation is television. Apart from the content of its programs (which I continue to believe is of dubious worth), television has shaped our perceptions (perhaps our very cognition) about time. After all, for most of history, time was amorphous, taking the shapes that the small social systems decreed. It did not dictate activities nor demand moment-by-moment compliance with its compulsive tempo. In fact, time was more a qualitative experience than a quantitative unit. Memories of times past took on the form of celebrations and religious festivals, or revolved around events that had a vital impact upon social life.

Within language, time seems to have been of less consequence than the experiences that shaped life, and tense in the development of language was of less importance than mood. Mood connotes meaning and feeling, and what was intended by the communicator was of greater concern than the time point at which it occurred. Even today languages among tribal communities in the world, and the Maasai of East Africa, notably, contain no future tense. Each generation is unerringly, and for the Maasai, no doubt enviably, a reproduction of the previous one. Tomorrow is like today and today is as yesterday, and generations are identified by the unending, eternal rituals that witness the successive transmission of the immutable customs to the come-of-age cohorts. But the clock and calendar transformed time, and it is now principally a commodity that has been fragmented and sequenced, and television programming has parceled out time into tight fixed frames that are quickly experienced and then discarded.[3] Program follows program, and within programs, viewing segments, encased within commercials, dictate our time frames. The television generations (my guess is there have been two distinct generations raised which have never known a time when there was no TV) have been habituated to a tempo determined by television programming which has become increasingly fragmented and unrelated. Shows are immediately obsolete upon viewing, and anticipation of the next show is the motivation for viewing. Unlike printed media, especially books, there is little need to recall or review. Indeed, neither is encouraged. Reruns are not scheduled to provide second chances to ponder important programs; they are simply the lucrative, less-expensive alternative to generating new programs.

Television as metaphor impacts viewers in a variety of ways. Perceptual fields are structured that extract specific stimuli from their larger, more-inclusive settings, and viewers are exposed unrelentingly to the intensity of these stimuli without the context in which they naturally occur. The intensity of the stimuli thus presented cannot help but heighten viewers' responses, and, after prolonged satiation, viewers require the increase in stimulus levels as threshold levels are raised higher. In part, this may account for the increased indifference and calloused disregard for the incidences of violence, sexual titillation, and general outrageous conduct both on television and in society. Not only have values been affected by the content of television, the perceptions and psychological processing of events have been modified by the technology itself.

We need not traverse again the psychological and philosophical terrain that critics of television have previously traveled. McLuhan's extensive treatment of media technology has identified fundamental shifts in the social psyche caused by the advent of the "cool medium" of television. However, one feature that needs to be underscored is the distancing effect produced by television. The term itself indicates viewing from afar, and all technologies that extend the neurological capabilities of the senses beyond their physiological limits necessarily distance the individual from objects or other people. Telephones quite obviously provide auditory access to people and events vast distances away, but in doing so, they not only depersonalize the exchange, they change the message itself.

Face-to-face interaction provides a message context with a corresponding response and accountability. It is difficult to avoid accountability for a communication that comes to us, person-to-person, immediately (that is, unmediated), even if we reject the communication itself. But communication that is mediated does not impose the same kind of obligation or responsibility or, of course, response. When we simply listen through an instrument to another's voice, we can say and do things we might not readily do when we are interacting face-to-face. We can obviously just hang up. We can put people on hold, or now we can provide answering services where a surrogate speaks for us. The ultimate distancing is the synthetic, computer-conceived voice that mechanically mouths programmed responses. It is the decontextualized voice alone that decrees our exchange, and it is easier to neglect or suspend values and courtesies. What may happen, and probably does happen, to a generation that has never been "telephoneless" is that the auditory perceptual processes are affected by the technology.

Children in the United States today are raised in homes where the telephone is a permanent feature (compared with emerging countries where telephones are still not available. Kenya, for example, plans in the next decade to have telephones within two hours of travel time for every Kenyan). The American child has been conditioned to distant, and hence impersonal, verbal communication (despite the reach-out image that's part of the standard television commercials). Telephones do not allow for face-to-face verbal exchange, and, thereby, negate the transfer to face-to-face visual contact. Conceivably, contextual clues in face-to-face communication that permit a more-transparent and interpretable exchange may be modified, distorted, or lost when auditory perception is shaped by this medium. A stutterer typically does not stutter when talking on the telephone, which indicates that the medium that depersonalizes the interaction reduces the anxiety prompted by face-to-face exchange, and, therefore, the person responds less authentically. I would identify authentic responses as responses that occur naturally and are unmediated, and reveal something of the self in the exchange. Mediation by technology of any social exchange or interaction must deauthenticate the exchange. That is not to say that there is not proper intention or honest motive, but the very nature of the technique, whether a telephone or a smoke signal, must by virtue of the distancing effect create a situation in which authenticity is reduced. This is not to say there is deliberate deceit or dishonesty in the transaction. Face-to-face interaction cannot preclude that possibility either, but what it does say is, deliberately or unwittingly, the distancing effect transforms the exchange inexorably.

The basic problem associated with all this is that in this generation where technology has established and decreed the modes of discourse and communication, particularly media which distort or redefine time, we have a situation radically new and distinct from prior periods in human existence. Successive generations become increasingly more detached from immediate first-hand contact with sensory reality. As the pretechnology generation disappears, along with the corrective (and perhaps prophetic) role it plays in alerting the new generations to the distortion with which they are dealing, the transformation will have occurred to the point where what is novelty (or an aberration), at least in terms of historical times, will become the established order, the status quo, upon which nothing is built but that which is self-validating and eventually self-extinguishing. Each generation will be an entity unto itself. And time spans will be reduced proportionately as data purport to double every two years (may not a future generation, then, consist only of two years?). Lack of precedent will lead to lack of principle. Recency will rule, and tangible contact with reality will be lost by technology.

This final point is for me the most critical and the premise upon which all I will say subsequently is based. Technology's genielike capacity for producing instant, decontextualized answers or advantages, typically at the push of a button, distances people from the critical need for unmediated contact with tangible reality. In education, increasing introduction of technology into and utilization within the curriculum and the school programs produce a second-hand approach to learning and to life. There are a number of fronts on which an attack on the excessive reliance of technology can be (and has been) made. Neil Postman's polemic against the degeneration of public discourse in a society that chooses to amuse itself (to death) indicts the frighteningly humorous role of television in trivializing, through its technique, the means and substance of the discourse that society needs to deal with fundamental social and moral issues.[4] Jacques Ellul's penetrating analyses of the perils of unbridled technology, and his warnings against the imminent dangers remained largely ignored during the 1950s, and although he continues to serve as the sentinel, untiringly alerting us all to the insidious, corrosive effects of uncritically accepted technology, his jeremiads meet with indifference.[5] Theodore Roszak's articulate tome on the cult of information provides a penetrating probe into the tortuous technology of the computer which, unlike any other gadget in prior generations, has so captivated our time, that its inextricable technological tentacles have locked its prey in its viselike grip.[6] Or to change the image to a more virulent metaphor, the technological tumor like a neuroblastoma has entwined itself about and penetrated within the very viscera of the social body. What began as an unnoticed and natural developmental stage has aberrantly, feeding upon a compliant host, metastasized throughout the system. A cell system gone wild with Frankensteinian fury threatens the very life it purported to serve, an obvious case of means becoming ends. A normal and promising adjunct to a system's survival and increased viability, takes over unregulated and the system capitulates to it, so that the point is reached at which the body will die if it does not comply.

   Peter Beidler, distinguished professor of English at Lehigh University, uneasy about the "astronomical increase in our use of technology" developed a new course, "Self Reliance in a Technological Society," to engage students in thinking about the complexities of the machine era. His proposal for the course captures tantalizingly the critical issue that causes many of us to view technology with a degree of unease:

The gothic novel *Frankenstein* was prophetic of twentieth-century life by showing the dangers involved when man creates a monster-machine he is unwilling to be personally responsible for. Contemporary human existence for most of us in America means moving from one kind of machine to the next. . . . The trouble is, however, that most of us do not understand the machines that we rely on at almost every turn, and as a result, we are at the mercy of these machines. . . . The loss of ability to do for ourselves is generally not examined in contemporary educational circles. . . . The course I propose would aim at examining some of the costs we pay for our highly developed role specialization in a technological world, and at demonstrating what can be gained by a more self-reliant attitude toward doing for ourselves.[7]

In the course, Beidler proposed combining traditional academic study and reading with a practical construction project with first-hand student involvement. He encountered some opposition but eventually persuaded the university to allow the course to go. He chronicles the construction process and its progress as well as the unanimous favorable student reactions to the experiences. Without dissent, they concluded that they learned to make something happen. It is this very notion that needs to be reintroduced into an educational system in which students have everything done for them; in which they are machine-reliant, not self-reliant.

The computer has become the icon of the age. Depending upon one's point of view, it is either the savior of the society through its ingenious capacity to transform a myriad of unmanageable data into meaningful information, and, thereby, provide a potent data base for effective decision making in a communication age; or it is a tyrannical ogre, a Nebuchad-nezzarian totem which we are obligated to venerate, or become fodder for its furnace flames of progress. Like the television, the computer is a technological artifact, now integrated into a social system which it was purportedly designed to help; but with the avarice common to technique, it now consumes what it was intended to feed.

One could point to other artifacts as well which have produced profound changes in societies. The automobile, most notoriously, revolutionized both the transportation and the social system. With the exception of remote colonies of reactionary social units (nativists, reclusive types, Amish, etc.), nothing has escaped the ineluctable grip of the car. A simple but critically important difference, however, between the automobile and the computer or television, apart from considerations of cost, is the "insideness" of the computer or the television. Automobiles are external extensions of people. The require external environments, and require some degree of effort to maneuver and control. They do not, in the same sense as computers do, distance people from their worlds. Admittedly, the aloofness of the driver within the steel cocoon does provide some degree of impersonality and unrelatedness; however, an automobile driver must attend to an external environment, and there is an "outsideness" that does not permit fantasy to intrude for too long without critical disastrous consequences (accidents).

Computers with their "insideness" promote an aloofness, and encourage fantasy flights which may be brief or prolonged without immediate negative consequences. The world of video games is designed for that very purpose. Fantasy is foundational for the success of computerized play. Children and adolescents (and adults who are adolescentized), mesmerized by the hypnotic appeal of such games, mistake the video screen for the real world, and the linkage between brain and terminal eliminates the context of social and physical reality which provides the corrective basis for sanity. Computer hackers, at least in their stereotypic caricatures, are represented as "out of touch" with reality. They are monomaniacally obsessed with their computer fantasy quest to subjugate the computer network. They seem to be on a sort of "star wars" excursion seeking new computer worlds to conquer.

It is this distance from reality that presents the great danger. A number of pedagogic approaches have sought to deal with the danger. Various types of programs, broadly subsumed under the rubric of "experiential education" derive their rationale from the regrettable bifurcation of learning and living that modern society fosters.

The arguments for experiential education are rooted in a concern for the total development of young people—social, psychological and intellectual. This development is seen as jeopardized by a social milieu that increasingly isolates young people from the kinds of experiences, encounters and challenges that form the basis for healthy development and that add purpose and meaning to formal education.[8]

In education, the distance between first-hand reality and student behavior diminishes growth potential and ego strength. The very task of education, which involves the total growth of students, is damaged if not jeopardized when technology is excessively enlisted in the educational tasks. The current mind-as-computer metaphor which pervades modern education, abetted by the information-processing model of the brain as Roszak has identified, much too simplistically insists upon learning experiences that mimic computer functions. Higher cognitive processes, not to mention metaphysical speculation, are reduced to input-throughput-output, and, even more disconcerting, the educational enterprise comes to rest increasingly upon the programming premise that leaves little room for imagery that is not couched in computer terms, virtually eliminating imagination. Utilizing an artificial intelligence paradigm, computerization of education deals a death blow to any form of creativity that does not conform to the computer's definition. Students are asked, yea required, to acquiesce to the computer's imperious dictates which will soon subdue the entire educational enterprise to its image.

Ontological considerations are inescapably involved in identification of the educational enterprise. Students, after all, are at the center of the activities, and it is for them that education exists. Bureaucratization of social functions including education runs the risk of elevating the means, the mechanism of education, over the ends—the goals of student learning. Max Weber was among the first to alert us to this danger.[9] Even the awareness of this potential for means subverting ends within schools, societies, nevertheless, acknowledge that each successive generation needs education to become initiated into social roles in order to function as worthwhile individuals. But the kind of people we see these students to be is, in part, determined by the technologies we accept within the educational process.

Pestalozzi's innovative approach to curriculums, for example, based on sensation and direct involvement with the sensory world was as much a function of his personal ontology as it was of the availability of resources. Competing definitions of human nature have given rise to competing definitions of education. *Homo sapiens* emphasized thinking, reflection, and intellectual processes; *homo faber* elevated the technical capabilities of mankind and coupled hand with brain; *homo ludens* provided a more whimsical, creative approach to learning focusing on playfulness. *Homo calcula* may be the next supplanting model reducing students to keyboard manipulators and video terminal perusers. In an age adrift from the stable moorings that secured the pre-1960s world to the unassailable verities of the past, it is not difficult to entice each generation with alluring claims of progress and prosperity. Prosperity itself has only recently become defined in material terms. For ages, changes in one's economic position was unimagined. Generation followed unchanging generation and for only a privileged few, fortune followed. With the celebrated advent of the industrial age when fortunes were there for the making, enterprising entrepreneurs, inventors, explorers, and risk takers sought to transform their meager holdings into incalculable wealth through cunning, investment, and ingenuity.

Technology's role in fortune making was undeniably critical. Manual labor alone could produce only limited change, but development of new techniques unleashed labor forces and energy supplies previously untapped and unforeseen. Technology's advance has been exponential with each new invention or development opening doors for rapid growth in development and pursuit of new markets for products and services. The interlocking network of social functions in advanced industrial societies disallows remoteness from the complex tapestry which the technology weaves. Education is invariably affected by commercial and economic advances. In the United States, certainly since the 1950s when the federal government began to play a larger and more-decisive role in education, change and innovation in education, as in all sectors of the society, have assumed national proportion. No longer have local or regional school concerns been afforded the luxury of such a limited purview for their publics. Eventually all concerns became national concerns, and with salient events such as Sputnik in 1957, and *The Nation at Risk Report* in 1983, the issues in education were made national in scope and no local issue was spared the disconcerting glare of the federal government's spotlight.

The rapid development of video and computer technology, through the initial impetus of the military-industrial complex, became top priority on the national agenda with the federal government leading the way. As education has moved into the national limelight, and as it has come to be considered the savior of a threatened society (a nation at risk!), the political agenda that invariably impacts education has moved technology training toward the top. The presumed perilous place into which America's economy has precipitously plummeted has prompted a funereal, mixed chorus of politicians, pundits, and vocal educators to chant dirges and sound death knells for America's schools. America's "unrivaled preeminence" in commerce and industry has been jeopardized, and unless radical reform liberates schools from the shackles of complacency, mediocrity, and inefficiency, it will lose its competitive edge and move to the back of the pack. In its desperate search for quick fixes and easy solutions, not to mention proverbial scapegoats, the chorus of reformers sings the praises of the virtues of technology. Computers to the rescue. Hence, the cry of computer literacy leads the charge with the new hardware and software specialists in the vanguard.

The contemporary educational agenda at all levels ranging from national goal setting to local curriculum development has decreed the priority of computer literacy, and as early as kindergarten, computers are introduced into the curriculum. Children are learning to operate computers before they are toilet trained. The Freudian implications are staggering! Distressingly, pupils will, through computer technology (allied to their early postnatal exposure to video technology), have their naïveté about the seemingly benign reality of life reinforced. Another Aladdin's lamp when rubbed the right way will immediately and automatically provide them effortlessly with quick fixes and ready-made answers.

The present generation in American society is unique in that it has never known a time when things were not effortlessly available. Affluence on a scale never before known has fueled the furnaces of capitalist gratification and greed, and showered the society with a plethora of conveniences, amusements, and diversions, all of which deceptively masquerade as necessities. In many cases, they are nothing more than gadgets of questionable use, and, in all likelihood, they will, in the end, be seen to be instruments of hedonistic decadence. With the exception of a few advances in medical technology (which are a mixed blessing by escalating the cost of medical services which makes them unavailable to a large segment of the population), all of the other technologies are of dubious worth. But medical technology too is fraught with fatal implications. Lionel Tiger has documented the distressing gender life-style consequences upon fetuses whose mothers have ingested medications prescribed for their comfort.[10]

Technology now intrudes upon the earliest phases of life, with incalculable ferocity shaping destinies and controlling personalities even before the children have the chance to interact with the natural world of experience. Even more gruesome is the scenario portrayed by Alice Miller who has spent decades of her life investigating the relationship between childhood trauma and subsequent adult development and stability. Her observations of contemporary dysfunctional European youth (which are undoubtedly generalizable to youth in the United States) suggest a clear connection between their maladaptive lifestyles and the frequency of technological intrusion in early life:

But if it is actually true that today's youth are becoming increasingly unstable, then I wonder if it might not have something to do with the advancing technology surrounding childbirth and the manipulation of babies through medication which make it impossible for newborns to experience their feelings and orient themselves in terms of those feelings.[11]

But education inevitably and uncritically buys blindly into the marketplace of technological innovation. There is a sheeplike subservience and a market mentality that brings about an unreflective acquiescence on the part of school people to anything that glitters, and they eagerly purchase the latest technological panacea that is being peddled. Understandably, school people are under pressure from constituencies and politicians to produce results, and the popular interpretation of results not uncommonly involves innovative technology. No one asks questions about the eventual worth. No one pauses to consider consequences of uncritical adoption of new fads. Education seems always to find itself driven by some sort of pedagogical death wish, assuming, like the proverbial cat, it has nine lives, and it readily accepts the naive notion that it's worth sacrificing a few of them on the chance that before they are all exhausted the elixir for eternal life will be discovered.

The high public visibility of education places it in a precarious situation. It does not enjoy the luxury of aloofness from the paranoia of the larger society. Whatever neurosis is current in society will infect the school. Whatever novelty tickles the fancy of a whimsical public must become part of the titillation of the educational program. In the United States, that is how the system works. Even private schools are being drawn aboard by the finely meshed web of government regulations. Local autonomy, the clear differentiating, historic quality of American education, has been eaten away by the voracious appetite of the federal government. Standardization and sameness have come to characterize a country that boasted of regional diversity and local uniqueness. Among its many flaws, one of the most insidious defects of technology is its tyrannical insistence on "sameness." Akin to its own undeviating electronic circuitry, technology clones its users. Television creates environments that bring about conformity and homogenize the culture. Whether that culture is within a nation or within a classroom, the inescapable reality that it presents requires a set system of perceptions and a set system of reactions. Perceptual parameters are determined by the visual stimuli that restrict the range of responses.

Computers, similarly, restrict. Despite the lavish claims made for the liberating potential of the new technology, their impact is quite the opposite. A questionable limitation of these technologies is the physical limitation they impose on students. Television must be watched in a restricted environment. Computers must be manipulated from a keyboard. Since the 1950s when affluence produced a generation of American children whose families could afford these inventions, the society has regretted the restricting impact they have had on the nation's youth. Children spend too much time indoors. A nation of overweight, underactive, and apathetic schoolchildren has required the creation of expensive and frequently resisted fitness programs to combat the ill effects of a sedentary life-style, in part, produced by technology.

It has been within my lifetime that America has been transformed into a technological tribe with its unique electronic culture and communication system. The quaint phrase "out-of-doors" has become passé, now part of American folklore. The place where children played, created new pastimes, interacted with both peers and elders in unhurried ease has virtually disappeared, and where it does remain, it takes on the form of highly structured, highly regulated, competitive interaction. For the most part, children spend their time inside in climate-controlled suburban houses where air and ideas are filtered of impurities. They are plugged into walkmen, or they are watching television, or interacting with their computers. Spontaneous, creative play, which a society that knew more about privation encouraged, has been just about lost. Commercially available, programmed and planned experiences control children's (and adults') lives, and opportunities for developing personal, cognitive, and affective capacities (not to mention physical) are diminished. The bane of technology, its most treacherous feature, involves the distance it puts between people and the real world of everyday experience. Each new device that springs from the mind of Madison Avenue and sees the light of the developer's day has its own nemesis; it may do harm in a number of unimagined and unanticipated ways. But it will, predictably, distance us from the natural environment and reshape our perceptions of the world.

The critical lesson to be learned about life, as psychiatrist Scott Peck has reminded us, is that life is difficult. Recognition of this obstinate fact can save us a lot of headaches and heartaches along the way. The problem is that we do not want to be reminded of that fact. Technology's appeal is that it opiates us and blurs our sense of struggle. Technology's creed is brazenly stated: Life is not difficult. Life can be made easy, and easy is better. Technology seeks to obviate this fundamental fact of human existence. Its seductive siren-song lures us into deep water which promises smooth sailing but provides no escape when we get in over our heads. Technology factors out the stress, the effort, the struggle, and the agony. That, of course, is the great appeal of technology: the so-called, labor-saving device that spares us the drudgery, and we fall for the fish bait—hook, line, and sinker. The fact is that we need effort, struggle, and agony. They are indispensable elements in growth and development. In schools, they should be fundamental ingredients in educational programs. Instead of seeking to eradicate struggle from schools, we need to ensure that legitimate struggle, in which students engage concrete, first-hand reality, constitutes the basis for curriculum development. We do no favor to our children if we provide them with facile, effortless education.

Technology, as I have redundantly insisted, plays this pernicious role. It makes everything too easy. It replaces legitimate agony with effortless interaction. Effortless education robs students of the only opportunities they can ever be given to grow. It is only in effort that students can, as John Dewey reminded us almost a century ago, test themselves against the real world and, thereby, be able to choose what is good and necessary and discard what is useless.[12] Identity and ego strength are neither gained nor developed without unmediated, agonic involvement with the real world of people and things. Nietzsche said it well a century ago: "A long obedience in the same direction; there, thereby results and has always resulted in the long run something which has made life worth living."[13]

The pages that follow constitute a plea for the reintroduction of agony into school programs. This is a cry as well as a call, an appeal as well as a polemic, for reconsideration of the way we carry out education in this technological society. It is not a reactionary manifesto celebrating the virtues of a bucolic age which can never be recalled. No one wants to return to and settle back into the past. Education of former generations produced its share of successes and failures. It was not a perfect program. But one thing education did do without the aid of technology, (and the successes bear witness to it), was to provide opportunities for some students to succeed because the necessity of struggle was an integral element of life. It is not that way now. Struggle is the missing ingredient, and true reform that will produce the type of students this society desires and requires must reaffirm the agonic element in education.

Not only are the philosophical and pedagogical ramifications of rampant technology frightening, the pragmatic considerations and costs are staggering. The increased need for a costly energy infrastructure to support the proliferating technology may bankrupt educational institutions. Present cutbacks and retrenchments could possibly have been avoided had we been not so hasty in adopting expensive hardware which we now are obligated to retain. A recent *New York Times* article contends that "the growing array of electronic accoutrements of today's college students is taxing the abilities of schools to provide adequate power." The president of Haverford College remarked that "the walls in some students' rooms look like the flight deck of the space shuttle." Haverford has had to increase electrical consumption by five percent a year to accommodate the appliances. The same article quotes the vice president of the Association of Physical Plant Administrators of Universities and Colleges who states that residential campus electrical use has steadily increased between three percent to five percent a year to adjust to consumer items, and this when general residential use in highly populated areas in the Northeast rose by an average of one percent.[14]

The increase in energy consumption is attributed principally to the use of computers, photocopiers, televisions, and VCRs in student residences. Haverford's president wistfully recalled his own college days as a student during the 1950s when he had a three-speed Victrola and a manual typewriter, and I could relate my own personal recollections when my peer-group population in the 1950s had none of these things—perhaps a radio but no other electricity-consuming appliances. And I doubt if our education was deficient in any critical areas.

And lest we are led to believe that academia alone is engaged in this energy-consumption and technology-wizardry madness, $20 million was spent in one year to help develop a "cluster of technologies known collectively as intelligent vehicle-highway systems," which presumably will help direct the maddening traffic flows that threaten to paralyze transportation arteries within the United States and other countries of high density automobile use. A recent study indicated that most of the populous areas of the United States have highway networks that are congested and cannot accommodate the traffic that uses them. Instead of finding ways sensibly to reduce the use of automobiles and trucks, and then developing alternative transportation modes, we assume that by applying technology to the problem, the problem will be solved. Do we never learn that with the proposed solution unanticipated problems, perhaps more threatening than the problem itself, will develop?

Futuristic fantasies about the beneficence of machines have beguiled each generation, and I suppose that the invention of the wheel was greeted with fanciful scenarios of a brave new world in which humans would be freed from the tedium of foot travel. The turn-of-the-century celebration of industry, extreme and visionary, was soon transformed into the holocaust horror about which a school principal wrote these words to his teachers:

I am a survivor of a concentration camp. My eyes saw what no man should witness: Gas chambers built by learned engineers. Children poisoned by educated physicians. Infants killed by trained nurses. Women and babies shot by high school and college graduates. So I am suspicious of education.[15]

Even in the hands of educated people, machines can be instruments of destruction. Berman underscores the potential for destruction that a misguided futuristic embracing of technology can bring.

The futurists carried the celebration of modern technology to a grotesque and self-destructive extreme. . . . But their uncritical romance of machines, fused with their utter remoteness from people, would be reincarnated in modes that would be less bizarre and longer-lived. We find this . . . in the refined forms of "machine aesthetic, the technocratic pastorals . . . the spaced-out high-tech rhapsodies."[16]

As a last newsworthy example of this naive acceptance of technology's beneficence, another *New York Times* article identifies a professor who boasts that he has developed a computer program that simulates evolution, and he contends that now his computer colleagues are closer than ever to creating "artificial life." Oxymorons are the stock in trade of technocrats who with facile fatuousness traffic in credulity. Such claims for the soteriological value of technology typically turn up to provide us with false messiahs whose brave new world turns out to be the empty old dream.

Chapter 2

Struggle and Civility

When writers seek a term to communicate the distress they experience in their struggle to spin golden prose from words of straw, invariably they settle on the word "agony." Few terms convey the weight and bathospheric burden that keeps the soul fettered, unfree to transcend the strictures of dulled articulation. The "agonies of writing" (a phrase by the celebrated editor Maxwell Perkins) have been likened by author Nikos Kazantzakis to "morning sickness" as the writer tries to bring to birth the creative work growing within his soul.[1] Whether physical, mental, or spiritual, agonic experiences, unlike any others, test our endurance, providing us with our peak, perfecting experience, or grinding us into dust. At these times, we are ground in the crucible as the pulverization reduces us to the quintessence of our sentient being. Our souls are stripped bare, and the electric current of existential awareness pulsates throbbingly like a naked, exposed wire. Only the word agony captures this sensation, and only the agonic experience does this to us.

Struggle is an inextricable part of life, and living. Only the dull, inchoate, insensitive existence that wraps itself up in the struggleless cocoon is immune from agony. The tests and trials to which we are subjected help to fashion us. We become the creative expressions of these sharpening and shaping experiences. Self-awareness and self-understanding emerge from the persistent, pressuring difficulties we are all called upon to endure. From time immemorial, societies and civilizations have faced hardships unquestioningly. That is, hardships, although inexplicable in their personal manifestations and often enigmatic when individuals seek an interpretation, have been, nevertheless, an integral part of the warp and woof of collective and personal life. "Man is born unto trouble as the sparks fly upward" is the simple and accepting commentary by one who has become the symbol of all noble suffering. Hardship, suffering, adversity, and a host of other equally expressive terms are used interchangeably and often redundantly as our feeble efforts at incisive description of our most keenly felt painful condition seek forms of verbal manifestation. We ransack our language scouring it for the right word, but nothing is quite satisfactory.

Agony, however, like its antonym ecstasy is the favorite choice of many in describing the extremes of feeling. If we took our often frivolous wishes seriously, we would desire to have ourselves freed forever of the anguish that life brings to us. But if we had the magic pill that Arthur Koestler coveted, a universal panacea for pain, we would find that we had diminished ourselves at the pivotal point of our being. Living in a lotusland of airy indifference, knowing neither pain of body nor of mind, we will have impaired the faculties that tell us who we are, and we will have sacrificed our soul upon a hedonistic altar. As Malcolm Muggeridge, the sage of the cynics, reminds us, pain is like the black keys on a piano. Remove them, and there is no music. Like the subtle interplay of flats and sharps is to melody, the magic mixture of pain and pleasure is to personal meaning.[2]

Technology's charm for this generation lies in its very appeal to rid our world of black keys, and personal pain; it is a simpler and less-distressing world in which to live but not a richer world. The value of human experience cannot be appraised (I almost said calculated!) solely in terms of its pleasure, in terms of its ease. As members of a society and, one hopes, a civilization, our goal is not the mere eradication of environmental discomforts. I trust we have not come to the point in our development that our purpose reduces itself to culture ease and mechanical efficiency. With every new technological wonder, we enslave ourselves to means which become relentless, unrepentant taskmasters. Engle's iron law of "quantity into quality" reinterprets the quality of life as a mere standard of living. The goals of Western education (indeed the very origins of education as we have known it) were conceived in the cultural womb of Greek civilization which sought to preserve and enhance a distinct way of life in which the quality of the human life within the social system was paramount. The *paideia* of ancient Greece, in which education and civilization were coextensive, defined humanity in spiritual terms (albeit, not necessarily theological ones) and elevated education to the pinnacle of civic functions. The institution of education was imbued with transcendence and a godlike character. To the ancient Greek mind, of course, unbreakable linkages existed with the Olympian pantheon, but the legacy bequeathed to successive generations within Western civilization, without accepting the mythical, dogmatic assertions, has enriched the ethical virtue-basis upon which education rests.

Culture in its most beneficent and magnanimous arrangement provides not simply the carefully selected and accrued artifacts for a more prosperous life; it constitutes, by its own appeal to the soul, a vision of transcendence upon which civilization must be built and without which the truly human within us is extinguished. Civilization requires more than the mere accoutrements associated with culture. Civilization, as John Nef prophetically noted decades ago, is in danger of demise.[3] In this technique-saturated world of ours, civilization is being eclipsed by sensation, and we must "re-search" for civilization, and restore it to its place of preeminence. The truly civilizing influences upon mankind, without which the race would revert to barbarism, are never to be found in mechanical aids and technological supplements. As MacIntyre says: "What matters at this stage is the construction of local forms of community within which civility and the intellectual and moral life can be sustained through the new dark ages which are already upon us."[4]

The industrial revolution wrenched (the very word is expressive) mankind from the organic matrix for which it was intended. Industrialism, viewed from a historical, sequenced-event perspective, is a Johnny-come-lately, a usurper, an upstart that defies tradition and arrogantly lays claim as the sole basis of power to territory that had taken generations to cultivate. Technique of any kind possesses this alarming, disruptive leverage. It can instantly displace customs, which have been centuries in the making, with seismic impetuosity, and restoration of the customs becomes virtually impossible. Like an erupting volcano spewing lava at whim, technology devours everything in its path, and the cultural landscape that had been formed by the thoughtful, deliberate accretions of custom is buried in an impenetrable layer of industrial ash (cultural trash?). The massive devastation caused by Mount Etna's eruptions over Pompeii (and more recently Mount Pinatuba in the Philippines) is tangible evidence of the impact a natural volcano can have upon a seemingly stable society. Within minutes, Pompeii was buried and life ceased. Similarly, and in some ways more dramatically, the volcanic eruptions in the Mediterranean in the fifteenth century B.C. brought Thera to a halt. Unlike Pompeii where people were caught unsuspectingly, Thera's population was able to evacuate; but excavations, only recently undertaken, have revealed a society that was prosperous and active, but which, in a short span of time, vanished from view. Today, both of these formerly thriving societies are subjects for the archeologist's spade and the tourist's curiosity. For some students of the classical world, they are objects of modest admiration, but practically, they have become quaint relics of a bygone era, which would have remained undiscovered without the efforts of inquisitive students who find the ancient world worth studying.

Technology's potency provides it with this kind of dislocating capacity. It can take the present and render it obsolete overnight. It can bury the hard-won benefits and carefully constructed values instantaneously under its avalanche of materialistic advancement. The twentieth century in general, and specifically since World War II, and certainly since the Sputnik event of 1957, has witnessed what may have begun as a modest movement within this sleeping seismic giant, and which has now erupted with full force into an uncontrollable fury. The speed with which it has dominated the culture has been unprecedented. Henry Adams perceptively wrote near the turn of the century: "The acceleration of the comet is much slower than that of society . . . the speed . . . [has] approached infinity and [has] annihilated space and time."[5] Technology has the uncanny capacity to annihilate. The legacy of generation upon generation is eradicated in the paper-thin time frame in which technology functions.

The word, generation, which conveyed pregnant periods when custom and culture were born, nurtured, and tempered over extensive time, lifetime upon lifetime, has been stripped of this fertility. The leisure that true culture and education require, when gestation and growth encourage the full formation of a mature civilization, is viewed as a nonfunctional vestige blown away by the frenetic assault of technology's tyranny. The maddening pace and frenzied speed by which technology functions distorts distance and compresses chronology. Speed and efficiency have been apotheosized. Whether television or computer, technology will not sit still for time. Time is an enemy that must be vanquished. And we must, through mediation, be continually removed, further and further, from contact with the creation. The only creations we own are the technological offspring sired by artificial insemination in simulated wombs.

Members of the generation that still spans the time gulf between the taken-for-granted technological world of today and the, comparatively, technologically naive world of four decades ago longingly recall a more-gentle time when life's hardships were filtered through a social membrane of neighborhood support and cooperation. Life has never been easy for most people in any period of time, and prior generations did not live in some primeval paradise of unabated bliss. The irony of the situation is that the present affluent society has prided itself on the great strides it has taken to reduce and eliminate hardship, difficulties, and even discomforts, but the consensus of social commentators characterizes the present time as one of the most confused, alienated, and addictive periods ever.[6]

Education, similarly, is under constant scrutiny and indictment for its ineffectiveness. We are plagued with seemingly unsolvable ecological, political, social, and personal problems. Innumerable critics carry on daily declamations criticizing present policies and practices, and prescribing their own panaceas, but nothing seems to work. For all the increase in specialization in the professions and academic areas with their techniques and tricks, the social situation continues to deteriorate.[7] It should be obvious to all of us that things are not getting better, and technology's promise of a better world has been little realized. If we would envision a scenario of the last four decades in which none of the major technological developments would have occurred, what sort of a world would be our present habitat? Speculations of these kinds may be considered, for some, the foolish prating of a child-mind seeking solace in the reconstructed innocence of the past, and for others they may appear idle exercises in nostalgia. But we do this kind of thing all the time with respect to future possibilities. We are encouraged to map out future worlds and propose futuristic scenarios. Some of the most influential social planners take their keys for projections from futurologists, that new breed of stargazers who fabricate from their cerebral crystal balls fanciful technological new worlds where problems are banished and privations are unknown.

We are beginning to reap a bitter harvest of social reality from the visionary seeds sown by these self-styled seers who, with arrogant disregard for contingencies, presume to control all the variables in a futuristic world. Ehrenfield has identified a number of these futuristic follies and laments the naive acceptance of programs of this cadre of technologists. Of course, the futuristic scenarios are all predicated upon human power, the presumed capability of collective mankind (led, of course, by a technocratic elite) to forge its way progressively into the limitless future. But human power has become the nemesis of the human race; its built-in, self-destructive force, which despite our bravado and incessant whistling-in-the-dark facade, threatens our annihilation:

modern society [has] opted, albeit unconsciously, for the assumptions of human power. The choice was understandable—the assumptions have long seemed, superficially to work and they certainly have been (and still are) gratifying to the ego. Now that the assumptions have manifestly gone sour ... [s]ome see technology's dehumanization of people and its destruction of the natural world as a departure from humanism, scarcely realizing that humanism itself has generated these tendencies. It is humanism that has spawned the apotheosis and worship of the machine and the human-as-imitator-of-machine culture which so many humanists despise.[8]

Ehrenfield equates humanism with the deified conception of mankind's ability to control everything. This type of *hubris*, which ancient Greek society dreaded, has contributed to the decline and dissolution of society after society. Is it not time for a new breed of "pastologists" (an awkward term I realize) to emerge to challenge the futurologists' much-too-rosy projections of technological brave new worlds? We need a renewed dialogue with the past.

I repeat the nonrhetorical question: What would the world today be like without the celebrated, technological triumphs of the past two generations? Admittedly, the mobility and maneuverability that new techniques have brought (I dare not say the freedom they have brought) would vanish. Time and space limitations would continue to regulate our lives at a more leisurely pace. Distances would be determined by personal, natural mobility (human and animal power), and life spans would be a function of the natural order. Technological advances in medicine, which would not be available, have had as many ill effects (no pun intended) as they have had positive ones, and, certainly a veritable Pandora's box of ethical issues (abortion, euthanasia, surrogate parenthood, etc.) has been opened. We could, of course, identify a lengthy list of changes that would not have occurred without technology, and even divide into two columns, good and bad respectively, the judged values of these changes.

Change, at best, during these two generations would have been incrementally deliberate, and circumscribed by natural parameters. We could expect then to see a world, apart from natural catastrophes which we are not always able to predict, that is manifestly similar to that world of four decades ago. An undeniable feature of such a world and society would be that people would have more direct contact with the natural reality, physical and social. The absence of these technologies would reduce or eliminate the mediation between people and their world, and the element of struggle, inherent in survival contact, would provide a now-absent opportunity for greater self-conscious awareness and personal connectedness with the natural sphere.

We need to return now to the notion of struggle and pursue it with greater and keener consideration. Any term which is part of the popular vocabulary necessarily suffers from confused definitions and acquires, over time with usage, associations which may not be intended by the user of the term. The etymology of the world "struggle" is uncertain, but there is a certain onomatopoeia about it. It almost needs no definition, for the tuned ear senses at its saying, with its double gutturals, an imputed effort of body and soul. It is the word we seize upon to describe the effort intensified. In English translations of his works, it is the favorite of Nikos Kazantzakis who described struggle as the goal of his life. We impute nobility to strugglers. Struggle is the stuff of heroism. Tales of endurance in which protagonists struggle against the odds in quests of various kinds create consonance within us. Empathy surfaces, and we feel a soul-kinship with the struggler, and especially when the confrontation is face to face. As man versus nature, or man versus man, we enter more deeply into the pain and pathos that's described. Man against machine normally leaves us unmoved or despairing. The appeal of the stories of tellers such as Jack London, and for the young, Walter Farley's *Black Stallion* series, lies in the gripping struggle of man and animal.

Struggle has always been the means by which the development of mankind has been accomplished and by which meaning has been found. The major trouble with technology is that it robs people of this basic good. In addition to the basic goods of the body (food, clothing, shelter), there is the basic good of struggle. Through struggle, life forms, at all levels on the phylogenetic scale, work out their development. Perhaps a case could be made that the higher up the life is on the scale, the more critical, comparatively, the element of struggle becomes for serious development. Nothing can reach its intended *telos* without struggle. Rob an organism of opportunity for legitimate struggle, and its viability is reduced. Examples from nature abound. Literary births similarly, according to their authors, come only after the anguish, the struggle. If one thing is incontrovertibly true, it is that growth and gain require struggle.

Chapter 3

The Agon Motif

As we now focus more specifically upon education and schools, the concept of struggle, which is the premise of this polemic and the basis for subsequent proposals, needs to be addressed with greater rigor. My contention is that without legitimate struggle within the educational enterprise, students will neither adequately nor fully develop into competent and effective people. The agonic element must permeate the educational venture or the students will not properly mature, and, as I hope to show in more detailed fashion, technology detracts from maturity by reducing struggle. Undifferentiated struggle without deliberate and contained focus does not necessarily facilitate growth and develop strength. Struggle may simply dissipate energy and deplete resources. Struggle must itself contribute to the renewal of resources; it must charge the battery as it draws on the energy source. Certain types of struggle, typically called stress (more accurately distress according to Hans Selye)[1] drain energy reserves providing no productive activity. Distress depletes stored energy resources while adding nothing to the supply. Eventually the supply may become totally depleted, and exhaustion occurs. Without reserves on which to draw, the organism will revert to inactivity and even death. So distress is a type of struggle but it is struggle that has severe negative consequences. Unabated distress debilitates. However, struggle can be a source of a continuing energy supply. Stress can be a conserver and replenisher. Selye calls this type of stress "eustress." It is energy-using but also energy-creating, and, like the alternator in an automobile, it can recharge the battery which would otherwise deplete its resources fairly quickly. Such

struggle (which requires stress but is not the same as distress) I call
agon-activity.

Agon is a venerated term whose etymology is rooted in ancient Greek
culture. Unfortunately, in my estimation, the term today is being used apart
from its etymological and historical linkage to the ancient agonistic Greek
society. An increasing number of journal articles, particularly in child
development, equate agonic behavior with negative, harmful aggressive
attacks. The studies and commentaries are almost unanimous in assuming
this association with the term.[2] Admittedly, the agonic element implies
both competition and combat. Inescapably, the term includes both of these
key components, but it is unjust, *a priori*, to assume these are deleterious
and harmful.

The word agon is intended to evoke an image suggestive of discipline,
endurance, tenacity, and struggle. Stephen Byrum, unwisely and unfairly,
I contend, places *agon* in contradistinction to *paideia*, both words from
ancient Greek civilization. In his analysis of administrative styles of
leadership, he contrasted the paideia style with the agon style, and adopts
both terms as metaphors for management styles. A paideia-oriented administrator, he contends, is a people-oriented, cooperatively engaged
leader who deals tactfully and humanely with subordinates in facilitating
movement toward organizational goals. The agon leader, on the other
hand, is a combative, win-at-all-cost administrator who cares little for the
morality of his methods. Byrum provides a superficial description of the
terms relying solely on Johan Huizinga's study of play. In fact, Byrum
erroneously equates paideia exclusively with play. Paideia only inferen-
tially means play, being derived from the Greek word for child which, by
extension, has come to refer to the spontaneous activity of childhood.
Jaeger's masterful analysis of paideia in the Greek culture, about which
we will say more, certainly bears little resemblance to the anemic definition Byrum gives it.[3] By contrast, Byrum defines agon as a nonplayful
metaphor of leadership style characterized by aggression and arrogance.
Similarly, Roger Caillois, the French anthropologist, appears to limit his
definition of agon to games that are devoted exclusively to competition.[4]
Agon, however, carries with it equally the notion of play, and Byrum,
I believe, distorts the meaning of the term. Huizinga's use of the word does
not dichotomize the terms the way Byrum's does, and the literature on
agonism does not stigmatize the term with blatant overtones of mere
self-serving assertiveness.[5] Agon involves struggle; it does not imply raw
aggression.

Assertiveness pertains to any management style by definition, and both
paideia and agon include assertion. Byrum unwisely adopts agon as a

strictly athletic metaphor, which it is not, and interprets athletics in the contemporary context of professional sports, particularly football, and legendary coach Vince Lombardi's version of football at that, which emphasizes "winning as the only thing." Historically, agon was not used so restrictively, and it is unfair to limit its meaning to that today. If Byrum for his purpose of differentiating leadership styles chooses paideia and agon respectively to dichotomize two discrete styles, he certainly is free to do so, but he errs if he concludes this is the only way the words can be used, or were intended to be used. The English word "agony" manifestly is derived from the agon. Agons were endurance contests staged in ancient Greece in which combatants demonstrated their skill through arduous competitive games. The most famous of these game were the quadrennial Olympics, but there were other contests throughout the ancient world,[6] and they included events other than those which were narrowly athletic. Musical and dramatic events were staged that were also referred to as agons.

Agonism is as much an attitude of mind and a social category of values as it is physical style. Burckhardt is credited with introducing the term to describe the Greek culture, and it was agonal in a competitive sense.[7] Raubitschek captures the term's intention more fully:

The agonistic attitude was from the very beginning not confined to athletic exercises but it constituted a code of conduct, the striving for excellence (areté) and for its recognition in the form of honor (timé). . . . Here lies the root of the Greek spirit of competition which permeates Greek culture and which is present in the world today. . . . Equality was conceived by them as by us as equality of opportunity which enabled every member of the society to enter into competition for success and happiness.[8]

In his scholarly study of the use of word "agon" in epic and classical literature, Ellsworth concluded that the term, although referring originally to an assemblage of people, always involved contests and competition and thus the term from its inception always involved activity.[9] These assemblages were at first principally religious festivals demonstrating devotion to deities, and eventually this was transferred to heroic figures within the culture, and funereal games and contests were tributes to deceased dignitaries. Over time, the term was generalized to a host of contests, not all necessarily physical or athletic, and agonic activity was identified as activity involving competition and effort in war, the courts, drama, artistic endeavors, and debates. Agon involved the place and the purpose of the contests, the goals, and, quite naturally, agon became synonymous with the struggle itself.[10]

All of life is a struggle. Technology attempts to deceive us by telling us it is not. This generation has forgotten the basic truth and wisdom of this reality. Psychiatrist Scott Peck, quoting the prophet, demands that we acknowledge the fundamental truth that life is difficult, a hard struggle. Once we admit and acknowledge this reality, we can then move triumphantly toward noble goals. De Unamuno expresses the tragic soul of Spain in agonic terms, and beyond the national spirit, he moves toward a clearer understanding of the universality of man's struggle in his quest to know.[11] Agony with a sharp needle weaves its way through the fabric of our lives. To paraphrase the sage, the agonic life is the life alone worth living. Identity and meaning can only come in this context, within the cauldron of agonistic dilemmas and enigmas.

It is unfair to define agonism solely in terms of its aggressive element as though it were bestial and barbaric. Greece we must remember brought us civilization. To engage in the agons, a contestant had to have undergone discipline and privation, and this required the cultivation of a civilized sense of valor. Agon could not be divorced from valor (*areté*). Without areté, agon may degenerate into shameless self-aggrandizement based on the win-at-all-cost attitude, but agonal activity imbued with spiritual sentiment provides the dynamic for success. The concept of areté requires further elaboration for it lies at the root of classical Greek culture. Jaeger identifies areté as the "central ideal of all Greek culture."[12] Although it does not translate well into English, it combines the concepts of excellence, virtue, and honor, although each of these may have its corresponding Greek equivalent. Excellence may be the best synonym for areté, but it is not excellence at any price; it is not the ruthless oppression nor the disregard for civil rules. Achievement and accomplishment without areté would not be success. Blatant disregard for the civil code and chivalrous code, which found their way into the courtly medieval valor of the knight, would discredit anyone from claiming success. Agonal striving must always be regulated by the balance wheel of areté. Civilization must be benignly governed by the rule of areté. Mere competence or worse, mediocrity, as the regulating principle will inevitably lead to society's dissolution. Areté is the preventive for entropic dissolution. And, as Castle, along with Livingstone, inform us, areté is not limited to Greek culture, nor was it in fact the creation of that culture; it is the instinct of the human race.[13] But instincts always run the risk of being modified or weakened, and technology whose very function is to render human propensities unnecessary or obsolete, by transforming or replacing them, can repress instinctual apparatus of such a sensitive nature.

Within education, areté must ever be the critical controlling factor.

Diminish it even modestly and education suffers. The debasement of education in American society today, as the proliferation of polemics tells us, is due in no small measure to the neglect of areté. A perverse form of equality has pushed areté to the periphery of educational concerns. Despite the incessant rhetorical references demanding excellence in education and American life generally (*The Nation at Risk Report* was presumably a cry for the return to excellence in American commerce), education is awash with every virulent strain of this subversive pseudoequality. One rule for the tiger and the lamb, as Richard Weaver informs us, is not equality; it is tyranny.[14] Areté allows individuals to strive for maximum attainment, but it also recognizes that differences in ability and aptitude will result in different levels of success. This is not elitism; this is simply the only way that excellence can flourish. Lowering the ceiling is not the same as raising the floor. Compensations for inequality of opportunity will never guarantee equality in outcome. Superiority inevitably surfaces at higher levels unless unnatural limitations are imposed from above.

Chapter 4

Agonism in Education

We need to discuss agonism specifically in the context of education. As I have attempted to show, the term, unfortunately, is being used with scant reference to its original meaning, and its present usage has been divorced from the cultural context which Burckhardt has brilliantly elucidated. The ancient Greek soul could only flourish agonally. To strive to be successful, to strive to be the best, to struggle for success and above all—excellence— filled the Greek spirit with the intoxicating nectar of the gods. The accomplishments of ancient Greece bequeathed to Western civilization can neither be understood nor appreciated apart from the enriched realization of the agonal dynamic that propelled them. Agonism permeated Greek life. It was not limited to physical activity or athletic encounters. Drama, the arts, public discourse, civic accomplishment, and certainly military conflict were linked by the unbreakable agonal chain.[1] The Greeks were vigilant against sliding back into barbarism. The Greeks, of course, considered all non-Greek speakers barbarians (*barbaros* was the uttering of non-Greeks), and they were, thereby, excluded from participating in the Olympic games which were, after all, the definitive agonal activity.

The cultural hard-won gains of Greek civilization which, according to Jaeger, constituted their paideia,[2] were as lasting as each generation made them. The cultural wheel would need to be reinvented with each subsequent generation if the gains were not preserved and augmented. The agon was a cultural tour de force which initially involved personal gain and accomplishment but eventually was generalized to cultural accomplishment and continuity. Civilization must be forged on the anvil of struggle, but struggle of heroic proportion. Heroism allied with honor, agonically displayed, determines success. In the video society of today, where everyone, as pop-culture commentator Andy Warhol has said, will be a celebrity for fifteen minutes, popularity is mistaken for heroism, and the word hero with its etymological godlike qualities (again from the Greek language) is bastardized by synthetic anomalies which technique permits and creates. Video technology "cools out the mark" (to use Erving Goffman's trenchant expression), and the most grotesque forms of failure are redefined as success. Agonic cultures will not permit travesties to masquerade perversely as paragons.

The lack of an agonic emphasis in modern society and in its educational programs contributes to both passivity and complacency, conditions that are conducive to the harmful growth of antiheroes. A nonagonal milieu, which intrusive technology fosters, unbalances the delicate natural relationship among the constituent elements of a culture. Struggle, certainly at basic survival levels, serves in part to provide equilibrium within the system and provides a natural prophylactic against the intrusion of debilitating foreign bodies. Once struggle is eliminated, the social body becomes a receptive host for disease. Technology has the unruly capacity to bully its way into any system, but an agonic system is better prepared to detect the intruder and provide a defense against it. In technological societies, honor becomes a liability. Ethical issues that honor insists upon raising and addressing are annoyances to technology.[3] Technology prefers and professes to possess ethical neutrality, but the claims it makes are bogus, for its peculiar ethic is power, and all other considerations are obstacles to its advancement. There is little wonder that Parker Palmer insists upon recognizing epistemological and ethical concerns together and at the outset of new educational quests.[4] Knowledge is never neutral. Technologies are forms of knowledge, and they intrude, irrevocably shaping outcomes at the very inception.[5] When nonagonal systems provide no defense against this intrusion by virtue of their acquiescent posture, they defer to an ethic that technology determines. Trying to sandbag the river banks of technology with ethical restraints once the river has flooded the territory is futile.

Achievement, and especially achievement determined by a predetermined criterion of excellence (areté) has historically been the quest of education. Injunctions to become the best one could become provided motivation for people in every stratum of society and for youths of all cultures. Circumstances and situations have never been uniformly conducive to achievement, admittedly, but irrespective of the starting point, excellence, if only relatively reached, was the goal. Dissonance, according to Leon Festinger, is the starting point for new learning.[6] When there is cognitive equilibrium, incentives for new learning are absent. Piaget's concept of equilibration comparably suggests the need for tension if new schemata are to develop, and the dynamic between assimilation and accommodation implies such a tension.[7] The proximal zone of development posited by Vygotsky supports an agonic learning prerequisite in cognition.[8] Greek culture encouraged what Marrou terms the "noble discord," a dialectic tension which was a manifestation of the agon.[9] Learning environments devoid of agonic tension, where legitimate struggle is factored out and obstacles that require effort for removal are absent, retard development of skills, perceptions, and attitudes that build strength. Modern education with its emphasis upon technical proficiency views the time-consuming agonic interactions as cumbersome and wasteful. The cult of efficiency, which Callahan identified several decades ago,[10] like the proverbial mustard seed, has rooted, sprouted, and branched out within the groves of academia and now dwarfs all other species of life. Efficiency's high priesthood of technicians with their esoteric coding have little time or patience for the slow growth of normal life. They want a clean, uncluttered, and that means unnatural, environment for their artificial intelligence to function.

The ancient Greeks in both their physical and intellectual pursuits viewed struggle as an integral element realizing that time needed to be "taken up" in the process. Technology seeks to bypass or negate time. Without some chronometric form, time takes amorphous forms dictated only by the presence or absence of sunlight. The timepiece, for all its aid to developing incrementally defined and determined sequences, dictates and controls time. When societies rely solely upon solar and lunar indicators, the flow of life is not maniacally regulated by time. Time is at the disposal of people who decide priorities and programs. Schedules serve only to facilitate the fulfillment of agreed-upon tasks. Effort is not only energy-consuming, it is time-consuming, and in a culture that considers time's value in its conservation not in its expenditure, technology's contribution consists of reducing task time. A secondary problem, which is not germane to our discussion but deserves brief mention, involves allocation of all the newly acquired time. But technology never likes a time vacuum so it will generate new, and frequently unnecessary, things to do, a variation of Parkinson's law. The host of gadgets that appear routinely are eagerly accepted and soon become coveted because they convert the "time" when there is nothing to do into hours of endless viewing of television, listening to walkmen, driving automobiles, and so forth. Boredom and its companion impatience are products of excessive time when the natural, time-consuming activities have been eliminated.

I received a revelation during my school-teaching days in the 1960s when the word "bored" was ever on students' lips. I don't recall my own pretechnology generation using that word very often. Boredom is a function of excess leisure.[11] Too much time, especially time made available by technologies that eliminate time-consuming effort, creates unhealthy moods which cannot tolerate unscheduled time. When a culture alters the natural tempo and rhythm which nature prescribes, pathological dislocations occur. Alterations in biorhythmic patterns which cause metabolic distress, sleep deprivation, and other organic disorders have been documented. Psychological maladjustment results from disharmony with the natural order created by seasonal variations and survival tasks. Intrusions caused by technology disturb the cultural flow that provides a sense of life's rhythm, and both the pace and the patterns of the social order are upset.[12] Anyone from the hectic, time-driven West who has visited the pastoral peoples of East Africa, notably the Maasai, cannot help but envy their unhurried, uncluttered pace and the organicity of their relationships. The meager technology that's permitted within their culture (a few handmade implements) does not detract from the synchronization of limited life-patterns. Cattle, housing, family, and tribe constitute the totality of their lives, and contentment is manifestly present.

Our mechanized world is asynchronic. The digital watch has become the metaphor for a pace of life that is lived calculatingly, beat by beat. In prior eras of analog watches, the leisurely pace of the minute hand was the regulator while the drowsy rhythm of a fluid sweep hand allowed the cycles of life to embrace us. Today's pulsations of digital watches that pump numbers into view and as quickly devour them tell us time is racing onward, and each number we ignore could have carried some discrete bit of datum. Rousseau may have been closer to the truth than he knew when he invited us to waste time, not preserve it. Technology makes us paranoid about time. We arrive at the end of the day guilt ridden if we haven't "managed" our time well. That's another term with which technique has burdened us.[13]

The control obsession of technology is accompanied by management compulsion. Leisure is the lost commodity. The mystics of the Middle Ages whose sights were on eternity, not time, even took the time to contemplate the number of angels on the head of a pin, but such metaphysical questions in a far too pragmatic world are impractical. Medieval scholars (and academic scholarship has critical links to that period being spawned in part by it) realized that profitable thinking required quality time and hence, "school" is derived from the rediscovered Greek word for leisure. Technology will not allow time to stand still. Schools, which should be casual, relaxed places, move at a frenetic pace where tyrannical schedules are controlled by the dastardly clock.

While teaching in a large high school years ago, I suggested a modest modification of the class schedule. Students were shuffled from class to class, from assignment to assignment with little time for the rhythm of life. I suggested we suspend classes for twenty minutes each morning and afternoon, and provide a schoolwide "coffee break" during which students, faculty, and staff could mingle, converse, relax, and engage each other in nontask activities. It would have untold benefits, I advised. It would certainly break the maddening pace; it would defuse antagonisms that may have mounted; it would provide a hiatus when there were no expectations; nothing had to be managed or controlled. Within the understandable, institutional constraints of the school imposed by law, this time-out would allow for social interaction or personal introspection. The plan was vetoed. It was neither efficient nor productive, the administration contended, and it would be a "waste of time." Of course, they were right. It would be a waste of time; exactly what I intended.

A fundamental irony has arisen in this society in which naturally recurring activities indigenous to pretechnological societies have had to be recovered and programmed within our own. Health clubs, spas, and other formal commercial establishments catering to the neglected physical needs of a fashionable but overworked "leisure class" are phenomena unique to this generation. Gymnasiums have always been available and popular, but gymnasiums have been geared to games and athletic competitions. The new faddish health spas serve an exclusive and wealthy clientele whose life-styles are increasingly sedentary and indulgent. Exercise and cardiovascular activity, which are normally undergone in the course of typical agonal survival, have been cavalierly brushed aside as machines now replace the natural modes of transportation and labor. Consequently, a generation of overweight, malnourished, and unconditioned, indulgent technocrats suffers from a host of diseases caused by a nonagonal culture.

Children are transported from home to school by bus, chauffeured to a host of activities, and spend endless hours sedentarily viewing TV or playing video games. The President's Council on Physical Fitness, alarmed at the tragic state of America's youth, now enlists the aid of sports celebrities to promote exercise and fitness. Even school curriculums have created a new breed of educator and a new brand of college program: recreational studies. Agonal societies quite naturally encourage, indeed force, their citizens for sheer survival purposes to be physically active. School programs generally and increasingly have erased the agonal element from education. The principal culprit in this conspiracy has been technology. Unwise acceptance of new technology has made it unnecessary for school students to expend appropriate physical and mental energy. Many school tasks now require less time, and the combined result has dramatically reduced student effectiveness.

It would be irresponsible to jump to hasty conclusions and contend that an agonal society never becomes an addictive society, but what is the appeal of drugs and other addictive disorders? There will always be a fringe element in any society that will experiment with novelties to find new thrills and adventures. There will also be an element that continually seeks inner escape from what they see as constricting circumstances and lives that offer little prospect of anything more positive; for them, addictions are appealing. But people engaged in the ongoing, agonic competition within life to bring meaning to life have little need for the artificial stimulation that addictions provide. Today's society, which is a creation of technology, has introduced unnatural sources of stress, and chemicals become, for some, the quick solution for coping with these stresses. Addictive options need not invariably be chosen, for hosts of people engaged in similar social arrangements rendered unnatural by technology have found "positive addictions"[14] as constructive alternatives.

Gardiner in his analysis of ancient Roman society contends that the agonic demands of daily toil engaged the farmers' energies completely. The stock of hardy farmers had little need for organized diversions. Neither were they inclined to the dissolution nor the dissipating excessive pastimes: "all their energies were occupied in a grim struggle with the forces of nature and in wars with their neighbors. Fighting, hunting, the work of the farm provided them with bodily exercises: they had no need of organized training like dwellers in cities."[15]

Urban life has its unique pathologies. Rural living undoubtedly may shorten life when the personal resources are inadequate to cope with the incessant survival demands. But in cities where people are eaten away by the "acids of modernity," the decreased demand for struggle also renders the organism more vulnerable to the virulent strains of urban pathology. Without glamorizing the agrarianism of a former age or ignoring much of the mythology that has grown up around it, there is, nevertheless, truth in the stereotype of rural, rustic self-reliance contrasted with the enervated, urban life-style. It was in Roman cities that enervated, indulged citizens concocted decadent pursuits and pastimes to fill the vacuum hours rendered meaningless by urbanization.

The crucial distinction between games for mere amusement and contests inspired by nobility and heroism is involved in the meanings of two words used by both Gardiner and Huizinga. Gardiner differentiates between *ludi* and *agon*, and in doing so demonstrates the differences between the ennobling activity of meaningful struggle and the debilitating indulgence of commercialized play:

The difference is implied in the very word "ludi." The Greek meetings are never described as games but as contests (agones) . . . and they exist primarily for competitors. The Roman games are ludi, amusements, entertainments and the performers are slaves or hirelings; they exist for the spectators.[16]

Although Huizinga takes issue with scholars who more rigidly categorize agon as something other than playful amusement, he, nevertheless, accepts that ludi and agon are not identical; although agon would, for him, be a variation on the ludi theme. Greek culture, according to Huizinga, was inventively playful, and games and recreation of various kinds permeated Greek life. The "competitive impulse" within Greek life, which is often interpreted as a serious, competitive struggle for victory, Huizinga includes within the "general, all-embracing, and logically homogeneous play-concept."[17] Even though the agonic contests, which formed the core of Hellenic social life, "were fought out in deadly earnest. . . . The essential oneness of play and contest, however, still peep[ed] through."[18] Play, as Huizinga employs the term, is never synonymous with any single, isolated feature of play but is a comprehensive notion that refers to a generic, human propensity (hence the appellation *homo ludens*).

Play manifests itself in the instinctive, random, self-satisfying behavior of children even when the contests, socially structured and socially valued, are athletic contests requiring specialization and excellence. The Greek concept of paideia, for Huizinga, deriving as it does from the word for child, denotes the playful expression of any culture, and carries with it a more whimsical, and less-combative connotation.[19] However, it would be unfair to interpret agon as a ruthless, assertive, nonplayful impulse. In this regard, Byrum is incorrect in his reified use of paideia and agon. The terms do not stand in stark contrast; they are complementary. To place the terms in the kind of opposition he does in his description of leadership style, I believe, is an unwarranted liberty, and the etymological basis he employs for this distinction cannot be justified. Paideia came to be a larger, more-inclusive concept that included agon, especially as civilization and urbanization eliminated or reduced the uncivil, barbaric aggressiveness, and necessitated a socially structured outlet for aggressive play.

At the time of the decadence and decline of the Roman Empire, even play had reverted back to an institutionalized barbarianism in the gladiatorial contests which, Gardiner maintains, were brutalized events catering to the cravings of a debauched society which found the Greek events unappealing.[20] Once agonism becomes detached from areté, the noble urge of competitive striving toward excellence degenerates into a brutalized striving for mastery and control. Stripped of the heroic and valorous element, agon may be transformed into a form of terrorism. In Greece, the moderating virtue linking agonism and areté was *philotimia*, which was "the desire to display and gain recognition for one's excellence in character and especially in deed."[21] "Honor above all things and honor in all things," was the creedal cry of noble agonism. Striving, exertion of will and might in quest of the recognition not only for accomplishment and success but for respect in everyone's eyes, prevented the struggle from being debased.

All noble, Greek struggle involved this love of honor. Homer's heroes could only be rightly heroic if their deeds were prompted by philotimia. Selfish, ruthless revenge or self-aggrandizement were not considered legitimate reasons for gaining public acclaim. This only came about when society's values were usurped by a debased needs-system built upon hedonism and savagery. Are there not similarities to this situation in contemporary society satiated as it is with a kind of sedentary voyeurism that demands increasingly stronger doses of brutality in sports and entertainment to satisfy its voracious appetite? One rather lamentable but poignant description of our own times reads like this:

The puzzle is why so many people live so badly. Not so wickedly but so inanely. Not so cruelly, but so stupidly. There is little to admire and less to imitate in the people who are prominent in our culture. We have celebrities not saints. Famous entertainers amuse a nation of bored insomniacs. Infamous criminals act out the aggressions of timid conformists. Petulant and spoiled athletes play games vicariously for lazy and apathetic spectators. People, aimless and bored, amuse themselves with trivia and trash. Neither the adventure of goodness nor the pursuit of righteousness gets headlines.[22]

The homogenized and cosmetized culture which engulfs us today elevates the synthetic experiences above the real. Appearances have become all important. Impression management has become the marketable commodity abetted by the visual media that assault us on every side. Cleverly designed images dazzle a generation that has been denied opportunities for true trial, for true testing of self against a necessary, albeit often, harsh reality. Technology has relegated honored tradition to the quaint archives of antiquity. Venerable traditions have become museum pieces which are brought out only on special occasions when nostalgia is in vogue. We are a nation of voyeurs insisting upon ever-increasing titillations as our thrill-seeking thresholds are raised.

"Videoism" is the voyeuristic pathology of the age, which craves, like an addictive disorder, larger and larger doses to keep us high. Videoism provides a vicarious experience through identification with cult figures created out of thin air by the media. Overnight celebrities and sensations are required to feed the insatiable appetites of a sensate culture which has given itself over to "carnivorality." The lack of first-hand agonal experiences has turned us into a nation of vicarious thrill seekers who are willing to pay the costly price for second-hand sensations. Education similarly has capitulated to the "fun ethic" that turns all serious academic struggle into game shows and schools into TV studios. Neil Postman with characteristic wit and wisdom rightly reminds us that television and school are antagonistic curriculums. The technology of the former imposes "three commandments that form the philosophy of education which television offers." The three "thou shalts" are (1) Thou shalt have no prerequisites, (2) Thou shalt induce no perplexity, and (3) Thou shalt avoid exposition. In other words, according to Postman, television and related video-learning equate education with entertainment.[23] Not only have we reduced students to a passive spectatorship which relies heavily upon technological sensory extensions, we have encouraged within students a misplaced passion. Passion (and we need to be reminded that the word in its Latin derivation implies suffering and struggle) has unfortunately become virtually equated with sexual titillation or with some superficial, emotional feeling. Deep passion has acquired an erotic connotation reinforced by the voyeuristic habits that television forms.

Courtly qualities, most manifested during the age of chivalry, when the agon had been transformed into a code of honorable conduct by which knights lived, are now laughingly derided by the antiheroes of a deformed culture. The high ideals of noble character, the valorous crusade in the cause of right, the unflinching dedication to demonstrate oneself worthy— all these, unassailably, constituted the vital core for heroic accomplishments. Agonic cultures encouraged, recognized, and created the conditions for champions to emerge, but not champions as they are defined today. Not the self-serving, egoistic, media-indulged sycophants, lionized and irrationally adulated by an adoring, infantile public which derives vicarious fulfillment from the fabricated exploits of their superstars. When true agonism erodes in a society, pseudoagonism takes root and feeds on the cultural carrion of a decomposing civilization. The evidence of such decomposition is all about us. The ubiquitous voices crying in the cultural wilderness are calling us to reconsider our programs and reevaluate our priorities. The chorus swells daily with dirgelike declamations.

Education is intended to serve civilization. Without rationally designed, value-laden, systematic education, society reverts to barbarism. Jaeger equates civilization and education. Paideia provides the animating spirit of civilized people, and agonism is an integral element. Education that is not animated and enlightened by paideia soon degenerates into barbarism. Self-appointed sentinels who vigilantly scour the horizon for signs of the ever-menacing barbaric hordes have sounded their alarms warning us that the invasion has begun. In fact, we may have already been vanquished and the capitulation may have begun. Schools certainly seem to have been captivated by the blandishments of barbarism as evidenced by the alacrity with which these schools jettison the structures of the past, and readily adopt the innovations of the present. Technology has led barbarism's charge in this assault. That has been the basic source of the educational enigma. Education by tradition and of necessity must be reluctant to relinquish the gains and accomplishments accrued over time. By its very nature, education is a conserving institution and change must always be viewed skeptically. Of course, change must occur. Life requires growth, and growth requires change. But developmental life changes are something different than changes inappropriately and unwisely conceded to power alone. Power of any kind, from any source, of sufficient magnitude can push aside the present and impose its agenda almost immediately. But power that insists on change must be perceived as legitimate. New ideas should not be entertained simply because they are new. Novelty is always suspect.[24]

Ideas must bring with them their authority. They must be scrutinized, analyzed, and debated. All innovation must undergo public scrutiny. If the proposed change can sufficiently command an audience, and after critical examination, demonstrate its worth, then and only then should it be given recognition. Technology's impertinence lies in its power apart from such legitimation. It is intrusive, intractable, impervious to expulsion, and arrogantly prescriptive. As Ellul has told us time and time again, if you give technology a foothold, you will never dislodge it, and the system into which it enters will be immutably altered almost immediately.[25] The new barbarism could not have occurred without the intrusion of technology. The educational edifice, formed and fashioned over centuries with appropriate but modest modification as new ideas and practices commended themselves, has been assaulted and battered by a formidable technological onslaught. But this is not an original observation. Whitehead prophetically warned us even before World War II that if "in the troubled times which may be before us, you wish appreciably to increase the chance of some savage upheaval, introduce widespread technical education and ignore the Benedictine ideal. Society will then get what it deserves."[26]

But, as we often do, we refused to heed Whitehead's sage advice, and now have opened the gates to the savage upheaval of the invading marauders. Within a span of several decades, the course of culture has been dramatically reversed. The hard-won gains of civilization, which had provided a bulwark against the encroachments of a persistent savagery, have suffered the seismic shock of technological upheaval. The cultural moorings at one time solid and secure are being swept away by the inundations of technology's tidal wave. Society has viewed these invaders as saviors, and education has embraced them as emancipators who have come to free us from the stifling traditions of the past, but the irony is, and perhaps the eventual tragedy will be, that both have mistaken new fetters for new freedom. Above all, the glaring deception that has blinded society to all else has been the blunder of believing that no gods are better than ancient gods. The tragedy of sightlessness may produce compensation when other senses take over the missing function. But a generation dazzled by the glare of shiny machinery mistakes the glare for a new glory, and thinks then that it can see better. Darkness and dazzle equally prevent clear-sighted vision. The true danger of the latter is that captivation by technology's glare renders needless quests for all other worlds. This brave new world—this new educational order—is sufficient and self-legitimating, and the transcendence which always told us that our imperfect copy needed to be corrected by something beyond it has, therefore, been eradicated.

Chapter 5

Transcendence
and Technology

Transcendence and technology are antithetical. By their very nature, they compete against and seek to vanquish each other. Technology is rooted in present, empirical reality. It both draws its substance from and demonstrates its superiority in the manifest, material world. Transcendence, on the other hand, points beyond the immediate and the mundane. It refuses to rest content with ephemeral, albeit tangible, realities. The world which science creates, the sphere within which science operates, and the methodologies that science employs are amenable only to sensory exploration. Science limits itself to matter, and technology is the application of science to the transformation of that matter. To be allied to technology is to be constrained, as well, solely by the senses. Technology takes us only as far as the senses permit, but admittedly, in this day of expanding technological horizons, the journey is an increasingly longer one. Nevertheless, we can only tread sensory terrain. We must remain forever within the sphere of the senses, and we must remember that the reality we encounter, however exotic it may appear, is always within the space-time continuum.

Technology has promised improvements and amelioration in our way of life, and, to a large extent, it has delivered on those promises. Incontrovertibly, humans have been freed from servile labor, from drudgery, and from dehumanizing toil by the accomplishments of technology. Information, entertainment, and a variety of new sources of stimulation have come through scientific advancement. It would be both inaccurate and unfair to indict technology as an ogre that has hidden behind a benign mask but which has revealed its true face only in the crises it has created. Thinking people acknowledge the debt to technology and the comforts and conveniences it has provided. Of course, the point must be made, before we proceed further with our discussion, that we did not need what technology provided. After all, life on this planet has survived for millennia without the technology that this generation has witnessed. Life would undoubtedly have continued, and generations would have succeeded their ancestors, and the pace of life would have moved along, although admittedly, more slowly and evenly. Technology is not a prerequisite for human survival. When it has come, it has ameliorated, not saved, the human species. But the thesis of this portion of my argument is that technology has altered human life in ways that will forever render it irremediably damaged.

We need at this point to examine technology in terms of its intrusiveness into the affairs of human life and living. We need to focus specifically upon technology as an invader that has assaulted the social and psychological as well as the physical world. Without the invitation or consent of society, technology was, in a sense, sneaked in through the back door, and soon took over the house. The conspirators in this melodrama, who were not always the inventors or originators (the father of the twentieth-century computer saw only a limited role for science in meeting the deepest level of human need),[1] dressed their aliens in attractive garb and made them appear "user friendly." They came simply to "help with the dishes, to wash the windows, to scrub the floors." And soon they displaced the owners, took over the house, and transformed it into a high-tech center. Technology is a means that rapidly and without much opposition becomes an end in itself. It generates its own mandate and obviates philosophical, reflective consideration of the use to which its devices should be put.

Technology, which in some ways is a fancy word for machine (although as Ellul has said technology and technique are different),[2] dehumanizes any human enterprise. Education which, if anything, is a human enterprise of the most solemn and exalted status has been demeaned by the reckless intrusion of machinery, whatever form that machinery may take.

Measurement is a machine operation that employs numbers to gauge performance. Numbers, without which technology could not function, assume, ipso facto, the significance of evaluations (which, of course, they are not). Numbers have come to possess self-signifying merit. Schools rely on numbers to tell them what to do with students. These numbers tell schools the importance of students and eventually determine what is important in education. Machines and numbers are a perilous combination. Cryptotechnical esoterica turned out by machines is vested with oracular powers and is then slavishly obeyed. Lionel Tiger tells of the testing business, spawned by Educational Testing Service, that provides measurement professionals (psychologists, psychometricians, educators, etc.) with efficient means of testing people. The respondents to the test questions simply punch in replies in a computer-controlled program and eventually the machine hums out pages of analysis that purport to profile the important characteristics and abilities of the test taker. Of course, there is no evidence that any of it is valid or worthwhile. Tiger concludes: "Surely this is madness of a sort, unmitigated by the smooth impartial hum of the efficient machine."[3] And there is no more-fitting word for it than madness, but a fine madness that has been regarded now as sure sanity by a technocracy that calls the shots and defines the conditions of reality. A number never gives anyone the right to decide anything. Humans are humans because they are able to deliberate, imagine, value, and engage in a host of human processes, and to defer to a number is betrayal of humanness. Tiger tells us about his apprehension over the situation:

[M]y concern is with the ease with which technical descriptions, through numbers, of often extremely complex and perhaps fugitive social and psychological circumstances, have come to be taken seriously as realities of life, not as notations of it. The pleasing logic of counting is combined with the reassuring formality of bureaucratic classification and procedure to produce ways of describing reality more rigid and mechanical than warranted by particular cases.[4]

Wisely chosen goals must be the basis for any worthwhile educational program, and goals that are clearly in keeping with the value system of the society. If the goals are not deliberately determined and the values explicitly articulated, then, by default, the means themselves will create their own conditions and establish their own agenda. Agonic education highlights the role of transcendence. Today's materialistic society allows little room for transcendence, and that may explain the existential neurosis that plagues this generation. Jean Paul Sartre referred to an "infinite reference point" as being critical for survival. Given a "why," we can find a "how," Nietzsche has echoed. But we are so preoccupied with the "how" that we pay little notice to the "why" or the "what." Transcendence, of course, leads us inescapably to the realm of metaphysics, but epistemology not metaphysics intrigues the information age. Stanley Jaki's fearless frontal assault on contemporary philosophy and science addresses this very tender spot.[5] The patronizing tone of philosophy toward metaphysics is the consequence of philosophy's being enamored with science. As philosophy's methodology has aped science, epistemology has eclipsed metaphysics. Without a metaphysical awareness and particularly a keen, ontological perspective on reality, a crude preoccupation with epistemology centers simply upon technique.

Within education, a similar mind-set has developed which discounts ontological issues. The present taken-for-granted technological society obscures all other considerations, and the aims of education are reduced to questions of new knowledge. The theme of control, which is paramount in a technological culture, requires ever-increasing data bases and information sources. Epistemological issues, redefined as information needs, drive the educational enterprise. As Ellul has stated with clarity and conviction:

Education . . . is becoming oriented toward the specialized end of producing technicians; and as a consequence toward the creation of individuals useful only as members of a technical group, on the basis of the current criteria of utility. . . . And education will no longer be an unpredictable and exciting adventure in human enlightenment, but an exercise in conformity and an apprenticeship to whatever gadgetry is useful in a technical world.[6]

Behind all of this obsession with technology and control lies an academic arrogance which, incidentally, like the ancient *hubris* threatens to cave in upon its advocates. Science offers nothing for the soul. If we equate sensation with satisfaction, we create a world that defines itself in terms of matter alone, and the physical displaces the metaphysical. More than a generation ago, Bell cautioned against the corrosive effects of unbridled scientism. Applauded as the new savior, science then, as now, was viewed as the hope for the future, but in destroying the historic structures built through labor and struggle, science restructured the social underpinnings that now threaten to collapse under science's own weight. Bell did not indict all scientists, but he saw even then the arrogant, superficial few who were willing to sacrifice civilization's hard-won accomplishments for a few trinkets that dazzled their generation:

The great minds in science know physics deeply enough to perceive the need of metaphysics. But the great scientists are few and they are reticent people. Meanwhile the air is vocal with the noise of hangers-on, the laboratory technicians, the merely engineers, the cocky young instructors. . . . Under their leadership we proceed scientifically to examine matter. There can be no doubt that the result is apt to be devastating to the courage of almost all of us.[7]

Transcendence provides the critical vision that separates treasures from trash. The relics of technology, apart from the feeble efforts at recycling, are mere discards. Yesterday's latest attraction is today's trash. The landfills testify to the technological trivia. The promises of greater labor-saving and life-fulfilling wonders become landfill fodder, and apart from the monumental and perplexing task of finding places to put all this stuff, the harm inflicted upon unsuspecting psyches and souls is incalculable. The insatiable appetite of a technologized society feeds omnivorously and rapaciously upon that novelty. It is impossible to go back to that saner time in society when changes, introduced incrementally, could be leisurely digested and assimilated. Our capacity for dealing with newness then was, thankfully, small, and social as well as environmental transformations were generally accommodated consensually. It is no longer that way. The very economics of the society, of themselves, do not permit us to have such a relaxed and rational view of change. Dislocations, socially and psychologically, have produced addiction states with each new generation accelerating the rate of change and augmenting the size of change. We no longer taste and sip; we gulp and stuff. But to what are we referring when we use the quaint, and almost archaic term, transcendence? It has acquired a distasteful association with meditative states, and for some people its only reference is to occult encounters. The popularity and appeal of these borderline, quasi-religious practices, at least, affirm the disenchantment by some with the merely mechanical approaches to life. Peter Bien detected this disenchantment soon after the troubled decade of the 1960s when the elite of that generation were dropping out. According to Bien, the disenchantment was fostered by the dull technology that was dominating the times, and killing the spirit.[8] Plunkett concurs in identifying the cry for meaningful, holistic education as "the fruit of the 1960s, of the protest movements against an overly technological view of the world including the technologies of social control."[9]

Nativistic returns to nature and the "greening of America" phenomenon lured the cultured to an asylum outside the culture. The dead weight of technology was dragging spirits that sought to soar into more elevated and ethereal zones. Reductionist theories of human nature harnessed to behavioral-analysis techniques sapped what little life remained in that generation which had suffered the loss of "autonomous self." The search for transcendence drove that generation to seek a god within, and the "Jonathan Livingston Seagull subsociety" was born.[10]

When technology diminished the agonic element and robbed people of purposeful pursuit, there was no place for many of them to go but "within." The increasingly popular appeal of self-psychology, which relies excessively on passive, self-affirmation, reduced, even further, the agonal quality of personal and social life. In desperation, perhaps to affirm meaning, that generation relinquished the natural, confrontative drive that is requisite for acquiring personal identity, and chose instead the diffused, distant, nonagonic acquiescence, mistaking alpha states in the brain for cosmic awareness.

The unpredictable and exciting adventure of human enlightenment, which education is meant to be, when traded for technological tyranny seeks, perhaps in disguised forms, some wings for its flights of fancy. The human spirit cannot be indefinitely caged behind the restricting structures of science; it cannot be reduced to a microchip. Even if it risks melting what may in effect be wax wings, it must soar like Icarus into the sun's sphere of light and heat. But this is not the talk that is welcomed in today's education. A friend who works for an international company that develops, manufactures, and sells new technologies commented that he heard at a convention the statement that if education had kept pace with technology, students could learn in a day what it now takes them a decade to know. By know, of course, the presenter meant merely technical knowledge and expertise. I irately asked how the accumulated wisdom of time could be reduced to a floppy disk. A prepackaged, synthetic, and aseptic amalgamation of information is what the presenter had in mind. Education is more than, yea different than, acquisition of technical expertise. By his definition, this is the only generation that is or could be educated. Transcendence is reduced to an irrelevancy. The focus and obsession of technology is control. All things are subordinated to this self-aggrandizing and pervasive principle. And epistemologies based on control (which technology demands) lead, inevitably, as Huston Smith has declared, to the destruction of transcendence. Smith's definition of transcendence will serve us well at this point: "By transcendence, I mean something superior to us by every measure of value we know and some that elude us."[11]

Epistemologies centered upon control preclude the presence of transcendence. They are mutually incompatible. As Stanley Jaki puts it so wittily: you cannot catch angels with a butterfly net. We must accept the notion that there are things beyond us, and that these are the most important things; and if they are, they, and they alone, must be the basis for determinations of education, society, and values. Transcendence reintroduces struggle into the human situation because the gap between the potential and actual can only be bridged by agonal effort. But a modern society enamored with enticements of convenience and complacency has almost no interest in anything that is not immediate, titillating, or sensually appealing. The chronic complaint of students at all levels of school stems from the perceived lack of relevancy of studying anything that is neither new nor of immediate utility. To be called modern is a flattering designation, and by it we mean whatever is current, fashionable, faddish, and starkly contrasting with whatever isn't. And modernity, as sociologist Peter Berger contends, is that phenomenon of social life that has a loss of transcendence.[12]

Without a belief in transcendence, life will lose its meaning. Without transcendence, a social entity will ride the bandwagon of popular, present priorities and will fragment itself into a collectivity of unrelated, divided parts, each seeking its particular and peculiar agenda. "Now" becomes the fashionable word. Shibboleths take on the vivid coloration of a narcissistic intensity where stridency rules. Transcendence mutes the acerbic, vociferous chanting of a monotonous chorus of self-seekers. The recognition of a reality beyond the present and the immediately practical gives us a certain reason to pause, and to ponder, and then to propose. Permit me at this point to introduce a term that receives little attention from technology, and, when it does, it is employed simply as an emotional ally for salesmanship. The term is "love." The ancient Greeks called it *agapé*. Agon and arete are linked together in transcendence by agapé. Unless its meaning is reduced to narcissism or simply an expression of pathological codependence, love is only explainable in terms of transcendence. Why would anyone be motivated to jeopardize oneself for the salvation of another, for as psychiatrist Victor Frankl insists, "salvation is in and through love."[13] The "Oxbridge" don, C. S. Lewis has captured the quality of love which frees us from the temporal and permits us the rare and rarefied view of relationships that love offers:

In love we escape from ourself into another. In the moral sphere, every act of justice or charity involves putting ourselves in the other person's place and thus transcending our own competitive particularity. In coming to understand anything we are rejecting the facts as they are for us in favor of the facts as they are. . . . Obviously this process can be described as an enlargement or the temporary annihilation of self.[14]

Education's agenda painfully reveals its all-too-ready acceptance of a temporal mind-set locked into a so-called practicality that shapes curriculums and orders programs. Education needs a reassertion of transcendence's role.

Parker Palmer's conception of true education requires a grace of acceptance:

Openness to this sort of grace has been vital in the development of all knowledge. It has often gone by other names, like "serendipity" or "flash of insight," but it is grace nonetheless, breaking through our preconceptions and allowing truth to speak to us.[15]

In technology, charisma is routinized (as Max Weber reminds us), and grace plays no part. There is little room or encouragement for breaking through fixed, inflexible routines. Routinization must rule and technology's hegemony must remain unchallenged. Precision and predictability are the exalted virtues. Spontaneity and serendipity are the twin vices. But when charisma is tamed and grace is excluded, wisdom's rule is similarly and woefully diminished. In order to penetrate the mist of self-imposed artificial illumination, an aperture open to transcendence is needed through which light can filter from another source. We join in Helen Keller's cry: "Light, give me light!" It is here that Parker Palmer enlists spiritual resources, for it is from the spiritual realm that the purest light comes. When education relies solely on mechanized modes for vision and direction, there is energy only for labor, little for light. That energy is quickly consumed and with the depletion comes a loss of direction and a distortion of purpose. But regenerative, spiritual energy sources for labor and illumination, continuously renewing themselves and never burning out (like the biblical bush that Moses turned aside to see), enlighten and refresh. The true teacher will seek and tap into this source.

The true professor is not one who controls facts and theories and techniques. The true professor is one who affirms a transcendent center of truth, a center that lies beyond our contriving, that enters history through the lives of those who profess it and bring us into community with each other and the world.[16]

Richard Weaver addressed this crying necessity a generation ago and with a prophet's vision sketched out for us what now has come to pass. Weaver takes a long look back and sees the ogre emerging in the fourteenth century when the naive, newly emerging scientific mind with its penchant for empirical reality was beginning to settle for a reality that went no deeper than the senses. The "fateful doctrine of nominalism" spread its roots wildly throughout the beginnings of the modern cultural landscape, and flourished in a field that was being cultivated with nutrients of a new science. This doctrine would in a short time cover the earth, displacing medieval mysticism at every point. The abandonment of the "belief in the existence of transcendentals," upon which the "age of faith" had been nourished, withered the roots of universalism and witnessed the demise of an ideology and cultural tradition that had dominated for a millennium and a half. "From this," Weaver says, "directly flowed those acts which issue now in modern decadence."[17] The loss of transcendence was a loss of wisdom, and science, inevitably followed by its offspring technology, replaced wisdom with information and knowledge. The society of the wise, which honored careful deliberation, rational reflection, and reverence for the traditions of the past, was swept away by the inundations of an overpowering empiricism.

Transcendence has a rightful reverence for the past. Pragmatism, the philosophical heir of empiricism, preoccupied as it is with change only pays homage and sacrifices the future. Present human experience becomes the sole criterion for social determinations. What is presently workable, applicable, meaningful, and desirable dictates social and educational agendas. "The denial of everything transcending experience," Weaver remarks, "means inevitably . . . the denial of truth."[18] Man becomes the measure of all things, and by "man," he means contemporary, pragmatic man. It is then a short step from (although a quantum leap to) the acceptance of nominalism to scientism, materialism, reductionism, and technologism. The slippery, precarious pathway downward leads to a debasement (and to the basement!) of human values and life. At the bottom where the walkway is level, movement is easier and more egalitarian, but the view is the lowest, the company stultifying, and the values base. This is the home of moles; eagles soar in the rarefied atmosphere of transcendence. The subterranean dwellings are not proper habitations for the soul, let alone the body. The soul shrinks, becomes emaciated, and soon shrivels into a lifeless vestige that occasionally reminds us of what we once were but what we can no longer be if we choose to remain where we are.

Technology inexorably drives us downward despite the promises it provides for liberation. Souls are manacled by oppressive weights, and we find ourselves shackled again to cave walls mistaking video images and computer scans for reality and truth. Dehumanized and sedated, we no longer struggle toward the illumined aperture that leads outward to freedom. We find a certain perverse pleasure in the tranquility of passivity. Like opium users, we are content to let technology narcotize us. For this generation, as Szasz in his refutation of Marx has correctly understood, "opiate is the religion of the people."[19] And as Weaver tells us, "one consequence of this debauchery . . . is that man loses discrimination."[20]

The sign of educated, reflective people is their capacity for discrimination. Differences exist, and excellence demands that differences be identified and distinctions be clearly drawn. The ancient Greeks understood this, and their culture based on areté testifies to this aptitude for critical discrimination. How else can achievements be determined unless criteria exist to distinguish between bad and good; good and better; better and best. A folly of this generation, which may become its fatal flaw, is the artificial egalitarianism that refuses to specify proper qualitative distinctions. Everything is reduced to an amorphous, homogenized ethic which permits all possible behaviors and endorses all productions. Transcendence tells us that there are irrefutable standards for judgment. Technology diminishes or obliterates those standards or distinctions. Education, thereby, becomes the hapless handmaiden of technique, further obscuring categories of discrimination. It makes no difference now whether a musical composition is the creative, agonic expression of originality conceived and brought to life by the labors of a genius, or the artificial, effortless artifact of a synthesizer. The computer is in this instance the great culprit because its programming capability allows it to synthesize millions of discrete bits of data and reduce the time needed to compose to a fraction of the former requirements. And still the results are not original, imaginative expressions of art or creative enterprise. Mechanical assemblages are not synonymous with masterpieces. In the final analysis, a simple "twinkle twinkle little star" which results from the creative, cognitive, agonal transformation of thoughts into verse is superior to the synthetic permutations and products of extensive inputs of data.

It is a basic thesis of this work that technology militates against transcendence. Their very incompatibility means one or the other will have to leave. The ideological town is not big enough for both of them. But they are unevenly matched. Technology always deals in quantities, and wherever it is introduced it will entrap the most sublime thought within its web of quantification, and, thereby, reduce verbal thought to numerical computation. It digests formulae and devours thought, churning it into a measurable commodity. Without being crude, the digestive metaphor is not too far afield for the health of an organism is often determined by the absence of illness, and symptoms of disease are examined. Consequently, the waste discards are studied for diagnosis of illness. Qualitative thinking conforms to a health model, whereas quantitative statements are rendered in terms of statistical analysis that seeks to fix the range within which errors or illness will be tolerated. Postman suggests something similar in his facetious appeal to educationists to adopt a medical model that would make teachers "treaters of stupidity."[21] Certainly, analyses involving hypothesis testing and measures of significance require confidence levels for exclusion of doubt. As Wilkinson states: "It is, in fact, the essence of technique to compel the qualitative to become quantitative and in this way force every stage of human activity and man himself to submit to its mathematical calculations."[22]

Contemporary society seems to be oblivious to this desensitizing aspect of technology. It has been given free sway to do what it wants. Merton observed that "restraints on the rule of technique become increasingly tenuous. Public opinion provides no control because it too is largely oriented toward 'performance' and technique is regarded as the prime instrument of performance."[23] Again we are confronted with a social dichotomy in which there is unequal leverage. Pensive versus performance. Being versus doing. Identity is today largely a matter of performance visibility. One is what one does. One is important to the extent that one's performance has public notoriety. One is rewarded to the extent that performance is big, boastful, and boisterous. Contemplative, reclusive people who engage in unspectacular pursuits are ignored or scorned. Teachers, unless they engage in novelty that brings them popular appeal, are not among the upper echelons in the occupational hierarchy. Helping professionals generally, despite the rhetoric of social respectability, do not make much money, nor are they given much air time on network television. But the entertainers and athletes (the two groups whose coverage is inversely related to their worth) are redundantly paraded before us, and their inarticulate utterances are quoted *ad nauseam*. Society applauds the public performers and awards them its rich, lavish prizes. Acts of mercy and humanitarian compassion performed by unheralded, self-effacing servants receive little recognition or reward. Celebrities, creatures of technology's high visibility, are accorded recognition way out of proportion to their contributions to true culture.

I am not denigrating performance, per se. I insist that performance is critical to creativity and success. Agonic struggle is implicit in performance, but I maintain that selfish and self-centered pursuit lacks the nobility of areté that the Greeks so wisely recognized as indispensable for a society to prosper. The redefinition of education, contrary to its historical and traditional understanding, now equates learning and schooling with a dehumanized apprenticeship. Training is important. Skill acquisition is necessary. Competency in specialized technical areas must be acquired. But all these are not the same as education. And the more technologically based the educational program, the more likely it is to lose the *sine qua non* of education—the development of personhood.

Transcendence as a philosophical category involves the recognition of and striving for excellencies beyond the temporal and sensual. Society has no mooring without a firm anchor of tradition to hold it and a star of transcendence to guide it when it begins a new voyage. Life has little purpose without transcendent goals. Education today suffers from the modern malaise of purposelessness. Education rides each new wave of fashion that breaks upon the social shore, and threatens to be flooded by the volume and velocity of the novelty. What is true socially is true for each individual. The social and psychological crises that plague this society feed on the carrion of decimated custom and dead creeds. We have murdered our culture, the single thing that sustained sanity, and we wonder why each generation roams rootlessly in search of significance. Alienated from a past they have been told is laughably irrelevant, fearful of an ominous future, the members meander among the burned-out, discarded remnants of a scorched culture and find no place to settle down. They seek meaning and find amusement. We promise them education and supply entertainment. They unwittingly seek transcendence, and technology offers itself as the panacea for their plight. Transcendence is not very attractive to this generation because it requires complexity of thought and design and struggle to soar to its heights. It is so much easier to let our lives be run by things, and be programmed by science, and to conform to a superficial culture that promises convenience and control and offers nothing for the soul. Education similarly likes to "line things up," and we "cover material" rather than discover outer and inner reality. Parker Palmer has noted this characteristic of conventional pedagogy which

persists because it conveys a view of reality that simplifies our lives. By this view, we and our world become objects to be lined up, counted and organized and owned rather than a community of selves and spirits related to each other in a complex web of accountability called "truth." The conventional pedagogy pretends to give us mastery over the world.[24]

And it is all simply pretense, for we soon find we are the hapless victims of a social philosophy and educational system which limit our options, destroy our sense of self, and distance us from each other. A pedagogy of transcendence will recognize complexity, refuse to sidestep the ambiguities that cause us tension, and embrace the inexorable agony which comes in this exalted quest for meaning.

How dare we talk about aims and goals in education and ignore transcendence's role? Philosophically, transcendence is akin to the social and personal vision that crowns effort with noble accomplishment. It is the good of and for the social order that Plato's philosopher-king acquires through arduous study and labor. We need to remind ourselves that the experience of the senses must be, at best, an imitation of the ultimate reality. Nature, for all its wonder, does not contain the "principles of its own constitution and behavior." Jaki, exposing the pretensions of modern philosopher-physicists, has convincingly demonstrated the deficiency of a cosmology that starts and ends with cosmos.[25] The source and significance of its being must be found beyond itself. We dare not commit the unpardonable folly, about which Weaver warns us, of mistaking nature's reality for all of ultimate reality, which, of course, is the pernicious folly that seems to have a perennial appeal to the "popular" mind. So Weaver says: "Whereas nature had formerly been regarded as imitating a transcendent model and as constituting an imperfect reality, it was henceforth looked upon as containing the principles of its own constitution and behavior."[26] But "there is a transcendent pattern of truth, beauty and goodness which man by means of rational effort or inspiration is capable of knowing and experiencing."[27] Technology blinds us to this vision and, thereby, tells us what we feel within is simply a function of programmed emotions or enzymes. But if the heart has reasons that reason knows not of, then transcendence has mysteries that technology could never know (per Thomas Campbell in "To the Rainbow" [1869]):

> When science from creation's face
> enchantment's veil withdraws,
> what lovely visions yield their place
> to cold material laws.

Transcendence thrives on mystery and mystique. Technique and mystique clash incompatibly. Video games are nothing more than anemic substitutes for fantasy and fairy tales, and without controversy, considerably less. They are distortions and perversions. Power is the name of their game. The game transcendence provides, the true ludi, gives wings to flights of fantasy. Education loses its enchantment when it is engineered. The human is naturally playful. The spontaneous play of childhood should tell us something about the fundamental condition of human nature. Curiosity and creativity spring spontaneously from the unrepressed spirit. Control only becomes important as nature is seen as something that needs to be harnessed. Rousseau, for all his naive sentimentalism, was wise enough to know that the onset of formal education, when defined as a process of conformity to a control mentality, should be delayed as long as possible. Where is the delicate magic of education that still startles the unjaded schoolchild? In my own school days, with all their privations and poverty and desperation, children saw school, with all its grimness and gloom, still as a place of possibilities. School was a place where something startling may happen. The plain, even stygian building, was entered, admittedly fearfully, but expectantly. In this place with these people, we told ourselves, something ultimately good will happen to us and for us. Of course, it did not always. Perhaps it seldom did, but we approached the portals with unquenchable optimism, a sense of urgent expectancy, and in that world of that day, when there were no other options for most of us, the vision unfolded. We experienced enchantment if only within the covers of a borrowed library book. Even the uninspiring classroom could not keep out the serendipitous awakenings that caught us so much by surprise. The absence of oppressive technology, at least, reduced the barriers that excluded outbreaks of ecstasy, and as George Leonard knows, "education at best, is ecstatic."[28]

Transcendence need not be conceived only in grandiose metaphysics or described with philosophical flourishes. Personal transcendence liberates the self and the spirit from both the social pressures of performance and their own private preoccupations. Transcendence should lead us out from ourselves and upward to new levels of accomplishment and awareness. Technology entraps the spirit, encasing it in a steel cocoon of control and predictability. Science and technology cannot function apart from specific parameters and unerring prediction. Prediction requires precise measurement, and it is sadly assumed that whatever is incapable of being observed and measured is incapable of existence. Only the observable, according to the Heisenberg principle of indeterminacy, is amenable to measurement, but it is erroneous, as Jaki contends, to conclude that "knowledge of reality [is] equivalent to measuring it." Transcendence is a nonmeasurable means of knowing reality. Transcendence is not chaotic, nor is it confusion; rather, it refuses to conform to the conventional assumptions of control. It is more serpentine than linear; mercurial and more like a mosaic which is not always easily measurable. It is filled with surprises and serendipity, and is not amenable to traditional measurement. If it needs to be assessed, then qualitative assessment, akin to Elliott Eisner's concept of "connoisseurship," should be used to determine its course and effects.[29]

It would be unfair and elitist to say that only those who have experienced the liberation of transcendence can identify it. This would be much too esoteric and would communicate an unintended image of the experience, but a cultivated, qualitative inquiry by people who are at least open to other dimensions of reality and truth than those which science provides is prerequisite to any apprehension of it.[30] When an experience is not reducible to quantitative analysis and measurement, it is assumed to be only part of an individual's idiosyncratic world bordering on the bizarre and irrational, but it is possible to produce a validating consensus apart from quantities alone. How else have cosmologies managed to survive unless they are seen to be more than aberrations produced and perpetuated by society's shamans? Even the sociology of knowledge tells us that our social orders are fictions that we choose to create and affirm.[31] Huston Smith points out that social perceptions change, and a particular one (or ones) is chosen at a given point in cultural history to be the dominant framework for ordering reality.[32] The control mind-set of Western society since the fifteenth century has ruled and overruled imperiously for half a millennium, but it has not succeeded in vanquishing the stubborn tenacity of transcendence that periodically recaptures a place of recognition in a slavishly scientific world.

Abraham Maslow and third-force psychology have reasserted, in opposition to behaviorism, the primacy of "openness to transcendence." Skinner and his breed of behaviorists, armed with the paraphernalia of the laboratory technician, captured the field of psychology even as the physicist captured the field of philosophy. "Generic man," that is human nature, was stripped of its metaphysical properties and reduced to a laboratory subject for behavioral analysis. All behavior was explainable in terms of environmental factors, and hence the specter of "autonomous man," which smacked of transcendence and which was assumed to be merely a vestige of a more-credulous age and a medieval mentality, was dispelled like the ghost of Hamlet's father by the dawning of a new scientific day. Maslow, initiated into psychology through behaviorism, separated himself from it forever, declaring it bankrupt and sought explanations for behavior and solutions to misbehavior in the natural-growth needs that humans have. Capping the pinnacle of his frequently modified hierarchy is the much-popularized "self actualization" which involves a quasi-transcendence with openness to experience and oceanic feelings.

Maslow freed humans from the cages, mazes, and boxes that delighted Skinner.[33] The "self" was not simply the sum of conditioned responses to stimuli. It was more than and maybe other than the complex of contingencies, responses, and reinforcers, and certainly not merely a repertoire of behavior appropriate to a given set of contingencies, as Skinner defined it.[34] A dynamic growth principle—different from Freud's blindly and wildly driven id, and Skinner's controlled behavior responses—sought expression moving from level to level as it found need satisfaction, ultimately questing for self-fulfillment. But even Maslow's improved conception of the self suffers from the limitations of nature-as-reality. It took Victor Frankl to add the missing piece to Maslow's truncated pyramid and, thereby, redesign it adding the critical element of transcendence to the ego's edifice. Self-actualization if allowed to remain an end in itself would soon degenerate into self-gratification. It could ironically become the unwitting accomplice in technology's plot to turn everyone into a compliant consumer.

Self-actualization, instead of being a springboard toward greater growth, runs the risk of becoming a cavernous hollow clamoring for new things to fill it up, and unhesitatingly, technology would gladly oblige. The opportunity for growth through struggle and exertion would be lost to greed and satiation. Frankl, sensing the inherent contradiction in Maslow's structure, warns us about the danger and declares that self-actualization can only be a means, never an end. Self-actualization can only be a by-product never an end-product. To make actualization an end in itself will create its distortion and bring about the self's downfall. Self-transcendence must complete the pyramid, and, thereby, assure the actualization of self. It is only by going beyond ourselves that we realize ourselves. Hence, the old adage that life is gained as life is lost. A greater goal than self and a more-worthy cause than satisfaction must attract us if we are, paradoxically, to know ourselves and reach success.

Only to the extent that someone is living out this self-transcendence of human existence, is he truly human or does he become his true self. He becomes so, not by concerning himself with his self's actualization, but by forgetting himself and giving himself, overlooking himself and focusing outward. . . . What is called self-actualization is and must remain the unintended effect of self-transcendence; it is ruinous and self-defeating to make it the target of intention. And what is true of self-actualization also holds for identity and happiness. It is the very "pursuit of happiness" that obviates happiness. The more we make it a target, the more widely we miss.[35]

Education has been snared by the twin traps of technology and stress-less, self-actualization. The two serve each other in a symbiotic but pathological way. Without the aid of technology, or more correctly technique, traditional patterns would continue to prevail and change would come only after careful, thoughtful consideration. The needs of individuals and the needs of society would be weighed more evenly and a more-judicious balance would be maintained. Moderation, which was the hallmark of Greek rationality, would be the fulcrum upon which an equilibrium would be established. But technology quickly transforms want into need and need into greed, resulting in the "me generation," spawned, according to Tom Wolfe, in the 1970s. And where there is affluence, the satisfactions can be obtained with relative ease and effortlessness. They acquire a sense of urgency, and they are readily purchased from an all too accommodating economy. Style usurps the role of character, and impressions are mistaken for identity. The price tag and the label become the signs of success. Students' sense of success is molded by what's fashionable and what will yield a material payoff. Skinner accelerated the process by insisting upon an incentive-reinforcement which was immediate and tangible. Educational technology bought into the system *in toto*. Rewards are not necessarily improper, nor need students always be required to defer gratification; but rewards should come only after effort, and there should be a contingency relationship between the two.

Seligman's seminal studies on learned helplessness demonstrated that there must be a contingency relationship between actions and consequences if character is to develop and self-esteem is to accrue. Individual abilities, he maintains, must be matched "to a harsh standard" if ego strength is to emerge. "A sense of worth, mastery, or self-esteem cannot be bestowed. It can only be earned. . . . If we remove the obstacles, difficulties, anxiety and competition from the lives of our young people, we may no longer see generations of young people who have a sense of dignity, power and worth."[36]

The contingency paradigm provides a feedback feature, and behaviors can be quickly assessed in terms of the consequences. Behaviors that are ineffective can be modified through critical analysis, and application of a suitable alternative strategy can lead to solutions of problems. Students must see clearly the cause-effect relationship, and must be given, with supervision, the directions and resources to make the necessary corrections.

Maturity by definition involves the delay of gratification. Growth of character requires that present benefits be deferred for greater rewards later, based upon that growth. But when character is considered a quaint anachronism which better fits a Victorian setting, there is little incentive to wait it out. Hence, we witness the rationale for imprudent condoning and distribution of birth-control devices to students within schools. Students, we are told, will engage in sex; ergo, we should provide them with protection. Whenever the issue of abstinence is raised, a condescending and amused smirk crosses the face of our self-styled "trashers of tradition," and they tell us that that's the way it is. But if the way "it is" is not the way it "should be," are we justified in engaging in duplicity by providing a preventive means for a prohibited end? Without technology, prophylactics and abortions would not be available. If we did not have these preventive and abortive means, would we so cavalierly consent to a practice? If anything, it is a banality to raise moral questions of practice. Morality like metaphysics has been rendered passé. We are a culture interested only in control of dire consequences which, of course, we find we are, after all, incapable of controlling. We care little for the act that precipitates the crisis as long as we can escape any serious consequences. But the tragic misunderstanding that deludes us is that consequences are inescapable. Once we decide to do anything, the consequences are out of our hands. We set in operation a series of events that can neither be controlled nor completely predicted. The flaw in our reasoning, perhaps the fatal flaw,

involves the naive and arrogant assumption that we are capable of anticipating outcomes unerringly, and we can predict consequences accurately.
The mystique of science and the cockeyed optimism of a gullible public
combine to produce a conspiracy of uncritical consent to the futuristic
manifesto that's promised to us. We have played into the hands of master
manipulators whose clever concealment of potential disasters has lulled
us into a collective complacency about the unfolding and potentially
frightening futures they may create. Only scenarios of progress and
promising futures are being presented to us, driven by the new technologies that will shape society like a *Walden Two* plan book. Panegyrics of
a computer-controlled paradise proliferate. Computer technology, we are
told, will eliminate planning error, will forecast with uncanny accuracy,
and will produce perfect physical and social environments for our brave
new world.

A recent article from a local newspaper applauds the promise of "roads
to the future" where driving will be left to technology. Computerized
highway systems promise to eliminate traffic congestion, its accompanying pollution, time waste, and psychological energy-consumption problems. "Successive stages of escalating sophistication" when in place, we
are told, will eliminate one of the great urban burdens—traffic jams.
Another scenario of the promised land where systems engineering made
possible by computer technology is added to the dream book. But we've
heard all this before, and it becomes another case of the cure becoming
worse than the illness. The technology that has caused the traffic disarray
in the first place is now touted as the new solution.[37] Little wonder that
cynicism has become the malaise of this computer culture. Promising
much, delivering little. Daydreams for a better tomorrow soon change into
today's nightmares.

Because we have allowed ourselves to believe, perhaps out of desperation, the lies of past promises, we no longer recognize truth. We accept
the masquerades of modernity. Masks are mistaken for faces so we settle
for appearances. The grand, extremely well staged, extravaganza is both
entertaining and promising, so we settle for the theatrics. But when the
curtain comes down and the lights go on, we will be face to face with an
unavoidably painful and inescapable reality. What do we do then? Seek
and accept another play?

Transcendence can save us from the perennial peril that technology
presents. Unless we are driven by a death wish, unless we are bent, like
beached whales, on leaving our natural environment where we only can
survive, we must struggle through this technological jungle in which
electronic and mechanical monsters threaten to devour us. Transcendence

alone can lead us to truth. Technology can only claim to make us happy. Technology cares little if at all for truth. Truth comes to be defined functionally, and the test for truth is always a pragmatic one—does it work? And technology's great affirmation is that it does work. What technology offers us is always offered on the basis of a better life, a better standard of living, a more convenient and comfortable lifestyle—in other words, happiness. And self-actualization has been misconstrued as happiness. To seek to be self-actualized is to seek for happiness, so we climb aboard the technological merry-go-round confident that the gold ring is there for the grasping.

Happiness as the gift of science, according to Ellul, surfaced seriously after 1920, and for the next two decades, the genie of technology, liberated from its ideological lamp, got to work and transformed American society, most notably, by the mass production of accelerated means of travel and transport. It also dangled before us the allurement of a visual medium that now keeps us transfixed to the tube.[38] When happiness becomes the goal of life, individually and collectively, we begin to submit to the dictates of whatever provides that happiness, and technology clearly has the upper hand when happiness is equated with the reduction of stress and effort, the maximizing of pleasure, and sensory stimulation. Happiness then, according to that definition, excludes agonism. Anything that requires effort and struggle to produce or acquire is anathema. But there is the substitution of the pseudoagon in all this because an occasional twinge of conscience (a remnant from our moralistic forebears we are told) will not allow us to be the recipients of a free lunch every day. Somewhere along the way, we must pay some small price and so we have introduced the conscience-soothing substitutes for real effort. Aerobic workouts in demure settings as well as pleasure-pain activities (jogging, biking, etc.) are examples of acceptable substitutes, but the more flagrant manifestations of pseudoagon are seen in the walk, rocking chair, and dance marathons where nothing of substance is accomplished, but they are all events and activities legitimized with an air of endurance and denial. Rather than real work and honest labor to obtain funds to feed the poor, marches are organized and sponsors are recruited and people are "paid" to walk certain distances or dance for so many hours, and the proceeds go to charity. Perspiration and bloodshot eyes, thereby, testify to the effort expended; the money collected for worthy causes placates the conscience, and, after all, it was jolly good fun. But this is not the same as working at a job that is painful, and producing something of substance out of the labor which, in fact, may be done in isolation without the media recognition that makes the participants celebrities. Even this is a form of happiness and the sentimentality that typically accompanies these events reveals their shallowness.

There are very few people in our Western world today who have earned the right to address this generation from a prophetic posture with a clarion call for reform and rethinking. Affluence, indulgence, and self-pre-occupation have coöpted even the self-ordained, highly stylized pretenders to the prophet's role. G. K. Chesterton has been resurrected by an insightful few who glean from his trenchant (albeit chatty) writings a vintage harvest of wisdom. C. S. Lewis of Cambridge, and, more recently, Stanley Jaki have been influenced immensely by Chesterton. Malcolm Muggeridge, former editor of Britain's *Punch*, with his mildly cynical sensitivity and his acerbic style has been unafraid to declare that the emperor is naked. However, one of the few twentieth-century lives that has suffered the utmost agony, survived the unendurable, and lived to reflect on and record his experiences belongs to Victor Frankl, Austrian psychiatrist. His autobiographical *Man's Search for Meaning*, far from being a sterile exercise in academic banality, pulsates with agonic reality as he shares the revelations received from his encounter with barbarity in Auschwitz. Surprising it is that such intensely actualizing insights came in a place of utter destitution, of naked privation. Not within a well-equipped classroom with computers buzzing, media abounding, and conveniences abundant, but within a stark, stygian internment camp (how grotesque the euphemism sounds!) Frankl, in struggling to make sense of it all, grasped the true golden ring of reality. In a place that he describes as utter primitivism, he came to understand that "it was possible for spiritual life to deepen." Frankl describes a typical scene occurring just before dawn, when ill-clad, prisoners trudged through the darkness, fighting the bitter cold on route to the day's work site. A fellow prisoner commented about his wife.

That brought thoughts of my own wife to mind. . . . A thought transfixed me: for the first time in my life I saw the truth as it is set into song by so many poets, proclaimed as the final wisdom by so many thinkers. The truth—that love is the ultimate and highest goal to which man can aspire. Then I grasped the meaning of the greatest secret that human poetry and human thought and belief have to impart: *The salvation of man is through love and in love.* I understood how a man who has nothing left in this world still may know bliss be it only for a brief moment, in the contemplation of his beloved.[39]

Transcendence takes us out of and beyond ourselves; not, of course, in some astral projection or out-of-body experience. But we are liberated from the shackles of self and, paradoxically, are allowed to become our selves. We are freed to be ourselves, truly self-actualized, but only through self-transcendence. Schools miss the mark by stopping short of this essential goal of transcendence. Satiated, indulged, undisciplined, and bored students result from school programs and environments that make them the ultimate center of the enterprise and clutter their lives with the technological trivia and toys that keep them from ever having to face the true reality of their struggling selves. The classic blunder of the court decisions about religion in the schools is not that the First Amendment to the Constitution has been interpreted as excluding religious dogma from schools, but that it has become a mandate for the removal of everything spiritual. God doesn't need the help of pressure and political action groups to maintain a place in the educational program, but the extirpation of the spiritual and the capitulation to the narrowly secular decisively exclude transcendence from the very place where students are expected to learn the essentials of life. Technology has become the principal instrument of this exclusion process because it cannot abide spirituality. Technology depends upon and thrives in naturalistic soil. The ethereal spiritual atmosphere of transcendence is inimical to technology. It would be imprudent at this point in contemporary society's ideological agenda and impossible at this stage of economic development to endorse a wholesale abandonment of technology and a return to a more simplified environment. Such a true return to fundamentals and "back to basics" would be met with laughable disdain, and cries of reactionism. But I would not be alone in calling for a moratorium on the proliferation of educational technology, and a scaling back of the role of hardware and software systems within schools. Others, either from conscience or from fear, have joined their voices in the swelling chorus of Wagnerian apocalyptism.[40]

Frightful scenarios of technological plunder are so plentiful today that their number desensitizes us to our plight. Because hyperbole is the characteristic verbal image of our age, we assume that everything is presented out of proportion, and that worse-case scenarios are fabrications of doomsday prophets and nay-sayers. But Lasch has summed up the thinking of many and has honestly if pessimistically captured the mood of the age:

As the twentieth century approaches its end, the conviction grows that many other things are ending too. Storm warnings, portents, hints of catastrophe haunt our times. The "sense of an ending" which has given shape to so much of twentieth-century literature, now pervades the popular imagination as well.[41]

Dire forebodings as these should cause us to reconsider the enterprise in which we are engaged. A rediscovery, if that's what is needed, of transcendence, like a beacon light or better yet—a star—(a less-technological metaphor) can guide us out of this philosophical fog. Such a luminous ecstasy dawned upon Frankl during a gray day:

The dawn was gray around us; gray was the sky above; gray the snow in the pale light of dawn; gray the rags in which my fellow prisoners were clad and gray their faces. I was again conversing with my wife or perhaps I was struggling to find the *reason* for my sufferings, my slow dying. In a last violent protest against hopelessness of imminent death, I sensed my spirit piercing through the enveloping gloom. I felt it transcend the hopeless, meaningless world and from somewhere I heard a victorious "Yes" in answer to my question of the existence of an ultimate purpose. At that moment a light was lit in a distant farmhouse which stood on the horizon as if painted there, in the midst of the miserable gray of a dawning morning . . . the light shineth in darkness.[42]

Transcendence involves a vision. Students' eyes must be opened to the possibilities not just within themselves but beyond themselves. Without the beyond, the within becomes a blind alley without any light to guide them. If we content them with a limited horizon that goes not beyond the borders of video screens, they will (as they have) mistake the shadows for the reality. Plato warned us about this millennia ago, and he rightly regarded the transcendent vision as the only true means of spiritual liberation. Curriculums that are constructed upon pragmatic foundations can never reach into the realm of the spirit. As important as the applied areas of study may be for maintaining and improving the technological superstructure, more critical still is the moral and spiritual substructure that provides any permanency to the social order and personal psyche.[43] Are we equipping students to survive in the cultural Auschwitz they may encounter? Sooner or later, we all encounter a puzzling reality that is not amenable to solutions offered by more-sophisticated software. Greater scientific power does little for the doubts that disturb us and the demons that terrorize us. Power can make us go faster, jump higher, calculate more quickly, and conjure up electronic imagery to amuse us, but in silent moments of inner emptiness, personal loneliness, and self-doubt, it can be nothing more than a temporary pacifier. It offers no permanent solution for the agonies of the spirit.

Imagination, unless it too has been sadly trivialized to mean anything that is unconventional (as is often the case with its frequently bastardized twin—creativity), points us to something beyond matter and time. "The imagination and the heart, like the mind, have powers of transcendence which the body lacks."[44] Education must include imagination. Good pedagogy takes children beyond themselves; it gives the mind and soul wings on which to travel. Science can deal with the world of millimeters and microseconds; it can extend our senses to peer to the edge of the solar system and within the droplet on a microscope slide. But science says absolutely nothing about destiny, and values and purpose. B. F. Skinner sought to expunge purpose from human life, and the generation of behavioral engineers subscribing unquestioningly, as they did, to and functioning from Skinner's operant-conditioning paradigm succeeded in convincing educators that purpose was an atavistic artifact. But Stanley Jaki has concluded that the "ravages of reductionism" bred by logical positivism have led on to blind alleys,[45] and that there are unmistakable "pointers of purpose" even in something so blatantly naturalistic as Darwin's theory.[46]

Peter Berger has gone a step further, and in his sociological analysis of the rediscovery of the supernatural, he has identified what he considers to be specific "signals of transcendence." He suggests that there are within natural empirical reality "prototypical human gestures" that transcend the normal everyday world and alert us to a reality both beyond and superior to our sensory awareness. For purposes of our argument, it is worth examining these signals and analyzing their possible role in enriching the imaginative element of education. Berger identifies arguments based on these signals and contends that a cogent case can be made for transcendence.[47] These arguments are

1. order
2. play
3. hope
4. damnation
5. humor

Each of these signals points beyond a self-contained and humanly created cosmos. Certainly, they pierce the technological control-mania because technology precludes the presence of these elements. Order is artificially imposed by technology; it is not imputed. Ordering implies traditional patterns that continue to persist and to which, if only nostalgically, groups and cultures cling. But technology's task is to dissolve tradition; it must break molds and jettison age-old conventions that circumscribe behavior and impede progress. The only order technology cherishes is the monotonous, routinized procedures of the assembly line or the programmed regularities of the computer. Play is unpredictable, whimsical, and, as Huizinga points out, serves no purposes of immediate, material interests or biological needs-satisfaction but belongs more properly to the realm of the sacred.[48] By being spontaneous, true play is nonprogrammable. Technology has redefined play in the form of organized games which are something quite different. Even the agonal games which began with the ancient Greeks were playful in their singular devotion to deities. Games were agonal demonstrations of transcendence. Games fabricated by industry, with their most lurid manifestation in video games, are not in the least playful. They are principally diversionary; they take up time, but they are, nevertheless, inventions of technocrats intended for capitalistic gain. Play, as ludic activity, points beyond time and materialism and frees the person from both. Time is often lost sight of in play. Not uncommonly, children, particularly, lose track of time when they play. When they are merely "playing games," time controls everything they do whether in arcades or Little League. A rediscovery of real play would profitably rejuvenate education for children. The carefree playful experiences more common in agonal societies preserve the element and innocence of childhood. Postman's lamentation for lost childhood underscores the tragedy of a generation that has robbed youth of the transcendent wonder of play.[49] The premature induction of children into the adult world, or more correctly the adolescent world, is in part attributable to the lack of whimsy and the loss of wonder. Everything within the adult world is graphically portrayed on television and in the media generally and children are hastily escorted, typically for mercenary purposes, into the consumerism of adulthood. Children should be children, as Rousseau stated and Dewey echoed, before they are adults.[50] Adolescence has become the marginal shadow land where children are not permitted the innocence of childhood, nor are they required to fulfill the responsibilities of adulthood; and so they sample the elicit fruit of adulthood's savage garden, yet incapable of being held accountable for their forays into the forbidden land. Moratoriums are difficult to impose and more difficult to maintain, but wisdom would decree that children before the age of six should be permitted no television viewing and no computer contact, and only limited and regulated contact until the age of twelve. If we can spare them the inanities of the media and technology before that age, they may develop sufficient sensibilities to forgo them entirely.

Hope is a ship that sails into the future, but it is anchored in the past. Without hope, there's little use in planning and anticipating. Hope is the celestial star preeminently. We are required to look upward, and every time we do, we increase the likelihood that we will view the present as a little less important. Hope is not simply a future vision, it is an upward vision. The straight probing at ground level may try to see what lies up ahead, but it does not guarantee that when we arrive, we will have accomplished any worthwhile goal. Curriculums need to be predicated upon hope. Inner goals that can be realized only in the future and which require persistence depend upon hope. Children will not pursue goals, regardless of how appealingly they are presented, unless they believe they have a chance of reaching them. Frankl saw that internment-camp survival required strength that came from hope. If in that indescribable horror and privation, a prisoner had any chance to endure, he needed to be given "inner strength by pointing out to him a future goal to which he could look forward. . . . It is a peculiarity of man that he can only live by looking to the future . . . and this is his salvation in the most difficult moments of his existence."[51]

There appears to be consensus in society that we are a people who have lost hope. If, as Seligman has demonstrated, that at the personal level, hope is the psychological prophylactic against learned helplessness, then at the cultural level, hope is equally critical against social despair.[52] Alienation, normlessness, rootlessness, powerlessness—all of the pathologies which have been identified—are part of the modern crisis. The literature is replete with redundant references to the alienation crises of our times. Technology has ruinously deluded society into believing it offers a way of hope out of the present despair. It has said this since its inception, but the truth is that it undermines hope; it offers only "hype." Each new promise becomes a prelude to yet another crisis. The soteriological claims of technology have ended up as empty boasts. New techniques, like a modern-day Moses, promise to deliver us from our human bondage. They portend the dawning of a new day when our "Red Seas" will miraculously open on the social landscape, and we shall all stride bravely toward the promised land. Technology as soteriology has become the new theology, and the technocrats with their esoteric numerology and cryptic computer coding are the new priesthood leading the dutiful but deceived worshippers in paying homage to the latest god in the scientific pantheon. But we find the technological hype is another variation of hocus-pocus and behind the curtains containing the oracle is a sorry substitute for the Wizard of Oz.

Sociologists have warned us about the currently popular cult of mystification. Andreski calls it sorcery parading in scientific garb.[53] It is nothing more than mumbo jumbo. The most audacious kind of pretense imaginable is gullibly accepted as credible science. It's the adult version of "playing doctor." Costumes and paraphernalia give the appearance of importance and authenticity while self-deceived and self-styled experts pontificate on any subject. It is the sophist's game as old as civilization, but the difference today is it has become a tyrannical enterprise. Nothing can be prescribed without the endorsement of these experts.

Ellul has targeted these experts as has Andreski, and they both warn us of the disaster awaiting any group that defers without challenge to their pontifications. The loss of reliance upon personal capacity for scrutiny soon leads to loss of other important attributes. Technical expertise should be limited to things. When machines break down, qualified technicians are required to repair them. When the construction of desirable goods is needed, artisans should be employed to build what is necessary. But it is foolhardy to relinquish control of society to the technocratic elite and equally malicious to allow the structures for society to be placed in the hands of the makers of things. Education has been shaped in this half century by pedagogical technocrats who are ever refining their skills and proficiencies in the use of things, but who are woefully, scandalously deficient in philosophical reflection. Even as the governmental sphere laments the loss of statesmanship, substituting for it mere politicians, so education has mistaken management for leadership. Sir Richard Livingstone presciently envisioned the sad, unfolding scenario of an education that would mistake means for ends, and that would entrust the enterprise to "leaders" equipped with all of the managerial and technical expertise of assembling greater and more-efficient means but who had not the simplest understanding of the ends that should be pursued.[54] That continues to be the critical issue in society and certainly in education.

Toward what ends should we move? What are goals worth pursuing? Every phase of education, from national organizational levels to the school classrooms follows the managerial model. Behavior is managed; resources are managed; time is managed. Manipulative modes of interaction, based heavily on industrial and behavioral psychology, utilize time and motion studies, baseline data determinants, and narrowly quantitative categories for analysis and measurement. The dull, tedious, and barren terminology of the laboratory and the office (on-task, off-task, reinforcement schedules, management by objectives, ownership, etc.), that depersonalizes and dehumanizes, replaces the fluid, imaginative metaphors that inspire students engaged in creative enterprise. Artistry and animation are displaced by automation.

When education is constrained by canons of science, and when teaching and learning are construed as programming and processing, students become infected with a robopathic disease which saps their vital energy through a process of insipid conformity, and makes them function only effectively in a sick society. And we conclude with Wordsworth that we are "now convinced at heart how little that to which alone we give the name of education hath to do with real feeling and just sense."[55]

This may not seem to be a suitable forum for discussion of Berger's next signal of transcendence, namely—damnation. By damnation, he means that certain acts of utter outrageousness demand moral retribution. Reminiscent of man's inhumanity to man, violations against human dignity, that defy explanation, demand retribution. The very fact that we have the capacity for such acute consciousness and conscience alerts us to realities beyond the merely mortal; otherwise why would we be so indignant when atrocities occur? The most memorable for this generation are those associated with the horrors of the holocaust, and with war in general. But the increasing and alarming incidence of abuses, principally against defenseless children, strikes our most-basic sensitivities. But even in this arena, technology has dulled our sensitivities and calloused our consciences by cloaking acts of barbarity in seemingly innocuous and acceptable scientific costumes. Actions that would have outraged an indignant public a generation ago are not only ignored but often condoned. Barbarities, impossible previously except as a result of demonic collusion, are now, by virtue of easy technology, commonplace, unchallenged—even unquestioned. Most commentators credit Hitler with developing the first modern technological horror. And superior German engineering, scientific advancement, and applied technology made possible unimagined atrocities. Cremation ovens, genetic engineering, and eugenic selection, as well as the conventional military technology, provided the means for Hitler to carry out his diabolical schemes in Nazi Germany. But today, in many parts of the world including the United States, similar practices prevail, and we congratulate ourselves for our sophistication in applying these techniques to social problems.

The complacent claim that technology is neutral in all this is, of course, by now recognized by anyone with an ounce of perspicacity as fraudulent. Technique is never neutral. Parker Palmer has noted that every epistemology (and technology is an epistemology of power) carries with it a morality. Technology advocates the ethic that the means justify the end, or as some scientists declare that there is no difference between means and ends. It matters little what the eventual or intended outcome is; means have an inviolate claim irrespective of any anticipated or unanticipated consequences. Ellul, most vocal in condemnation of this arrogance, has now concluded that no means should be allowed unless there is incontrovertible evidence and proof that the means can convincingly demonstrate that only good will come from them.[56]

Education has become a means game. Educators, driven as they allow themselves to be by politicians and demagogues, are never satisfied with what is presently available. Surely, one would think, the economics of the situation alone with unmanageable expenses and nonfundable budgets should slow the innovation process and soften the strident rhetoric. The whole concept of construction within education, whether facilities or curriculums, is caloric and consumptive. Eat and heat! Gobble up everything available. Recycling would not be necessary if there was little cycling in the first place. Copiers churn out paperwork, much of which is unnecessary. Where chalk would be sufficient, computer graphics are now required. Where the sound of a teacher's voice would be both more efficient and humane, the expensive video apparatus drones on and distances.

We have deceived ourselves into thinking that retribution is an outdated ethic that was compelling only in educational days of the McGuffey reader. But it is catching up with us, and we may to our peril find that what we thought we banished from the scientific world will reemerge in a shiny, fabricated form. Toynbee told civilizations that they sow the seeds of their own demise. We have in our social and ideological laboratories created a virulent strain which awaits the suitable time to appear; a recessive gene that requires only the incestuous mating of technology with a non-transcendent view of life, and an epidemic of unimagined proportions will be upon us.

Finally, Berger sees humor as another pointer to the reality beyond. This may be the most sanguine and redeeming of his signals. Why do we laugh at all? How, in the face of imminent peril, can we find time to smile? This laughter is not the inane guffaw of a lunatic who is happy about the prospect of disaster, nor is it the diversionary comedy of paid performers. Genuine ludic laughter stares in the face of tragedy, and believes it is not the end or the ultimate. Laughter distances us if only briefly from the futility of all our efforts gone awry. Education should be a joyous enterprise, and laughter is a key element which keeps antagonisms from reducing the participants to adversaries. Teaching-learning is an advocacy relationship based on mutually perceived worthwhile goals and upon mutual respect. However, no pedagogical situation is without its annoyances, and antagonisms can readily develop. Laughter is the prophylactic that keeps the environment free from the enervating effects of antagonisms. Laughter loads the dice in favor of advocacy. William Glasser sees laughter as a psychiatric source of strength.[57] Laughter allows confrontation to be noncombative and alerts us to the temporality of all our efforts. Although education is undoubtedly a serious endeavor, it must inevitably meet at times with failure. Failure that is not redeemed can devastate the most-ardent student. Humor transcends the immediate, the moment. A teacher with humor, with a chuckle, communicates that the defeat is neither permanent nor insurmountable.

Technology is humorless. It provides a fraudulent, synthetic "laugh track" technique. It even creates dolls that laugh on cue, and computer software that amuses us. But amusement is not humor. Humor is a conscious recognition of the disparity between real events. It is not a denial of reality but the superimposition of a higher reality upon the immediate reality. Andreski's words about humor are relevant:

[L]aughter is a mental mechanism which enables us to face reality without falling into despondency or delusion. As people who have sunk into apathy seldom bother us by rushing into print, delusion (leaving aside deceit) constitutes the chief obstacle to the progress of our understanding of society.... A sense of humor is the most reliable external indicator of the likelihood of immunity from this folly, and of the ability to appraise social situations realistically.[58]

Chapter 6

Ciphering the Schools

More than two millennia ago Socrates said that the secret of life is to "know thyself." The key to success in life and in education is identity. A knowledge of oneself is prerequisite to knowledge of anyone or anything else. Augustine believed that we start with a knowledge of self and proceed to a knowledge of God. Everything begins with the basic understanding of one's inmost being. The ontological issue, most succinctly voiced by Hamlet, involves being and identity. To answer Hamlet's query (to be or not to be) in the affirmative requires a clear affirmation of identity. It seems so elementary that it should not require extensive discussion. Exactly who am I? What does it mean to have an identity? Technological societies are plagued with people whose sense of self has been underdeveloped, weakened, or damaged. The modern world for all its talk of fulfillment and self-definition has become a poor place for people to find themselves. In fact, the modern world is notoriously a place of lostness. The utterances of existential anguish take a myriad forms and voices in literature. It has become a truism, an obvious fact of industrialized society that traditional ways of achieving and maintaining identity are threatened by the intrusiveness of impersonal technology. Anonymity and anomie are the twin perils of modernity. Riesman's "lonely crowd" is all about this.[1] Durkheim's classic study of suicide links alienation and anonymity, and demonstrates the propensity of ciphered people for self-destructive behavior.[2] The common wisdom coupled with statistical studies have demonstrated that when industrialism comes with its fragmentation, forms of suicide follow. In preindustrial societies, identity comes from face-to-face (primary) relationships. Families, clans, and tribes prescribe relationships and circumscribe behavior. Even today, visits to non-Western or partially westernized societies reveal, not only prescribed roles in the social stratification, but an integrated network of underlying and organic relationships that gives each person a certain sense of personhood. The word "identity" finds its etymology in relationships and to be without an integrated social network is to be without identity. The abundant anthropological and sociological studies, as well as the popular perusings of social commentators, have examined this issue with intensity, and conclusively declare that identity is crucial for adequate social and psychological functioning. Isolates not only have few, if any, friends; they are friendless with themselves. The universality of social needs is by now an uncontested premise of civilization. The reclusive figure choosing isolation in a world of his own making (even the ascetic-monastic) is viewed quizzically and skeptically by members of society. Maslow along with other motivational researchers places the belonging-need fairly high on the human-needs hierarchy. The psychological literature dealing with deprivation of social contacts reveals subjects with psychopathological syndromes of depression, withdrawal, psychophysical symptoms, and suicidal tendencies—people of pain. Social environments that distance people from themselves and from each other promote distortions in identity.

Criticisms of schools as often sterile or pathogenic places that serve as breeding grounds for alienation are abundant and not without merit.[3] However, the corrective to this condition lies not in the incessant introduction of "bogus innovation" which has the similitude of science. Application of scientific principles, methodological procedures, and behavioristic models has not always enhanced the educational enterprise, and it has not provided effective means for students to achieve identity. Schools, in concert with other large impersonal institutions in this country, have become mechanisms for ciphering students. The "ciphering game" is recklessly reductionistic. Students become objects. Human attributes and qualities take on the mechanistic properties of variables. And measurement is equated with evaluation. We have become a society that worships numbers, and we defer to the technocryptic priesthood that mouths its arcane, gnostic nostrums. Behaviorism at its worst contributed significantly to this cultic pedagogy, but schools had already been prepared by the naturalistic value system begun with the rejection of transcendentals and fostered by the accretions of Darwinism, Freudianism, and Pavlovian conditioning. E. L. Thorndike played no small part in the conspiracy when he pronounced that all knowable knowledge is quantifiable and, hence, measurable.[4] It was a small step from all this to the technocryptic transformation of education from an enterprise in enlightenment into an exercise in management and control.

Qualities are not easily controllable. Qualities are illusive, mercurial, and abstract. Statements that project educational goals in transcendent terms are not readily amenable to measurement. The introduction of values and aesthetics into the educational endeavor is resisted by the scientific-management mind-set, because these intentions are not transferable directly to observable behaviors. Of course, this type of mentality (the word is used intentionally) refuses to acknowledge that the soul can see, and that intuition has its criteria for confirmation. Unless all expectations are stated measurably and behaviorally, accountability, presumably along with accuracy, is precluded. Simplicity and parsimony demand neat, succinct (even if unimportant) educational statements whose effects are immediately, readily, and objectively measurable. Invariably this means the development of a test—an assessment instrument.[5] The stage is now set for unadorned, unambiguous quantification.

Names are messy. Numbers are neat. Frankl observed the troublesome nature of names for the capos in the internment camp in which he was imprisoned. As he records it: "All that mattered was that one's own name and that of one's friend were crossed off the list of victims, though everyone knew that for each man saved another victim had to be found. ... It did not really matter which, since each of them was nothing but a number."[6]

Our world today is a world of codes and coding. The information-processing model of learning prefers a communications approach where messages are coded and decoded. Everything is reduced to a datum which has a corresponding number. Learning is then viewed as the processing of these discrete bits of data which are then stored and retrieved. Schools are inclined to consider education to be little more than the accumulation of these bits of information. All learning is, therefore, reducible to digits. Measurement techniques relying almost exclusively upon identification of these bits dominate education. The proliferation of standardized instruments makes their use unavoidable. The shrill cry for accountability in education compels administrators to insist on concrete, tangible, observable measurement data. Tests are ubiquitous agents, not only of assessment but of direction, for it is a maxim that "whatever measures mandates." The assessment cannot be divorced from the articulation of educational goals. It was an in-house joke in the department of the university where I did my doctoral studies that dissertations were determined by the availability of measurement instruments. Projects and problems were not pursued pristinely for their scholarly potential or profit. If empirical assessment means were not available, there was little likelihood that a student would pursue a topic, irrespective of its appeal or contribution to the world of scholarly endeavor.

All things are defined in terms of the operational means used to measure the thing. Operationalization requires a behavioristic, quantitative technique for determination of outcomes, and, therefore, demands that anything remotely transcendent be converted into a form that is directly and objectively apprehensible. The most notable and controversial example of this is the hotly and belligerently debated issue of intelligence. No variable is as critical to success in contemporary schools than intelligence, and there is consensus that such a thing as intelligence exists; but the debate heats up and threatens to become explosive when the means to measure it are introduced. Intelligence tests have been labeled discriminatory, elitist, and imperious because these instruments are not neutral but do, in fact, define the nature of intelligence, and are, thereby, necessarily prejudiced in favor of select groups within society. People who do well on tasks the test targets will gain higher scores (larger numbers) and consequently higher places in society. The number that the test yields eclipses all other considerations. Elusive concepts such as intelligence as well as other variables with which education is concerned are, ipso facto, defined by the means used to measure them, and this deceptive tautology dazzles the uninitiated and reinforces the privileged position of the people in power.

The single most influential culprit in the contemporary conspiracy to efface identity is the computer. All cults with authoritarian correctness create conformity among members, cloning their constituencies. Computer technology has achieved a cultlike status in society, and an unrivaled demagogic dominance. The nerve network of the social system is regulated by computer central. Nothing moves without a computer command. An ever-growing corpus of computer polemics has emerged as the peril of computer power has become more apparent. Weizenbaum's early warning shot was fired decades ago,[7] and since then volleys have been hurled. Jaki, an astute historian of science, sounded his alarm.[8] Ellul has been an insistent sentinel of the peril, and Roszak has unsparingly heaped scorn on the menace that no longer simply lurks at the door but has taken over the house.[9]

Modern society's early embrace of computer technology, like similar seductions by machines in other ages, and its enchantment with the new technology were motivated by claims of global enlightenment and a quasi-religious salvation—a soteriology of silence:

The computer, in short, promises by technology a Pentecostal condition of universal understanding and unity. The next logical step would seem to be . . . to bypass language in favor of general cosmic consciousness . . . the condition of speechlessness that could confer a perpetuity of collective harmony and peace.[10]

Now at the outset it needs to be said that computers have played a positive role as aids. Tedious and time-consuming computations have been reduced to manageable proportions. Computer simulations have aided in forecasting, and computer-generated models in medicine have made possible diagnoses that were heretofore impossible. All of these areas have benefitted from the advent of computer technology. Within schools, when educational technology, typically classified as audio-visual aids, constituted adjuncts and supplements, learning was enhanced, enriched, and even made more enjoyable. But all of this is decidedly different than having computers become the driving force behind the enterprise. Education has let the computer call the shots, and often these shots are deadening.

An article in *World Press Review* warns against trusting computers completely. In "The Trouble with Computers," attention is called to the numerous critical instances in which computer mistakes threatened lives and whole societies. One expert in computer safety is quoted as saying that "the more we rely on computers, the more drastic the accidents will be."[11] Faulty software programs created disaster situations at nuclear power plants, national railroad lines, banks, and businesses. The increasingly complex programs increase the probability of computer error with corresponding disastrous possibilities. Horror stories abound of computers out of control—variations on the Frankenstein fiasco in which the object of study achieved a life of its own and became an uncontrollable terror. A brief article I wrote for a local newspaper was entitled "Frankenstein: Computer Literate?"[12] It was simply intended to be a caveat for the public about the ingenuous overreliance upon computers in schools. I was amazed at the negative reaction by my academic colleagues who saw what I considered to be a rather harmless item as a challenge to their professional prerogatives. But I stand by what I wrote. Even if we dress up the technology with terms like "user friendly" in hopes of disarming hostile reactors, we cannot dismiss the danger inherent in this ubiquitous intruder. Are schools really legitimate places for computers? In particular, is the elementary school a legitimate place? Should young children be assaulted with computer technology in addition to the video technology that has already rendered them passive spectators?

My call is for a return to agonic education, education that forces students to confront their environments and worlds in creative struggle-conflict.

The dearth of confrontation with the enigmas of life deceives children into believing that all difficulties can be readily resolved by pushing a button or pressing a key. The television and the computer share similarities in their technologies. Both of them deal with images on screens and demand constantly-changing imagery. Attention for protracted periods of times (such as reading a book or listening to lectures requires) is discouraged. Speed, visually attractive imagery, and participant passivity are common elements. Television has promoted passive learning and shaped a generation of learners who are generally incapable of initiating activities or engaging in spontaneous play. Despite claims to the contrary, so-called interactive television and computer software programs require reactions rather than interactions. The program parameters limit respondent options and do not encourage or permit creative, spontaneous initiations. Studies of the effects of television on children tend to agree in their assessment that children in contemporary society have been cloned into a colony of unanimated beings who seek titillation but avoid trial.

Computers distance students from the real world. Agonic involvement is eliminated and replaced with mediated imagery which is in effect a distortion of reality. Zajonc, a physicist, agrees: "the computer distances us from action. . . . it usurps important activities essential for the child's cognitive development."[13] He contends that the computer should be simply a supplement not a teacher surrogate. Students experience an "atrophy of feeling" when they are excessively exposed to any technology. The rich sensory life that initiates them into the joys and struggles of humankind is denied them, and the synthetic world of technology stunts the growth of identity and self-understanding. Douglas Sloan places the problem in keen perspective:

If we are to be full of life and fully alive, it is the increase in our capacity to be aware of the world through our senses which has first to be achieved. For the healthy development of growing children especially the importance of an environment rich in sensory experience—color, sound, smell, movement, texture, *a direct acquaintance with nature* (italics mine), and so forth—cannot be too strongly emphasized. And that fine sensitivity in discrimination which is the heart of emotional rationality arises in working and playing with the materials of the senses—through storytelling, drama, movement, music, painting, handwork, encounters with responsible, involved other beings. . . . The lack of such an education can produce only a society that, whatever its cleverness and power, becomes increasingly philistine, insensitive to life, and uncaring because incapable of truly knowing. And it becomes more and more a menace to itself and others.[14]

Some feeble efforts to justify computers as aids to social development, in my judgment, are unconvincing. Seymour Papert, inventor of the software program LOGO, claims that computers can facilitate social interaction. Several sets of studies were conducted by two researchers who concluded that computers acted as social facilitators, that students were more inclined to interact with their peers with computers, than those without them. They summarize their findings:

[R]esearch findings do not support the contention that computers cause isolation or classroom disruption. . . . Evidence from all of the research reports reviewed here indicates that the introduction of instructional computing has no deleterious effects on social and cooperative activity in the classroom and that positive social interactions are often enhanced.[15]

Several deficiencies surface in a perusal of the article. The studies seem to have been done with very young children in early grades. At this level, children are naturally curious, socially active, and typically need little prodding to engage in and sustain social interaction. Would similar results be obtained with older children? The article does not address the social-ization of students into the computer culture of the classroom. It is one thing to engage in playful activity involving the novelty of computers; it is another to be immersed systematically and longitudinally into an educational environment in which the computer is the icon. What will happen to students over time? The television may appear as an innocuous instrument that excites and titillates children; they even gleefully engage initially in social interaction. But over time, the passive engagement with television and the all-consuming appeal of the programming eventually render viewers passively isolated spectators. Computer hackers are not notoriously social beings. W. I. Thompson provides an unflattering portrait of the computer cadre at MIT as "insensitive, unsensuous and possessed by abstractions" whom he contends are unfit to be the "inventors of the future," a future which would serve the "military-industrial space stations serving instant coffee in carcinogenic Styrofoam cups where as much attention will be grudgingly paid to the body as is now in a restroom or restaurant in an American airport."[16] The favorable research findings endorsing computers for young children were published in a journal sympathetic to technology and computer-assisted instruction, and presum-ably would receive less-critical acceptance by peer reviewers who eagerly seek such opportunities to silence the chorus of critics who have assaulted their academic sanctuary and who threaten their credibility.

Echoing Ellul's lament that education has become an apprenticeship to gadgetry, computers, like cancer, metastasize the culture in which they are embedded. A lethal "network" (the term finding increasing currency in contemporary parlance has origins in computer technology) interfacing all facets of the social environment demands (indeed compels) compliance with its technodynamics. The computer becomes an idol within the classroom, creating a cultlike atmosphere redolent with sorcerer's incense and mystical incantations. Classrooms are transformed into techno-idolatrous temples of devotion to the wonders and worship of science. Perhaps temple is too blasphemous a term to associate with the much-too-worldly rites and rituals technology undertakes. Just as the glittering and now distant industrial world of steel and concrete and plastic and glass has turned into weed-infested, decaying, deserted landscapes and abandoned eyesores, so "the culture of hackers, engineers and cognitive scientists . . . brings forth a very peculiar and most unsensuous world of abstract, laboratory ugliness and an electronic umwelt of noisy, fluorescent lights and cathode tubes."[17]

Education should encourage intelligent critique of these new techniques rather than conformity and capitulation. The religious aura that surrounds the creators and operators of these machines and the wisdom that is attributed to the computers are akin to idolatrous worship. Soon, I suspect, along with the presumed (but fallacious) artificial intelligence, computers will assume artificial wisdom. Computers will take on oracular status. There is an uncanny and frightening similarity between the Delphic tradition of Apollonian enlightenment in which the sibyl, mesmerized by hallucinogenic vapors arising from the sacred aperture, pronounced the verdict of the gods and the mysteries of technology as unriddled by the coterie of computer devotees with their esoteric programming language. The whirring, dervishlike, technological gyrations of the computer and then the oracular pontification! Children in the classroom, naive and unsuspecting, accept the pronouncements as the inerrant utterances of an infallible deity.

If the scenario I present appears too extreme and radically "theological" perhaps Robert Sardello's assessment will be more agreeable, for his analysis of the assault of computers upon students is based on the psychological. He states:

The computer, if it is allowed to infiltrate the very heart of education in the particular manner I will outline . . . , will destroy education; not because it is a mechanism and as such threatens to transform human beings into likenesses of itself; the destructive power of the computer is to be found in the fact that it transforms education into psychology.[18]

Sardello claims that the peculiar brand of psychology on which the present computer educational approach is based will produce a generation of psychopaths. He does not object to the utilitarian value of computers as aids in education, much like other hardware that reduces the tedium of computation and classification tasks. What horrifies him is the radical claim that children can learn to think by programming computers and, thereby, be relieved of "the necessity of formal classroom instruction." Seymour Papert with his system of LOGO opts for an artificial system of intelligence which dispenses with traditional structures and the conventional culture. The past, which is the critical element in all cultures, is, by the computer's facility, rendered needless and only the progressive, futuristic view of life in which everything is easily "debugged" is valued. As Sardello describes this emerging psychopathy:

[It] is actually a kind of programming in life, knowing how to debug life. The psychopath does everything effortlessly, freely without any sense of inhibition, restraint, or suppression. Nothing of the world makes a claim on the soul of the psychopath.... Everything is a game—feelings, emotions, courtesy, love, sympathy for others, expression of care... the psychopath can imitate any form of behavior without it's [sic] going through the heart.[19]

Lewis Yablonsky, just a few years before the maniacal onset of "computeritis" captivated the world, observed that a peculiar personality pattern was emerging, which he called "robopathy," as a response to the technological malady. Emotional distance resulting from depersonalization was a clear symptom of the illness. Computers dichotomize feelings and thinking, and create a schizoid mind-set where intelligence becomes machine-controlled and emotions are minimized. Yablonsky casts the matter in cold terms: "This dehumanized level of existence places people in roles where they are actors mouthing irrelevant platitudes, experiencing programmed emotions with little or no compassion or sympathy for other people."[20]

Sherry Turkle shares Sardello's realization that computers have attributed to them psychological as well as physical properties. She observed that young children experience a frustratingly opaque difference in computers whose workings are less intelligible and accessible than simple toys. Mechanical devices that operate solely and observably by principles of physics can be analyzed and disengaged. Children can open toys up and see the parts that constitute the whole apparatus and observe the mechanical logic of the works. But with computers, which are opaque and when examined reveal only computer chips and batteries, the animistic principle of operations is perceived as psychological. Size and complexity, or seeming lack of complexity of parts, are dismissed, that is, the physical properties are of little consequence. It is only significant that the computer-controlled object "remembers" or performs its psychological processes irrespective of the transparency of its operations. Turkle employs the aphorism that motion is replaced by emotion.[21] The traditional distinctions between machines and humans based on the standard definitions become blurred for young children, even to the point of attributing emotion and motivation to computers. Older children, near Piaget's formal operational level, presumably are able to maintain the distinctions of emotionality and recognize that computers do not engage in true emotionality. Nevertheless, Turkle expresses concern that children growing up and being educated in the computer culture will dissociate intellect and emotion, rationality and feeling, and lacking the critical awareness of the interrelatedness of the two, will reduce emotionality to something sentimental and superficial, and may even, as they find an inner void as a result of "dissociation of sensibility," confuse exotic mysticism with true human emotion.

Everything is done effortlessly. Programming factors out the agonal element. Mere manipulation through computer power renders the natural and necessary obstacles of growth and learning mere inconveniences that are easily bypassed or blipped. Education assumes the proportion of a game, a game played from a distance without psychic (soul) investment; hence, the accuracy of Sardello's contention that psychopathy develops. Students reinterpret education as manipulation, which eventually leads to exploitation. A culture, narcissistic in nature and ultimately exploitative in intention, assembled synthetically from the artifacts of ubiquitous technology, indifferent to the referents of the past, and preoccupied with power, will, with indulgent myopia, sacrifice virtue for utility. We will not be able to see beyond the computer terminal and video screen. We will mistake the images there for reality, and students will, perhaps unwittingly, learn that life is simply a series of images that can be manipulated, managed, and molded to their whimsical tastes.

Identity is supplied by the catalyst of imagination combined with effort toward goals worth achieving. We see ourselves grow and develop as we acquire the self-esteem that results when we agonize and struggle. It is with the real world of daily involvement that we interact and agonize. The unmediated concrete world provides feedback for the formation of character. The artificial abstractions of the computer world remove students from vital contact with the nature of things. Even John Dewey recognized the need for students to test themselves against the real world of people and things. What television began in distancing people from face-to-face contact by video technology, computers will complete. At least television, in its early years, dealt with real people and places, but even now through computer capability, video provides viewers with simulations and computer-generated images that parody the real thing. Abstractions, not as transcendent truths, but as technologized perversions of basic truth masquerade as truth and "learning does not celebrate the actual things of the world but turns away from the world in order to program an imitation world."[22] Computers commit a double fault for students who should be learning that they are not the center of the world. First, computers isolate students and, in common with video technology, viewing is a self-absorbed activity. Education has to have a vital social dimension. Dewey was quite correct in realizing that, but the increasingly idiosyncratic quality of education fostered by computers atomizes the environment and "interfacing" is student with computer. The excessively individualistic emphasis in education causes students to lose the comprehensive connection of life, the community concept that is the fundamental corrective to selfish behavior. Turkle's extensive, ethnographic studies based on hours of interviews and observations support the contention that computers isolate, and the stereotypic computer hacker illustrates the caricature of the loner who spends endless hours with his computer. Admittedly, the hacker culture may be self-selected, and hackers at MIT do, in fact, acknowledge the "nerd" role they have been assigned. But the socialization of very young children in school settings into the computer culture will aggravate an already distancing dilemma begun by the home-based television.

Secondly, the computer technique aggrandizes the individual ego. Computer involvement is a form of self-centered egoism and is based principally upon power. Adults along with teenagers who have become addicted to video games confess that the attraction that compels them to play endless and intensive games is the euphoric feelings of power that come. This is something more than the "voice of technological dependence" that Roszak detests. Ironically, the power of manipulation and control inherent in video games must in the final account produce the opposite effect unless the addict limits himself to the machine. It is from true control of human life that the machine distances. The rules of technology do not permit options or creative anomalies. Deviation from the prescribed program will prove perilous. Human reality requires just the opposite, especially for young children. Opportunities for exploration, trial and error, creative encounters, all with the natural environment are the more normal way to learn and grow. Of course, young children need parameters to protect them from the consequences of extreme peril, but everyone needs that. I am not advocating a no-holds-barred, free-for-all with the elements. Certainly in education, Dewey's realization that the teacher's task is to "reconstruct experience" is of critical concern. But the world as that which is encountered should provide the starting point and should be the vital element in every phase of education. Simulations and software are poor substitutes for unmediated contact. Piaget's cognitive theory of development has told us at least to provide sensorimotor experiences in all formative education endeavors. Bruner similarly prescribes "enactive modes" of encounter as the basis for other learning modes. This does not mean that we are seeking a return to the naive notions of Rousseau or the impractical pedagogy of Pestalozzi, but the erosion of the bedrock sensations and immediacy of agonal encounter threaten all existential sources of strength. Roszak offers his impressions of the emerging computer, school scenarios that find acceptance in education today:

Some people relish the image of schools where ranks of solitary students in private cubicles sit in motionless attendance upon computer terminals, their repertory of activities scaled down to a fixed state and the repetitive stroking of a keyboard. I find this picture barely acceptable. . . . My own taste runs to another image: that of teachers and students in one another's face-to-face company, perhaps pondering a book, a work of art, even a crude scrawl on the blackboard. . . . It is the unmediated encounter of two minds, one needing to learn, the other wanting to teach. The biological spontaneity of that encounter is a given fact of life; ideally it should be kept close to the flesh and blood, as uncluttered and supple as possible.[23]

Uncluttered is a key word. Technology, invariably, by its nature intrusively insists upon a buzzing, whirring, anesthetically discordant cacophony of mechanical sounds to conduct its operations, and in as sterile a place as possible, a climate-controlled, aseptic environment for the prophylactic exclusion of pollution. Machinery, and certainly sophisticated computer machinery, cannot run the risk of assault from contaminants in the air. The technology malady of computer viruses presently plaguing the culture and threatening to reek havoc on expensive and highly sensitive information networks testifies to the germ-free prerequisite of environments. The psychological dimension is equally reduced to the noncontaminable logic that drives the software. Roszak's scenario describes stygian and sterile environments where isolation is critical and spontaneity is detrimental. Education is, if anything, human, and often unpredictably spontaneous and serendipitous. The charm of learning involves the whimsy that the noncalculable provides. Teachable moments, unprogrammed and unpredictable (not of course without solid preparation) encourage the "eureka phenomenon" and the "aha" of educational wonder.

The computer creates its own culture. The computer-imperative brings all activity within its sway and under its domination. Computers cannot sit idly by, as books can, waiting for a curious explorer to finger its pages, and decide to peruse its passages. Computers are on, booted up, ready for action with their omniscient eyelike monitors, insisting upon attention. Their appetite is omnivorous. They must incessantly be fed data. They crave attention and they are consumptive. Books, by contrast, are unobtrusive, compliant servants who are willing to yield their secrets to the diligent, but they never voice, in vociferous fashion, their pleasures or their pains. But computers dominate the room. Like the television, they need to be turned on, and tuned in to.

One additional word about books. The printed page clearly created its own world, and transformed the culture of Western civilization as numerous scholars (McLuhan undoubtedly the most visible of them) have pointed out. The oral culture was modified, not eliminated, by the written culture. Books have become ubiquitous in the Western world, but there are places around the globe where illiteracy rates are still staggeringly high and where books are unavailable. But books are not an intrusive technique. Books do not dominate the way the television and computer do. And books are in abundance so no one book, even best sellers, monopolizes the market. Books are leisurely unobtrusive and benignly obliging. And they require agonal effort. Reading, particularly of good books, is difficult. It requires more than simple information processing. One mind engages another in a book, and a dynamic tension arises. Of course, the effort needed to profit from the book may not be reciprocated and the benefit is lost, or in an age of available inexpensive books, much that is of little value comes into publication. But even here, agonal discernment is required. The mind must engage itself discriminatingly to decide whether there is value in the reading effort. One can stop at any time and discard the book. But the genius of literature is that one good book reproduces itself in an ongoing lineage of inquiry and rich reading. Reading is not simply production; it is reproduction, and it is possible to trace the extensive progeny a masterpiece has sired.

Computer literacy is a horrid term. The term combination is oxymoronic. Technology that provides video-imagery is antiliteracy. The kindred term "word processor" is equally objectionable. As though words, the most elegant conveyors of human thought, can be categorized with food and other elements that are processed. Food processors grind things up. Word processors are contrivances—simply grand forms of typewriting. Even the one I am presently using is a form of an electric typewriter with capabilities for arranging, adding, and deleting bits that I determine. Words are not processed except in the same way that food is processed. I do not call upon this machine to do with those words anything other than I determine. To allow a machine to provide word arrangements merely by fact of its intricate and elaborate electronic capacity is an unconscionable abdication of human responsibility. A newspaper item within the last several months described the elation of computer technicians who contended that they could develop a computer-generated repertoire of music by using basic Bach paradigms. By extracting the essential musical structure from Bach, they could develop permutations by computer programs. Genetic engineering is dangerous enough. Genius engineering is loathsome. Bach's music is what it is because Bach was who he was. The audacity of second-rate musical minds with their technological gadgetry presuming to emulate the unemulative mastery of the masters!

Technology does not simply intrude itself in a way that its means eventually become ends, although that is true enough; technology produces new psychological and perceptual paradigms. Proponents of computer technology's accomplishments loudly applaud the transformation in the way humans think and in the new definitions of intelligent behavior. Turing's test, by now an established canon in computer mentalism, decrees that computers do indeed think. The academic bastions of "computerolatry," notably MIT, Harvard, and Stanford, boast an international coterie of subscribers to the new myth of artificial intelligence. Philosopher John Searle adamantly opposes the notion that intelligence is a function of machinery. He stubbornly attributes intelligence only to humans.[24] Although computers provide a pervasive psychology by virtue of their capacity for simulation and modeling, they nevertheless do not think. And without resorting to a naive Cartesian ontology, an invariant and species-unique property of homo sapiens is, nevertheless, the ability to think (IBM's parody on the cogito, notwithstanding: I think, therefore IBM). Metacognition (thinking about thinking) provides its own metaphysics. Science with its endless variations of pragmatism has been unable to eliminate the nasty metaphysical fly in its positivistic ointment. Ultimately, acceptance of any and all methods for certifying truth relies upon the acceptance of the intelligence that does the certifying. One cannot refuse to admit the basis on which all refusal is based. Even Darwin admitted, to his consternation, that the empirical evidence upon which his claims of evolution were based were themselves acquired, classified, synthesized, and validated by the intelligence of a human who was the evolutionary product of a nonhuman. No datum is self-validating in any system of science. The very methodologies that determine what is admissible as evidence are human constructs fashioned from human intelligence. Godel's theorem means at least that much, that no system can be self-referentially validated.

I admit my own presuppositions about the nature of human intelligence. Its origin I assert is noumenal not phenomenal. Just as language, as Noam Chomsky has demonstrated, is innate in and unique to humans, so intelligence is the peculiarity of human nature. It may be simulated by computers and even anthropomorphically ascribed to infrahumans, but it is not intrinsic to them. Language and literacy are the manifestations of logic and intelligence. Computers may paraphrase, process, and parody language, but they cannot *de novo* produce it. Yet a child, without all of the extensive data input, in a relatively short span of time, can communicate intelligent thought through intelligent speech. Artificial intelligence is, like artificial insemination, a joyless, a-erotic, passionless means of bringing together in an aseptic environment what was intended to be the reproductive result of the most-sublime sexual ecstasy. Stanley Jaki, alert to the claims that computer technology would make for itself, cautioned us three decades ago:

Among the various fashionable phrases which nowadays are often taken in some circles as genuine signs of scientific sophistication, reference to artificial minds or thinking machines easily hold a foremost rank. Fashions, as is well known, are obeyed rather than criticized; followed rather than challenged. . . . With most fashions, the best policy is to wait out calmly the demise of their usually ephemeral success. Scientific fashions are a different matter. . . . In our times the growing obsession with the idea of artificial intelligence is already heavily contributing to a weakening of critical sense, to a lessening of man's appreciation of intangibles, and to a growth of skepticism about human values. . . . To prevent such disaster one certainly should keep remembering the difference between machines, however marvelous, and their true source, the marvel of man's mind.[25]

We need to return to the question raised by E. B. Castle when he asked, What is the right paideia for a technological age?[26] It is a question that links the Greek past with the greedy present. In one statement we are asked to consider the fundamental features of culture and connect them to a society committed to consumerism. We are asked to relate the spirit of man to the science of man. Whatever the technology that presently captivates and controls, it must be subjected to the relentless spiritual scrutiny which alone can provide clear vision for the future. Fundamentally, the question about the good life must be asked and answered. Do we want to educate for good people or good technologists? The ancient civilization of the Greeks is not without relevance to these questions which are age old. A major problem for us, however, is that we have so divorced ourselves from the ages that we are not only unaware of the possibilities of superior answers from them, we are so blinded by the dazzle of our technological present that we cannot see to ask correct questions. Have we forgotten the lesson of Sparta and Athens? Has the frightful dichotomy of cultures disappeared? Caught up in contemporaneity and obsessed with the maddening movement toward more and bigger, are we no longer able to call upon the past to enlighten us? But, of course, that is one of the very evils of technology that I have been trying to emphasize. It erodes, obscures, obliterates the past. It severs all ties with tradition.

We must reflectively, reverently, as Castle and Weaver plead, reassert the superiority of the sacred over the secular, the mind over matter, the soul over the senses. In no other period of human history has culture been so pervasively conditioning (I would like to say educational). Where is the true educator, the poet, in all this? Why has the technologist been elevated to the pinnacle? Why does he presume to speak for this generation and to this generation? Homer educated a civilization and kept barbarianism in check. Today, barbarianism in its boorish manifestations has ascended the throne. It rules in prime time. Television is no longer simply a wasteland, it has become the social sewer. Prime-time television (aptly if facetiously termed "slime time") is a toxic site that infects the minds and morals of each successive generation with more perverse imagery than the previous one. This technology at least has brought a society down to its own level. Television exercises moral entropy. It is desynthesizing, deconstructionistic, and dehumanizing. The rhetoric about First Amendment rights, notwithstanding, there is nothing freeing about the speech on television, and the computer will follow the same path. It will barbarize. Without a paideia of principles and morality, Philistinism will be the best we can hope for in schools and society.

In one form or another, these pleas and this polemic have been trumpeted by others. What I say is not new, nor is it radical. But the expression I give it implies that the remedy will not come now without a high price to pay and a bitter pill to swallow. It is not simply a matter of foregoing options or of merely slowing the progress of the plague. It means reversing course; we must confess both folly and evil in our endeavors. It means we must call a halt to the maniacal march our culture has taken, charmed by the cadence count of the computer. We must admit the value dislocation it all has caused, and we must penitently reassess our direction and reappraise our goals. We must call upon the paideia of the past to come to our rescue. We must restore faith with precedents that we discarded, and mine the golden legacy left for us. It will be an agonizing task of unprecedented proportions. It will require the agon of an education that restores the virtues of morality, discipline, and transcendence. Are we willing?

Chapter 7

A Note About Narcissism

Each age seeks its title. Ever since historians and social commentators began the self-conscious act of labeling epochs and ages, we seek some symbolic rubric, a shibboleth, a caption that calls before us the prevailing mood and mentality of the times in which we are living. We need to know the overarching, prototypic pattern that seems to define our selves and our style, the frame of reference within which we can understand what is happening, and perhaps communicate to our posterity both its praise and its perils. Tom Wolfe seems to have set the tone when he stigmatized the 1970s as the "me decade." The pronominal identification has not abated since then and promises (threatens?) to be the shibboleth that will shape the remainder of the century. Technically, "me-ness" is termed narcissism, adopted from the fateful character of Greek mythology who pined away, pathetically preoccupied with his own image.

Williams and Patrick have provided a good survey of psychological and psychoanalytic literature that addresses this issue. They concur with Beldoch that narcissism is "the archetypal pathology of our age."[1] They trace the introduction of the term into psychiatric use to Freud.[2] Further-more, they contend that most of the therapies that seek to treat the pathology merely indulge narcissistic tendencies; however, Frankl's value-laden logotherapy is an effective treatment approach that does not pander to narcissistic perversity.[3] It is worthy of note that Frankl's therapy was forged in his struggle, in his privation experience of Auschwitz, and is one of the few that is open to legitimate agony, and one that seeks to find meaning in the struggle.

Lasch's jeremiad about the role of narcissism in an age of diminishing
expectations indicts society and its refusal to interrogate the past for
solutions to the present quandary in which it flounders. Lasch echoes the
undeniable theme that the fundamental source of contemporary social evils
is to be found in ignorance of and disregard for the past.[4]

The narcissistic personality that reflects the pathology of the times
focuses less upon transcendent goals and struggle to advance social
interests, and is less willing to avert one's glance from the mirror's image.
The one all-consuming question is: Mirror, mirror on the wall, who's the
fairest of them all?; and the one shattering fear is that the answer will be:
Snow White—not you! When we are bewitched by the perversion of our
projected image, we fear the image of innocence which "looks down"
without condescension even upon the dwarfs. Preoccupation with appearance blinds the mind and soul to true values and transcendent visions.
Technology is the creator of imagery that seeks to conform us to its mold.
We can never see ourselves as others see us, Robert Burns, notwithstanding. I am unable to see my own face except in a reflection. But it is the
reflection I see, not me! (Don't trust what you feel; reflections aren't real.)
But we are told just that and told, tirelessly, repeatedly that we are our
reflections: reflections of other people, reflections of the media, reflections
in the proliferating, cultural looking-glasses that are often expensive,
typically gaudy, and always ornamental.

Education today, especially in its emphasis on self-discovery, is narcissistic.
Prepackaged programs, computer and otherwise, define us to ourselves in
terms of the program's goals and design. Increasingly, education curriculums and programs are so heavily fabricated, engineered, and tailored so
that opportunity for making oneself is eliminated. Although inherited
temperaments and genetic predispositions contribute immutable thresholds of personality and identity, the large outlines of macroidentity are filled
in experientially as we encounter the real stuff of life, or as we are deprived
of real life experiences. Contrived, second-hand images are confused with
selfhood. Processed identities derived from technology not only create a
conformist, homogenized herd-think, they deform the social system by
reducing aspiration levels and achievement. Among animal species, there
is so little variety. Sheep all look alike; giraffes, lovely, exotic creatures
that they are with their distinctive markings, nevertheless, appear as
products from a mold; but humans are mercurially and enchantingly
diverse; however, media technology has converted generations to a clone-
like sameness. Teenage peer groups are indistinguishably alike. A visit to
a school soon reveals the prevailing, tiringly banal sameness of student

dress, talk, and culture. And the level of all this diminishes with each successive generation. The level does not rise; it descends.

Theodore Roszak has shown that technology takes us down to its level. Wisdom revealed in classic writings of inspired authors is sacrificed for the utterances of television personalities whose own lives are shallow and uninformed. And the nature of television demands a stunted level of discourse where neither deep understanding nor critical thinking are encouraged; in fact, they are liabilities which could serve to undermine the consumer-culture framed by technology. The only consensus that counts is the agreed-upon goal of devoting ourselves to desiring, coveting, and acquiring the commodities and images the technocratic elite has determined. Virtue is banished and all values are graded according to the consumer index. Little wonder that our schools have become the very instruments of a variation on the "publish or perish" creed: buy or die; buy out or die out. Even the introduction of Channel One, a daily television Program for Students, provided free to schools, has a commercial element. Students are indoctrinated with the belief that there is always a price tag tied to education. Education is equated with dollar signs. Its value lies only in what you can buy with it. Credit accrual, course completion, and school programs translate into career purchases. Students are what they buy. Community is replaced by consumerism. The cerebral must show a commercial side; a profit motive drives the enterprise, and at the heart of it all is the narcissistic preoccupation with self. The student-centered curriculum was never intended to be a self-serving, indulgent program by which pupils in atomistic aloofness pursue their own pleasure and profit. The nature and developmental needs of students were intended to serve as significant sources for selecting growth experiences that would allow the ultimate end, for which they were intended, to be fully realized. But this is a far cry from the shallow and selfish indulgence of whim or the fabricated futures based on materialistic exploitation that have been presented.

Prize-winning playwright Archibald MacLeish provides a poet's perspective on the technological problems in which "the process had somehow taken over leaving the purpose to shift for itself." He is principally concerned with the confusion over purpose in higher education, but his observations are equally applicable to all phases of schooling:

the renunciation by the university of an intention to produce a certain kind of man, a man shaped by certain models, certain texts, the university's concern with "man" as such has grown less and less and its concern with what it calls "subjects" has become greater and greater . . . and the ultimate consequence only too evident in the time we live in, has been the vocationalization of the high schools. The college no longer exists to produce men qua men, men prepared for life in a society of men but to produce men as specialized experts. Men prepared for employment in an industry or profession.[5]

Narcissism is a variation on the ego theme, but it is self-preoccupation to the neglect of all others. Television has contributed to the social narcissism of our times, and may itself provide a fitting metaphor for the malady that plagues a generation of self-watchers. Celebrities who are ego distorted manifest to a larger degree the narcissistic syndrome. They are products of the media and seem to reinforce their self-created and self-accepted image by parading in public. Television is essentially a voyeuristic medium, and personalities look into the reflective mirror and fall in love with that image. That television viewing is the major pastime for most American people is not without significance. The linkage between viewing and narcissism is not inconsequential. Videoism is the voyeurism of the age, but it is autovoyeurism—a condition looking always at oneself or at the image one desires of oneself. And education has drawn upon this compelling image to make students virtually paranoid about their appearance and performance. Schoolrooms have become too much like television studios where image is everything, and substance counts for little.

Agonic education releases the self from performance paranoia. By generating "flow" in the "autotelic experience," fueled by the physical and psychological effort of the activity, students can be at leisure from themselves. The activity dominates and not the self. Energy is focussed on the agonic task and freedom from the fear of failure or the need to save face imbues the experience with a nonnarcissistic richness that feeds back as strength for the student. Any activity that takes us "out of ourselves," as agonic education does, reduces the deleterious potential of education that pushes us to the platform on which the ego is displayed. Humans cannot interminably endure preoccupation with their own images. This is symptomatic of sickness. Popular cult figures who are forever inflicting their presence upon the public not only wear out their welcome with the public, they wear thin, and soon they are seen, and see themselves, as ciphers. Few things are so sad as the elderly seeking to cling to the worn, thin threads of youth. Maturity is to grow older and to grow up. Maturity means that we accept the paradox of a new self that has assumed this new form which is older. Self-styled celebrities, and celebrities of the public's making who seek to remain forever celebrated personify narcissism. Celebrations are periodic events not prolonged accolades. Christmas would not be Christmas if it came every day.

Narcissism clings to the ghosts of Christmas past and recreates daily a parody of yesterday. Agonic effort cuts the atrophied, umbilical cord that tethers us to the self-indulgent womb which we clutch with a Freudian ferocity in our refusal to grow up. Television would keep everyone a child. Television's regressive appeal for many is its fetal attraction for passivity and inactivity. When education is shaped by television's intractable technique and created in the image of the video, all effort is resisted. A resident of a small Mississippi town, and herself a Yale graduate, was lured back to her state to teach in the hope that she could inspire children who may be otherwise left unchallenged. She tried to "instill a thirst for knowledge" in her students, but she lamented that, when she insisted "they exert some kind of effort, it's like squeezing blood from a turnip."[6]

The mirror of narcissistic self-centeredness must be turned first into a window through which a real world is viewed, and then into a door through which students may march into a world of challenge. Schools simply must end this practice of catering to student whims. Certainly, sensitivity to real needs is imperative, but unwise indulgence that reinforces a sense of dependency is neither healthy nor helpful. One need not be a Mother Theresa to be nonnarcissistic, but, frankly, she isn't a bad model for students and teachers to emulate.

Education that turns students from themselves, from preoccupation with the interior, and the excessively morbid self-introspection, to engagement with the world and with agonic reality can spare them the pathology of narcissism. We need to peel the silver backing from the mirrors the world continuously holds before us and our students. It is only as we see "through the eye" (William Blake's words) beyond ourselves that we will experience significance and self-worth which we desperately need. Frankl is eminently wise in telling us that we need to "withdraw attention" from the problem and "forget ourselves." Dereflection, which draws our attention from ourselves, is "an implicitly anti-narcissistic technique, for it works only to the degree that one is able to forget one's self."[7] Agonic education succeeds in accomplishing that very thing.

Chapter 8

Agon and Motivation

The ancient Greeks, as the early teachers and framers of Western civilization, emphasized the significance of ends against means. Confusion between the two has been the frustrating source of many of our personal and social ills. Philosophy's task, until recently deterred by its repudiation of metaphysical concerns, has been the perennial preoccupation of moving mankind toward the Good. Plato's vision, and the educational program which derived from it, peered beyond the slavish limitations of sensations toward the ultimate value which alone could serve as society's guide. The duty of the philosopher-king, who through agonic education had apprehended that "good," was to guide society according to its premise and precepts.

A constant passion for any knowledge that will reveal . . . something of the reality which endures forever and is not always passing into and out of existence . . . [this] desire is to know the whole of that reality. . . . Another trait which the nature we are seeking cannot fail to possess—truthfulness, a love of truth, and a hatred of falsehood that will not tolerate untruth in any form. . . . Hence, besides our other requirements, we shall look for a mind endowed with measure and grace, which will be instinctively drawn to see every reality in its true light.[1]

Richard Weaver's masterful analysis of modern society and his trenchant prophecies concerning its suicidal rush toward destruction support this premise. With the rejection of transcendentals and with slavish deference to the utilitarianism spawned by an epistemology of control, naturalism established the metaphysical agenda resulting in materialism and psychological reductionism.[2] The entropic forces of ontologic decay destruct civilization into disorganization and chaos. The cumulative efforts of centuries, whereby virtuous civility creates order and form and reflects a transcendent reality, impose upon an atomized collectivity a true sense of social and civil identity. But the lessons of history, if they are learned, alert us to the relentless decivilizing tendencies that threaten every civilization, and eternal vigilance is not only the price of liberty but the only protection against the inroads of entropy. Such is the task of every true social paideia. Paideia must militantly defend against ontological decay by constantly reminding the society that true selfhood is defined not biologically but celestially; not in terms of mechanistic models but in the language of transcendence.

Motivation is a meaningless term apart from identifiable goals. Technology undermines this necessary philosophical infrastructure and, thereby, seeks to build everything upon a psychology of reductionism. Reductionistic conceptions of mankind, overly mechanistic and invariably simplistic, tend to negate growth, to emphasize control, and to elevate means to the place of prominence. The bankruptcy of behaviorism reveals itself in this preoccupation with research paradigms that are excessively manipulative. Having dismissed interior, motivational processes, behaviorism's focus on control requires contingency management and stimulus manipulation, and assumes that extrinsic payoffs are the only explanation for behavior. The emerging research in autotelic activity confronts this naive notion with contrary evidence having identified self-satisfying activity which relies upon no external incentive. The pure "pleasure" (even if, paradoxically painful, and indeed it often is) of the activity serves as self-motivating. The autotelic activities are characteristically agonic. Csikszentmihalyi's discussion of this concept and his identification of pertinent spheres of activity address the specific agonic nature of productive, self-enhancing, and transcending experiences.[3]

Autotelic activity involves experiences that are ends in themselves. They are pursued not as means, but as ends. They are inherently, although agonically, satisfying. Autotelic involvements are neither narcissistic nor narcotic. They do not mask pain, nor do they indulge hedonistic cravings; in fact, participants typically undertake arduous and often extraordinary extremes of effort that seem to defy logical limits. Some participants are by temperament "risk takers" who constantly seek to expand the environmentally imposed limitations, while others sense a need for unconventional but life-enhancing experiences. Autotelic behavior is characterized by "the underlying assumption that all such activities are ways for people to test the limits of their being, to transcend their former conception of self by extending skills and undergoing new experiences."[4]

Challenge is implicit in and an integral element of autotelic activity. People are provided opportunities to "explore the limits of their abilities, and . . . expand them."[5] In his treatise on discipline and freedom, John Dewey similarly identified the need for students to test themselves against the real world of people and things.[6] The testing event provides occasion for discrimination and discipline. Students are able to see what things work and what things do not work in guiding their behaviors, and they are then able, in the context of struggle, to accept or reject them.

But the appeal of autotelic activity includes a benefit that accrues from, but is not the initial purpose of, engaging in the activity; and that appeal relates to the "transcendent stage" or "flow" that frequently (and for some always) accompanies the autotelic activity. "People seek flow primarily for itself, not for the incidental extrinsic rewards that may accrue from it."[7] The "flow" phenomenon is comparable to the transcendent states experienced in a variety of contexts and reported in both the psychological and religious literature. Maslow's concept of "peak experience" and the "oceanic feelings" accompanying self-actualization have renewed motivational and humanistic psychology. Peak experiences are not necessarily limited to agonic effort in physical activity; cognitive and emotional effort can create comparable states of inner awareness and contribute to strength. One author suggests that peak spiritual experiences can be an object of curriculum analysis, and he cites his personal experience and the reports by students of their activities in classrooms when they experienced transcendent states prompted by cognitive activity and aesthetic awareness.[8] Effort, agonic activity, does appear, however, to be an element in creating or contributing to the experience.

William Glasser's intriguing concept of "positive addiction" suggests similar notions of agonic activity and the achievement of what he terms "a spinning out" state of being. His research with people who have experienced "spin outs" documents the potential for the experience and the psychological profit accrued from the state. Most notably, his investigation of runners has revealed that the agonic act of running readily and frequently creates the conditions for the spin out.[9] People who have diminished ego-strength lack the requisite resources to handle life's demands. Nonagonic education distances children from contact with the real world and dissociates them from an understanding of the need for tangible reality. May not the disorders of the age be products of the impact of technology as it has reduced contacts with nature. Glasser records the remarkable increase in psychological strength in previously weak people who undertake strenuous activities that are nonevaluative. Running, most significantly among a variety of agonic involvements, seems to give this heightened sense of self-awareness, while at the same time providing freedom from self-preoccupation.[10]

The pathology of excessive self-consciousness is inversely related to active ego-strength. The more we think consciously about ourselves and dwell evaluatively on our person, probably the less secure we are in our sense of personal worth. When we are able to accept ourselves and "be at leisure" from ourselves, we are capable of a more healthy, confirming attitude toward ourselves. But in order to achieve this strengthening posture, we need to have clear, affirming evidence of our personal significance. Typically, this comes from a network of social relationships in which we are accepted and affirmed, and from periodic accomplishments that provide tangible proof of our capabilities and worth. Weak people, and particularly negative addicts (as Glasser identifies them), lack both these elements, and, consequently, are plagued with paranoia and self-preoccupation. Strong people (and positive addicts are extreme expressions of strength) balance these needs equitably and rationally. While not disregarding their identities and legitimate needs, they, nevertheless, avoid the debilitating dependencies that make these things prominent.

Agonic activity, either mental or physical (or preferably both), is an indispensable element in the development of personal sufficiency and acceptance. The flow concept connects vitally with the agon. Csikszentmihalyi's quarter decade of research and writing about what he has come to term the "flow experience" captures remarkably some of the critical qualities of the agonic struggle. Flow follows from or is the crystallization in experience of the pleasure of involvement and commitment to an inherently satisfying task, but a task that requires effort.

The chronic complaint of this generation of students is expressed in the term "boredom." I don't recall my generation using the term. I can't recall as a child ever using the word to describe my personal psychological state. Perhaps we referred to specific activities as boring but we seldom, if ever, said that we were bored. Several possible explanations for this lack of reference to the term suggest themselves. Perhaps we were, phenomenologically, simply incapable of evaluating an experience or our inner state in that way, or our sense of selfhood could have precluded reflection on that aspect of our lives. In all likelihood the cultural conditions of the 1940s did not encourage children to be unduly preoccupied with this kind of introspection and self-analysis. Another plausible reason could have involved the nature of the environment and the social expectations for children in that day. Our activities, apart from school and assorted house chores, were not programmed. There was a dearth of social planning and community programs for children, apart from an occasional, limited recreational activity at a local park, or for the favored, the YMCA, YWCA, or similar organizations. Children quite simply and naturally were expected to find or provide or, typically, create their own pastimes. In my working-class community with large families, peers were abundantly available, and there were virtually no obstacles to assembling a group for a game. Although finances were limited in the extreme, and recreational resources were virtually nonexistent (certainly during the war era), imagination and determination together supplied essentials for activity, entertainment, and enjoyment. I recall quite vividly the eagerness of my cohorts and the creativity involved in our transforming local vacant lots, streets, and other unused areas into arenas for our made-up games. In a sense, we were forced, by privation, to provide for ourselves or perish. Technology was in its infancy, and apart from a local movie house and the radio, there was nothing else "to do," and yet we never complained of boredom. Enjoyment was indigenous to the activity.

Subsumed under the "elements of enjoyment," Csikszentmihalyi identifies eight factors that were described universally by people as being involved in the phenomenology of enjoyment. As I reflect on my experiences then (and even now), there appears to be a correspondence between elements of agonic activity and Csikszentmihalyi's eight factors listed here:[11]

1. The tasks we undertake are capable of completion. We view the activity as eventually coming to closure. Surmountable challenges, although involving effort, are realistically perceived as accomplishable.

2. Concentration is required. Focusing of effort and energy, physically and mentally, commend the task to our attention.

3. Concentration is possible because the goals are clearly stated. The task has well-demarcated parameters which allow us to function within a set of expectations and play by a prescribed set of rules.

4. Feedback conveys a sense of accomplishment. Feedback continues to emerge as a critical element in all activities that produce pleasurable results and which encourage sustained commitment. We need to know if we are making progress, if we are winning, if we are moving toward the goal.

5. A deep but effortless involvement removes the pedestrian concerns of life from consciousness. At this point, I would take exception to the definition of involvement as effortless. A transcendencelike state may emerge which phenomenologically reduces the consciousness of effort, but I believe agonic effort is inherent in the involvement, or elation does not result. The runner's

high is an example of Glasser's "spinning out" state during which reduced awareness of or indifference to the pain develops (no doubt biochemically induced by the secretion of endorphins). Mediation states require expenditure of psychic energy or mental concentration (as Scott Peck describes) and may produce signs of physical exertion (intense perspiration), but paradoxically, awareness of the intrusive concerns of everyday life is substantially diminished or eliminated.

6. People control their actions. Control is a critical factor in human activity. Agonic activity requires that contestants or participants are capable of controlling the circumstances of their participation.

7. A paradoxical disappearance of the self while a strong sense of self emerges after the flow experience ends. The literature on psychological disorders that are treated by involving patients in agonic activity testifies notably to this paradox. Running, again, emerges as an agonic activity in which this paradox prevails.

8. The sense of time is altered, and time's duration fails to be calculated in the traditional chronometric ways. Transcendence is not uncommonly described in terms of the suspension or absence of a sense of time. Flow experiences do not negate time; they transcend time. Psychological transcendence is phenomenological and perceptions are altered, although to an impartial observor the clock ticks at its normal pace. It is when time is dragging that boredom is experienced.

Schools suffer from the motivation crisis. The artificiality of the tasks students are often asked to perform and the involvement imposed upon them are perceived to be unrelated to their lives and irrelevant to themselves. The problems that plague schools and cause upset and disorder are in large measure simply by-products of this principal malady. All others are symptoms of this illness. If impatience is "seeing the moment as being without meaning," then boredom is perceiving the self as uninspiredly inactive. The flow experience represents the quintessential antithesis of boredom. When engaged agonically in autotelic activity, the self is actualized (in Maslow's term), is authenticated (in Rogers's term), and is transparent (in Jourard's term).[12] Agonic activity is inspiriting (Jourard's word) and is psychologically growth-stimulating. School students constitute an institutionalized population who, increasingly, in this technocratic society are wards of a system supervised by a corp of professional monitors and programmers. Serendipity is precluded by the obsession with control, and there is little occasion for the breaking through of nonlogical, nonlinear, cognitive experience.

The terms mystical and mysticism and their cognates are eschewed in modern education. In fact, to be modern involves the refusal to recognize these realities. Reality, more accurately, is defined in ways that preclude these possibilities. Epistemological obsession with positivism reduces reality to sensation, empirically validated and logically comprehended. There just is no place for the intrusion of mystery. Huston Smith, one of the most-ardent advocates of perennialism, and probably its most articulate spokesman, admonishes scholarship for its mistaken notion that one methodology alone is capable of discovering total truth. His analogy of the searchlight scanning the sky which may illumine a man-made space ship but lacks power to disclose hidden heavenly bodies aptly illustrates the limitations of empirical methodologies.[13] Because the instruments of investigation are incapable of identifying phenomena beyond their ken, it does not mean that those phenomena do not exist.

Reality is to a large extent defined by the respective methodologies that are used to study it, but as Andreski has somewhat acerbically announced, methodology is at best prophylactic—it can keep the germs out but it does not guarantee the genius will get in.[14] In other words, methodology can only guard against the unwanted intrusion of contamination in detecting truth, but it can never in itself discover and define that truth. Truth is an interpretation from data, and the absence of data is not to be equated with nonexistence of data. The methodology is fallible. But what is even more subversive of truth is that methodology is never ideologically neutral. Methodology gives shape to truth and champions an ideological agenda. A somewhat faulty but fair analogy would be a vessel into which a liquid is poured. The liquid will conform to the shape of the vessel. Indeed, the vessel determines for all practical considerations the appearance of the liquid. Water poured into a tall, thin, ornately crafted glass will appear more elegant than the same liquid poured into a clumsy bottle. It is the same liquid but its contours are transformed or created by the bottle. The sense of sight used to evaluate the respective contained substances gives preference to one or the other depending upon the predilections of the evaluator for shape and size. Of course, other senses may be brought into play in the evaluation (smell, taste, etc.) but the form of the liquid determined by the container will prejudice the evaluation. The ample body of research in sensation and perception suggests something similar. Therefore, psychology itself is influenced by methodology; by psychology, I mean the perceptual predispositions brought to the assessment of the object on the experience.

Imagination, except in selected pedagogical forums such as drama or artistic endeavor, is offered little entry into education. The measurement and positivist bias of current pedagogy "dis-enchants" education and schooling. Despite Jerome Bruner's plea for more latitude in "intuitive thinking,"[15] and the recent physiological focus on brain lateralization and "left hemispheric" insight, the logico-deductive paradigm continues to dictate educational programs.

Rigorous cognition, critical logic, and intense cerebration should never be dismissed from education. It would be foolhardy and counterproductive to dismiss with the wave of the hand (or wand) the legacy of two thousand years of Western education. But even here, the agonic element, which actively conceptualizes problems and discovers solutions, should be emphasized. Not the fuzzy "game playing," cognitive gamesmanship (which computer models present), but concrete, reality-based life situations that encourage creative solutions to surmountable problems must be developed and provided. Imaginative exercises should allow students to synthesize learning and extract from the complexity of learning elements that specifically relate to life situations; imagination may need to be tinged with mystery.

Mystery is too often confused with magic, but Huston Smith, as well as Mortimer Adler, contend that intelligence recognizes and accepts mystery, and intuition and illumination are, for them, admissible sources of truth.[16] Openness to information, to knowledge, and to wisdom (the last, of course, demands something beyond the unembellished intellect) from sources that are not narrowly cerebral attunes students to truth that is not accessible any other way. The ghastly sterility of modern society and its omnipresent and gratuitous materialism deaden the will and spirit. When school-budget constraints prompt officials to perform surgery on those school budgets, the arts are not uncommonly considered redundant organs that can be excised without ill effect. But ill (pardon the pun) is exactly the effect. Poetry, as a writer recently suggested, is the only antidote for technology and the spiritual paralysis it causes. We cannot, as C. S. Lewis reminded us, remove the organ and demand the function.[17] When mystery and enchantment are excised from the curriculum, as art and music are cut, we "kill the spirit" (to use Page Smith's trenchant phrase).[18] A classroom should be a place of magic, as George Leonard has noted, where ecstasy and education coexist and provide symbiotic support. The world, after all, is not made from matter but from music![19]

Chapter 9

Imagery of Agony

In a graduate seminar involving the study of complex organizations and organizational theory which I took decades ago, the text that we used was divided into two sections. The first part of the book was devoted to the traditional and rather perfunctory treatment of research data and their implications for organizational functioning. Topologies, taxonomies, and various research models and paradigms were developed, discussed, and applied to role functioning in organizations. The author, a noted researcher, both competent and literate, provided a coherent, readable, and profitable body of reading. This first section received extensive consideration in that seminar. The second section of the text provided, refreshingly, a qualitative treatment of organizational life and styles of functioning. This approach was a radical departure in those days from the traditional treatment of organizations. Rigidly empirical research was considered the only acceptable source of insight into organizational life. The author drew the notion of various perspectives on a single issue or theme from Lawrence Durrell's *Alexandria Quartet*.[1] The author, quite enchantingly, provided highly expressive imagery to illuminate the dynamics of organizational life, and to illustrate the nonverbal behavior cues that are often critically important in understanding organizations, but which typically are overlooked. This section of the text dealt with metaphors and imagery culled from fiction and drama as well as from art and sculpture.

It afforded me, at that point in my academic program, a novel and liberating look at human behavior which I had, in an academic venue, heretofore, been denied. I have sought, subsequent to that experience, to try to be a keen observer of the nonverbal, the seemingly incidental, the nonquantifiable, and the vaguely mysterious aspects of human life and behavior. I have been open to information and insights that the arts and humanities alone can supply, and have insisted that they, even when measurable data are clearly needed, supplement and inform all considerations and conclusions.

The abstruse and opaque jargon of education often obscures what it intends to illumine. Dependence upon quasi-scientific nomenclature and slavish allegiance to insipid journal-style form render educational writings unintelligible. The one redeeming feature of the rhetorical overkill of educationists is that what they have to say, which is often neither worth saying or knowing, is, thereby, rendered unintelligible to readers. In its rapacious quest for academic respectability, education often emulates the obscurantist style of the self-styled, scholarly research journals which are not uncommonly guilty of the unpardonable sin—incomprehensible prose. Elliott Eisner with good cause chides the educational establishment for its reluctance to include the qualitative language of the arts into its increasingly narrowly drawn purview of procrustean prose that insists upon embedding all discourse within the deforming limits of numbers and impoverished writing. Metaphorical discourse, he contends, aids in the "seeing" which is presumably the purpose of research and inquiry.

In this sense, educational critics and critics of the arts share a common aim: to help others see and understand. To achieve this aim, one must be able to use language to reveal what, paradoxically, words can never say. This means that voice must be heard in the text, alliteration allowed and cadences encouraged. Relevant allusions should be employed, and metaphor that adumbrates by suggestion used.[2]

The plea for literacy within the educational-writing community has swelled into a concerned chorus now crying for the return to saner and more literate prose by the practitioners of the craft. Let us hope that the educational community heeds Andreski's complaint against "nebulous verbosity" and pompous bluff, and all those cryptic pseudoscholarly publications.[3] A simple comparison of the writings of scholars of a former era (blessed by active engagement with the classics) with the corps of contemporary academics reveals a dearth of originality of many of the latter and certainly confirms the superior writing style of the former. A fertile field of cultivated ideas coupled with craftsmanship in composition produce things worth writing and worth reading. The dominance of unreflective, mechanistic rhetoric, such as predominates in too many scholarly publications, is both tedious and tendentious. Abstracts alone would suffice to state the purpose and results of much of the research. But in a social order such as ours in which mindless technology creates the mind-set, words will count for little except as the means to persuade a gullible public to purchase unnecessary products and adopt stultifying lifestyles.

Language, like fire, is the great gift to mankind, and it can kindle holocausts, lull us to sleep with its gentle warmth, or heat and light up our lives. In the wrong hands and mouths, language becomes another instrument, another technique to tyrannize and trivialize. Agonic education is best served when its imagery is derived from the elements of the living world. Not paradigms and models drawn exclusively from mechanistic worldviews and communicated with typographic tedium, but visions and images gleaned gracefully from the profusion of life's experiences conveyed by delicate metaphors best suit the purposes of the serious task of schools. We need to recover serendipity, and we need to be, even as Wordsworth was, surprised by joy!

The English word agony, which transliterates the Greek "agon," conjures up suitable connections related to struggle, intensity, emotion, duress, stress, endurance, and anguish. Harris identifies the term's use in ancient Greek athletics:

The reason is probably connected with a fundamental view of the aim of athletics that it was to gain the satisfaction of victory and a sense of physical well-being in return for hardship, exhaustion and discomfort, "ponos" as they called it; the resemblance to our word "pain" is not accidental, and our "agony" is derived from "agon," the Greek word for athletic contest. Here, as elsewhere in life, the price must be paid. They would probably have felt that there was insufficient of this element in a race shorter than a stade.[4]

But agony is better illustrated than defined; it is with imagery, rather than analysis, that the deep texture of the term is experienced. Agonic education, if it is to capture the qualities that agony suggests, must have its fitting metaphors to inform and impregnate it. We dare not reduce agonic education to a curriculum or program that is designed and constructed from industrial, scientific, or mechanical models. It should not resemble the assemblage of a set of tinker toys or lego blocks. It is not so much constructed as composed; not so much designed as dramatized. Agon is an interior entity that manifests and embodies itself in action; it works from the inside out. It is "autoic" by being a self-manifestation. The imposition of strenuous, struggle-experiences may produce beneficial results, but such activities do not of themselves constitute anything agonic. There must be self-investment leading to a sense of self-actualization, which is always a by-product of self-transcendence, as Frankl reminds us.[5] Agonic experiences partake of transcendence. The quest for successively higher states of ontological awareness and concomitant self-acceptance and success moves a being to struggle and sacrifice self for the paradoxical pleasure and profound realization of self. When individuals seek to add incrementally to themselves from the outside through passive engagement, the autoic, the "inner man," the "autonomous self" grows smaller and the true self is, correspondingly, reduced. The self is subordinated during the flow experience while a stronger sense of true selfhood emerges after the experience ends. The literature on the treatment of some psychological disorders by involving pa; ..its in agonic activity testifies to the therapeutic role these activities serve. The positive impact of running programs on helping depressed people, for example, has been documented. But effective implementation of educational programs based on the agon element will require environments that may be different than the conventional school settings.

Mechanical models that may impose rather rigid rules and regulations on the activity will need to give way to more fluid forms in which learning can take place, and a rich and heuristic imagery will need to inform and form the programs. The tyranny of "Engle's Law" (the passage of quantities into qualities and qualities into quantities) must keep us alert to the danger of transmuting a process so mercurial as education. It is at this very point that we allow ourselves a different language based upon different assumptions. A liberating language that frees both vision and voice to see and say unconventional things, a language rich with images and symbolism that is not reluctant to embrace uncommon, even eccentric, modes of speech, is more suitable for inspiring and invigorating an anemic endeavor.

It must be for education as it is for poetry (as John Ciardi suggests) a "language of experience" not a "language of classification." Metaphors, similes, and other figures of speech will furnish the vocabulary and give expression to school programs. Sterile goal-statements and pedagogical propositions are not the same as educational expressions, and it is through metaphors that we express our grand visions. Agonic education is an expressive activity and requires an expressive idiom. If we simply state it in inflexible, literalistic language, we mistranslate it.

My intention in this section is to peruse selective literature for images that convey the expressive qualities of agon. The references, understandably, are limited and reflect personal reading preferences; but nevertheless, the examples will, I believe, be reasonably representative; and more importantly, they will provide a robust imagery that is conceptually symbolic and affectively satisfying.

HEMINGWAY

Pulitzer Prize-winning author Ernest Hemingway, with his terse, virile writing style and his fondness for conflict and combat themes must be included within the writer's agonic pantheon. Whether war or sport, he accentuates the heroic in all he writes. He was, as Clark's learned study portrays him, "a man in pursuit of the agonal ideal."[6] The heroic qualities of toughness, risk, adventure, and valor weave their way, with the pointed needle of pain, into an agonal tapestry. Whether bulls in Pamplona, elephants and lions in Africa, or fish in the Caribbean, pursuit, for Hemingway, became akin to a holy quest and conquest—gaining the holy grail, or in the language and life of ancient Greece, he pursued areté— nobility and excellence.

Hemingway was revered as a celebrity in Spain, and he embodied the qualities admired in bullfighters.[7] The link between the bullfighters in Spain and the bull leapers on the Cretan frescoes reveals the agonal connection between the societies. The Homeric concept of areté, evident in the life-endangering valor of the contestant, prompts the applause and evokes the admiration of the spectators. Pure sport, athletic prowess, virtuous combat—all were manifestations of the agonal ideal.

One of the most compelling portrayals of the agon motif by Hemingway is in *The Old Man and the Sea*.[8] The old man, Santiago, "is the quintessence of the ancient agonal warrior."[9] His struggle against formidable odds turns to eventual triumph. The non sequitur references to New York Yankee baseball great Joe DiMaggio provide the meaningful model of areté—the paragon of athletes who embodies all of the inward virtues and manifests outward excellence: "I must have confidence and I must be worthy of the great DiMaggio who does all things perfectly even with the pain of the bone spur in his head. . . . Do you believe the great DiMaggio would stay with a fish as long as I will stay with this one?"[10]

As Santiago encounters the marlin and struggles with it, he recapitulates the epic virtues from time immemorial of all true agonists who risk life in the pursuit of excellence—in pursuit of the ideal: "In agonal warfare, the glorious struggle is the most significant facet of the ethic, and the true agonal warrior knows that he needs his brother for another struggle, that a worthy opponent should not die in vain."[11]

As in sport, so in combat, the agon was manifested only in noble and virtuous struggle. Excellence was the defining quality for noble natures, and fighting according to rules of civility was the distinguishing mark of victory. Hemingway wrote in his novels of the degeneration of warfare into savagery, and of the barbaric debasement of the modern soldier who is required to kill as a matter of compliance with commands. Certainly modern warfare with its destructive and annihilative techno-kill has erased from the military the last vestiges of any morality it may ever have had.

The old agonal warfare was between brothers; conducted according to rules; limited in objectives and limited in time, in a necessary alternation of peace and war; the brothers need each other in order to fight another day. The new warfare is total: It seeks an end to war, and an end to brotherhood.[12]

Professionalism in sport and warfare has corrupted the agon motif today. Hemingway lamented the corruption. To a large extent, the blame must be laid at the feet of the technical specialization now available that allows anyone to acquire the means of participation without serious and noble identification with the ends of the enterprise.

KAZANTZAKIS

Few authors employ agonic, literary imagery as frequently and as effectively as the celebrated Greek author Nikos Kazantzakis (although Miguel De Unamuno of Spain is similar in style and substance).[13] He is, in my estimation, the consummate agonist. Although he acquired notoriety through a number of areas of artistic endeavor, his fiction writing and essays provide a cornucopia of vivid metaphors of struggle and transcendence. His cherished Greek historical and literary legacies created an enviable and emulative heritage for him, and quite naturally predisposed him to the agonic life. Kazantzakis conceptualized life in terms of struggle. The ancient Greek society furnished the classic concept of agon, and the continuous, perennial struggles of Greece, both politically and socially, imposed upon it, in part, by an often unsympathetic geography, transmitted that agonic awareness to contemporary Greece. Kazantzakis's homeland of Crete became, for him, the archetype of all arduous struggle. The "lordly island," as he called it, with its fierce, undeniable attraction as both companion and object of conquest could never avoid being the cynosure of avaricious empires which resulted in Crete's constant conflict and foreign domination. Its position in the Mediterranean Sea and its proximity to imperialist powers gave it a special, exotic appeal much like a seductress to a sensuous man. But additionally, its mountainous topography and sea-bound isolation contributed to the harshness of life of the people even as they, at the same time, could not resist its sun-drenched warmth and fertility.

Man is forever engaged in struggle, Kazantzakis contends, a struggle which, philosophically, seeks to transmute flesh into spirit. Flesh symbolizes the base and human constraints, the world of sense reality which, although necessary for life and for fulfilling meaning, must ultimately be transcended if true being is to be attained. The ontology of agony demands that students, while never ignoring or disregarding the tangible, present reality, must, nevertheless, never stop there. Materialistic philosophy and convenience-technology based on scientistic, nonmetaphysical assumptions inadequately explain life's purpose and man's being. Fulfillment, as it is used philosophically, psychologically, and educationally requires a goal, a transcendent point, a reachable level of aspiration above and beyond the routine of everyday life. It is this Kazantzakis has in mind when he contrasts the flesh and the spirit. Transmutation implies transcendence, and agonic education orders a learning environment with the "hard stuff" of life that engages the student holistically, but never in itself purports to be the final end.

Kazantzakis is fond of life cycles and growth stages expressed in living things as representation of his views. Grubs through struggle transform themselves into butterflies. Guts become gossamer. Cocoons are places, not for indolence and complacency, but environments in which the wonder-working transforming labors occur. If schools are cocoons for students, they are so only to the extent that they constitute a stage in this transformation process when as pupals (what a charming, serendipitous similarity to "pupil": etymologically there is a similarity in terms from their Latin derivations—girl and boy), they are engaged in growth and the eventual emergence from the chrysalis (etymologically "gold") reveals a complete, mature, functional being. Schools, whatever their design, if they fulfill their mission, are intended to be places where, in leisure (but not idleness), students are grubby and are transformed into gold.

Michael Brown, a human-resources consultant who advocates experiential education programs for all students, feels that such programs serve as facilitator for transformations. He likens the process to which students are exposed to a metamorphosis, "a permanent shift to a higher level of operating," but he acknowledges that this transformation by love "is a delicate and fragile process that is difficult to achieve." He explains:

The metamorphosis of a caterpillar into a butterfly must happen at the right time, must take place within the safety of a chrysalis, must be directed by an internal guiding principle, and involves a fundamental restructuring of its basic form.

Right timing, safety and an inner guiding principle are also necessary to achieve a comprehensive restructuring of basic patterns within the human psyche. . . . Wilderness and backcountry settings—free from many of the cultural and social influences of the regular world—can offer an ideal context or chrysalis for transformation to take place. And transformation, to a very significant degree, must be guided by an internal principle unique to each person, not simply forced from the outside.[14]

The reconceptualization of education in symbolic, metaphoric terms can "provoke regenerative effects" in students. The encrusted forms of schooling shaped by mechanical models, linearly constrained and geometrically designed, in which schedules conform to bells and buzzers and a host of hardware and software can profit too from transformations. The artist's eye and the poet's ear can provide newer visions and more-natural voices to express and echo the soul's desire. Softness and gentleness with contours, and serpentine shapes; pastels and portraits on the walls; mosaics and murals and music of the masters; poetry printed all about and time to stop and read it; cloistered silent places for meditation and reflection; open areas for talk about subjects worth pursuing, worth the time it takes to tell about them; quadrangles of hallowed, respected grass where macadam and concrete are not allowed, and ducks may waddle by, and birds are invited to feed and bathe; floral and fragrant gardens and whispering waterfalls, and springs that flow lazily covered at points by wooden bridges guarded by gazebos. Statuary surrounding us with remembrances of ages past and of people we should know. If there must be vending machines, allow them to sing us a song, or tell us a tale, or refresh us with strains of Mozart or Beethoven, Liszt or Brahms, Grieg, or even an occasional Gershwin.

Why must schools be all plaster, steel and glass, vinyl, concrete and cinder blocks? Pragmatic paint, durable but depressing. Insipid architectural styles, rectangularly the same. Design buildings with an eye to history and mystery, with intrigue and interest and enchantment that flows from imagination. Make the inside like a hospitable home, not like a doctor's office or factory or supermarket. Learning yearns for the warmth and wonder of places with texture and timeless charm, places we love to enter and hate to leave. And grow trees in the hallways, have fresh flowers in the rooms, and tell-tale signs that people live here. Make the schools loving places.

When educators with poetic appreciation for life are allowed to design schools and develop programs, perhaps then the harshness will soften, and children will seek out schools, seeing them as places in which they're welcome. Can we not couch our constructions within these metaphors?

Can we not use the inner vision to invent? Are we in such short supply of "poetic grace" (as Eisner calls it) that we are dominated by unfeeling, technological law? To paraphrase Browning: A man's speech should exceed his gasp or what's a metaphor.

Still, the fact that all linguistic expression is and remains "metaphorical" expression is proof that the capacity for objective representation can never become completely dominant in the domain of language. Metaphor constitutes an indispensable factor in language in its organic wholeness. Without metaphor language would lose its lifeblood and stiffen into a conventional system of signs.[15]

Spermatic and maternal metaphors are favorites of Kazantzakis. He speaks of Crete as clay which is always with him, a kind of maternal mud that he caresses affectionately; but in *Zorba the Greek*, his most celebrated novel, Zorba protests against the exclusiveness of mud. But where is the seed, Zorba demands to know. Nothing can grow without seed. Life within the seed is delicate and capricious, and the assurance of the life's survival and growth relates to its robustness in the struggle. The fragile life-form timidly tests the strange environment in which it finds itself, and if the surroundings repel the seed's advances, the seedling will retreat within itself. "Feelers" that encounter hostility or indifference will fear to probe further, and the inchoate form is stillborn. Germination will be proportionate to the seed's capacity to push away "pushable" obstacles. Seeds will be dwarfed if they meet no resistance. If the chick's shell is unnaturally and prematurely (even if sincerely) hatched, the chick will be dwarfed and deformed and may soon die. It is the legitimate struggle, the agonic engagement with that necessary tangible environment that allows that creature to emerge, at that stage, maturely. But if the eggshell is obdurate, through interference or aberration, the chick can never get out "of its shell." So children in schools must be given opportunities at each successive stage to test themselves and engage their natural world and come out of their shells. Well-meaning teachers may unwittingly deter the growth process by eliminating all legitimate obstacles to growth and, thereby, deform the pupils who never develop adequate coping skills, or by erecting unnatural barriers to growth which students are developmentally incapable of overcoming.[16] The concept has been succinctly explicated by Bull:

The new life demands new forms and the question is, are we going to retain the old forms and squander the new life or are we going to let the new life determine everything and allow it to work out its own forms suited to its own development? . . . It is the form which that life at the present stage of its development had adopted and from which it cannot be separated if it is to continue. If we destroyed that form the plant would never grow. It is essential to the life of that plant at that stage of development. As the life develops, however, we find that at a certain stage this form begins to be discarded. . . . Later, however, the form again changes its appearance. . . . The important principle remains, however, that the earlier form, although a product of the life force and essential to its expression at that stage of growth, must ultimately yield to the more mature form.[17]

Teachers if they are not creators of life are certainly cultivators of life within the classroom. The concept of garden for the growth of seed life need not be restricted to the Froebelian notion of the kindergarten. But gardens, perhaps surprisingly, are places of struggle. Fruits and flowers, fertility and fragrance are ultimately expressions and products made possible by and only enriched through struggle. Who has not observed the emergence of a plant of some sort which defied all odds to grow and prosper? I recall in our own yard, several years back, the annual growth of what eventually revealed itself to be a peach tree. Unplanted, a discarded peach pit found suitable soil, and, what was undeniably an effort that defied odds, grew into a productive, fruit-bearing tree which both startled us with its vigor and delighted us with its fruit. Admittedly, this phenomenon is unusual, perhaps even rare, but it demonstrates the resilience of life in the face of seemingly insurmountable odds. Even so, schoolchildren survive the hostile, unsympathetic environments in some schools, and, in fact, a brand of student may even thrive in that hostile environment; but it is better when deliberate preparation and planting of the seed occurs and the normal struggles of life alone are endured.

The imagery that we bring to education predisposes us to adopt certain teaching styles and methods. The ubiquitous references to engineering, programming, and mechanistic models (computer input-output, industry processing, etc.) in education, I contend, biases the enterprise in unhealthy ways.[18] Rich, expressive, organic metaphors such as leaven Kazantzakis's writings provide more-profitable points of discourse. Transcendence, as I have stated earlier, is not fashionable in education or society, but its neglect has, I believe, impoverished the educational process and stunted children's potentials. Thankfully, perennialists, like Huston Smith, have reintroduced the term into a part of the philosopher's vocabulary today, although, regrettably, he has not prompted a revolution in this type of rethinking.

Kazantzakis seizes on the dolphin symbol to communicate this concept. The flying fish is a favorite symbol in the ancient Greek texts. The palace at Knossos contains mosaics featuring the dolphin, and extant Egyptian carvings similarly highlight the dolphin. The dolphin among the sea animals is unique not only in its fondness for humans and its delight in engagement with people, but it represents a life-form that seeks to transcend its species' environment. Dolphins are displayed leaping from the waters into the air above. Seaward to skyward, they free themselves, if but temporarily, from their natural environment. It is this aspect that Kazantzakis attributes to transcendence. Although the everyday reality in which we move or swim permits us to survive and grow, that reality, we sense, is never finally fulfilling. Education that only seeks to accommodate us to our environment deprives us of developmental possibilities and of a fulfilling purpose. Learning that is merely life adjustment turns into a narcotic which dulls us into acceptance of the expedient and immediate. Hence, my personal dissatisfaction with narrowly vocational curriculums, and my protest against contemporary, reform movements (from Sputnik to *Nation at Risk*, et al.) which settle simply for skills that will be useful in a technological world.

I am not asking that we shed our skin. A radical transformation is not the object of my personal polemic. But knowledge, understanding, and wisdom that transform us, enrich us, and take us beyond the level of sensation and accommodation to a programmed environment will, with the technical skills, make us not only better equipped to survive, but will make us better people, and being better is always something we desire.

As students swim through the opaque waters of the curriculum, they need periodically to "come up for air" not simply to catch their breath, but to experience the vital awareness of an environment in which they may and should eventually live. Of course we dare not take the comparison to an extreme but the aquatic analogy Kazantzakis presents is appropriate for the school to consider. Water is obviously the natural environment for aquatic life, but certain species seek to transcend that environment. In their refusal to be confined to what appears to be the ordinary, agreeable realm of activity, they demonstrate both an awareness of and a desire for involvement in a sphere of being that presently eludes them, but which may ultimately be the basis for their survival. The effort involved in breaking through the barriers and leaping joyfully into the air may very well have a salubrious, self-enhancing impact on dolphins. The imagery is applicable to children in school.

A suitable, felicitous metaphor, in kinship with the dolphin, is the dance. Terpsichore was the muse of choral singing and dancing, enlivening life with artistic expression. Classrooms need choreographers—teachers who compose and conduct, who arrange the elements artistically like a symphony or a ballet. Life is drama and dance, and although Erving Goffman has in his scientific studies of social-exchange theory related the drama metaphor to life, dance has been only incidentally employed.[19] Typically the dance-of-life image has been applied to the biology of growth and development, and has served simply to capture the whimsicality of living things. Seligman seeking to explicate the relationship between environment and human growth chooses "dance" as the image that reflects the delicate, and, at points, capricious character of the movements between the two. The outcome of the dance of development, which begins in infancy, determines, he contends, the degree of mastery or helplessness which an individual achieves throughout life.[20]

Kazantzakis is fond of the dance metaphor particularly embodied in his most-celebrated character, Zorba. Zorba is at one with the universe. I never tire of reading the novel and usually permit myself the indulgent luxury of an annual rereading. In fact, I have taken the book to Crete, the place of its setting, and have lived and read the passages *in situ*. Few things are as pleasant, as Kazantzakis himself confessed, as sailing the Aegean Sea in springtime or autumn and imbibing the beauty of the ancient islands, inhaling the intoxicatingly sweet fragrance of the fabled red-wine sea, and being immersed in the agonic ambience of the lordly island.

Happy is the man, I thought, who, before dying, has the good fortune to sail the Aegean Sea . . . to cleave that sea in the gentle autumnal season, murmuring the name of each islet, is to my mind the joy most apt to transport the heart into paradise.[21]

Zorba tunes his santori and with careless abandon dances the day and night away. He calls upon the muses to translate him into their realm as, beneath the rich sun and lambent moon, upon the timeless sands:

He threw himself into the dance, clapping his hands, leaping and pirouetting in the air, falling on to his knees, leaping again with his legs tucked up—it was as if he were made of rubber. He suddenly made tremendous bounds into the air, as if he wished to conquer the laws of nature and fly away. One felt that in this old body of his there was a soul struggling to carry away his flesh and cast itself like a meteor into the darkness. . . . At last Zorba crouched on the ground out of breath. His face was shining and happy.[22]

George Leonard has established himself as an observer and reporter who possesses a unique perspective on life. Dissatisfied with the traditional, banal understandings of human behavior, Leonard has brought a fresh vibrancy to the discourse about the meaning of things. His description of a classroom is more a coloration than a characterization: "A classroom, any classroom, is an awesome place of shadows and shifting colors, a place of unacknowledged desires and unnamed powers, a magic place."[23]

Classrooms, schools, society, yea the very universe, for Leonard are places in which a dance is unfolding, a dance aesthetically satisfying and agonically fulfilling. From the minute mechanism of an atom to the sprawling, incomprehensible universe, a cosmic dance, a silent pulse is resonating, and when we sense ourselves moving harmoniously with the rhythm, we are then alive to life's full possibilities. One does not have to be a follower of fashionable, human-potential movements or be-all-you-can-be fads to appreciate the power and the perfection that such notions of symmetry and harmony present.

The dance metaphor above all offers itself so pleasantly, so appealingly to us because pulsations are the sticking points, the trysting places of our very being. We are vibrating beings who seek vibrancy, who wish to lead vibrant lives. Our vernacular has accepted the notion of "vibes" as expressing a life in touch and in tune with the rhythm of life, "the rhythm of relationships," as Leonard terms it. The reason so much of education is irrelevant today is that it is not tuned; it does not resonate with the fundamental condition of human life. Humans are more than makers and thinkers and do-ers; they are dancers!

The truth of the matter is, the human animal was born a singer and dancer. Rich and complex cultures existed for at least a million and a half years without pyramids and cathedrals, and we can perhaps conceive of a future without high-rises. But a humanity without music is not just inconceivable; it is impossible.[24]

Schools should be studios of dance. Athletics, to the extent that they are fulfilling and enriching, are themselves forms of dance. Not surprisingly, many university departments today which had formerly been devoted exclusively to physical education and recreation now include within the departmental curriculum the area of dance. What is as pleasing as the enviable ease of the long-distance runner, with gazellelike grace, caught up in the flow of the chase, not, however, without the agony of labored breathing, and accelerated pulse, and muscles stretched and tendons taut, and sweat-drenched skin glistening vibrantly. And we know this is a dance, a dance of distance, an internal metronome keeping time, ordering the rhythm. Wrestlers encircling each other on the mat, clasping and unclasping, getting an advantage, losing it, and finally the pin. This too is dance. Tempo, rhythm, vibrato, pitch—all terms musical and terpsichorean capture the spirit of the enterprise.

And there are other parallels, other dances. What is the recent appeal of figure skating in the winter Olympics? Why has that event achieved premiere status? Poetic flows of rhythm, acrobatic leaps and spins, defying gravity, chasing the wind, the uncluttered simplicity of the human form frictionlessly transcending the limitations of weight and the ice's unforgiving chill, achieving what George Leonard calls "perfect rhythm." Gymnastics, elegantly precise movements that mesmerize the spectator, sinuous forms flipping and cavorting like dolphins, breaking through invisible barriers, emerging into sunlit auras. And swim is a lateral dance. Sleek, sculptured bodies slice through water as through air, economy of motion, unwasted effort, flowing like a fish. Everyone a dancer keeping tempo, harmoniously blending with the elements which make them active, but with every stroke, with every breath, the struggle to transcend the elements and achieve areté.

Schools are staid and safe places. Safe in the sense that the risk and the thrill have been factored out. Schools more often resemble asylums and hospitals and factories when they should be studios and arenas and battlefields. Students must transform the "fear of falling into the joy of flying." Leonard relates a personal drama of his involvement in the martial arts which tellingly, vividly describes the dance quality of the contest.

From the very beginning, it was apparent that something extraordinary was occurring. It was like one of those sporting events that are later memorialized . . . during which every last spectator realizes at some level that what is happening out on the field is more than a game, but rather something achingly beautiful and inevitable, an enactment in space and time of how the universe works, how things are. . . . Everyone . . . noticed the shift of illumination. . . . Some people also began seeing an aura—some described it as golden, others as clear plastic. . . . the speed and intensity of the attacks increased, and yet there was still a general sense of time's moving slowly, an unhurried, dreamlike pace. . . . The exam continued in this spirit, like a long, hypnotic phase of music. . . . Richard seemed to become denser, brighter, unmistakably golden. The genius of aikido is to transform the most violent attack, by embracing it, into a dance and it was the essence of dance we saw there on the mat.[25]

Teaching and learning should together embrace each other as a dance, as the DNA spirals dancelike, as the unfolding of flowers warmed by the sun, as athletes in rhythm with themselves and nature. Overly calculated, stiffly cerebral, tyrannically technologized schools fragment life instead of allowing it to flower. The dance is ingrained in all of life's movements and should be reflected in school activities.

At the start of each semester, I have college students engage in a brief activity which I term an exercise in empathy. In pairs, they present themselves to each other, and they are asked, in a sense, to dance. One of the pair is a mirror and the other views himself in the mirror. As the viewer looks, he is told to begin to move, dancelike, small facial movements at first and then larger movements until the whole body is involved. The mirror is to reflect empathically what she, the viewer, does until eventually the two are in consonance, in harmony with one another and dancing. At first, students are awkward and embarrassed; they find it difficult to initiate or respond. Some, however, do achieve a dancelike quality, and it is pleasant to watch their unified movements.

To have this kind of ecstasy, this exuberance, this enchantment in the classroom would be transforming indeed. Of course, not every school day can be so exuberant. Tedium goes along with the task. But if we could reconfigure the classroom in terpsichorean terms, visualizing it as a developmental dance where student and curriculum engage each other in style and rhythm sinuously and robustly, we might create conditions for joyful education. Why must the curriculum be so linear? Why must we conform learning to blocks and squares and categories that never relax? Mechanical and engineering models with well-honed, precisely planed, and unmistakably matched parts, so unimaginatively mitered, are manageable and manipulable and certainly fit nicely into a technological world, but movement inspired by dance, and elegance enriched by spontaneity, attuned to what life is, address the fundamental qualities of the spirit, the qualities that not only must endure, but which, ultimately, define human nature.

Dance as an expression of play has no redeeming value except its service to the spiritual. Dance does not bake or buy or bury. It will give us no gadgets, will not take out our garbage, but it will teach us that we must live in harmony with the world about us. It teaches us that there is a rhythm by which we must abide if we are to live well. It teaches us that we are not solo acts, for it takes two to tango, and even the ballerina in all her singular splendor needs, at some point, her counterpart. Dance will teach our spirits to be in tune with our bodies. Aristotle prescribed dance for kinesthetic awareness, and for appreciation of the aesthetic quality the body can have. Dance, like athletics, attunes the person to poise and refinement of character, although unlike sports, dance is discursive. Not surprisingly, the psychomotor taxonomies list as the supreme, most-complex physical skill nondiscursive communication such as dance exemplifies.[26]

The experiences constituted within curriculums must be predicated upon the ontological reality of the student's being in this world. Both physical and social realities must be considered in the construction of

curricular activities, but additionally, self-transcendent opportunities are
required. Aesthetic and artistic expression will probably be the curricular
domain most suitably designed for the effecting of transcendence, but
sadly, these very areas receive the least attention in curriculum development; and in a technocratic society, leadership refuses to give a fair share
of the student's curricular time to this realm. Flach's contention that
resilience, which is the capacity for strength in times of stress, needs to be
nurtured in schools, and the aesthetic areas of the curriculum, now,
unhappily reduced, are the garden plots in which resilience grows.[27]
Neglect or dismissal of the curricular realm of the humanities and arts,
aesthetics as such, irreparably damage children who are then restricted to
the cognitive-mechanical realms of the curriculum.

Robert Bersson, instructor in art education, identifies the flaw and
fallacy in a curriculum devoid of aesthetic experience. The contemporary,
technocratic society, he contends, militates against "sensuous immediacy"
and rationalizes aesthetic experience, imposing upon it a prefigured
paradigm that is "rational, scientific, purposive, control and mastery-
oriented."[28] Phenomena are not directly perceived or, more critically,
directly sensed. Aesthetic experiences are increasingly mediated and
overly cerebralized. This is the kind of school, akin to cultures created by
computers, which, as W. I. Thompson contends, is "most unsensuous."[29]

My personal concurrence with this observation indicts the excessive
reliance, generated in part by the control mentality of the Western mind-
set, on mediated experiences. A sensuous, nonmediated experiencing of
the environment and world provides opportunities for agonal awareness.
Tangible, tactual, visual, auditory, and kinesthetic experiencing of
concrete, unprogrammed, and prefigured reality allows students to develop a
taste for life; they can envision as well as see; they can get a handle on
life. These concerns in art education, suggested by Dewey and reechoed
by Eisner (and in all education), do not belong exclusively to the realm of
humanism and holistic education. Maslowian, third-force psychology
allies itself to this perspective but does not claim authorship or exclusivity.
One need not subscribe to the excessive sentimentalism of the 1960s or
even Rousseauian romanticism to recognize the importance of direct,
agonic experience. The modern mind-set, which Huston Smith so articu-
lately critiques,[30] has elevated, even deified, the technocratic control
approach to education and social life. The cultural advances occur, however, when the social and educational context encourages the spontaneous
and spiritual pursuits; but when technology dictates conditions, aesthetic
and spiritual claims are dismissed as superstitious, nonutilitarian or
unproductive luxuries. And so Bersson notes:

Unfortunately, our technocratic capitalist society remains tied to a cultural code that demands strict predictability, conformity, and "rational behavior." Sensuous aesthetic behavior, which by its very nature is unpredictable, spontaneous, and uncompromisingly personal, appears to most of us as incomprehensible or even bizarre.[31]

Critics of the present, technocentric education feel like they are talking into the wind when they raise questions about the direction in which we are heading. Despite the credible testimony to the technocratic folly all about us, despite the peril in which we have placed the planet by our wanton disregard for things of the spirit, despite the Philistinism that permeates this "cultural-less" culture, this society flagrantly thumbs its nose at the artistic temperament, mocks all educational efforts that do not have a technical payoff, and promotes cultural barbarism. Bersson is right when he says, "in the increasingly conservative, technocratic educational and social context . . . it will require courage to educate students to experience aesthetically."[32]

But courage may not be enough, because courage often leads to ostracism by the society; and the technocratic elite that controls school boards and budgets will dismiss aesthetic concerns as incompatible with the realistic demands of a consumer society. And, of course, they will be right, but they will be addressing the wrong issue; they will have asked the wrong question. Should consumerism constitute the criterion for education? So we come back to Livingstone's questions: What is the goal of education? What is the goal of society? Consumerism is an appropriate goal only for a society that is adrift, for a society that has lost its moorings, a society that identifies people as statistics or ciphers factored in to a gross national product.

Chapter 10

Agon and Creativity

Clearly, creativity is a crucial element in the struggle to succeed. Effort alone never guarantees success. Although effort is a vital ingredient in learning in every aspect of life, and its absence will thwart the growth process and undoubtedly produce a dwarfed specimen, effort must be controlled and directed creatively. The type of effort that is needed for successful life in school is based upon strength, certainly physical and cognitive, but equally importantly, psychological and moral strength. Psychiatrist William Glasser opts for the term strength in identifying the *sine qua non* for successful living. Equivalent terms such as self-esteem, confidence, effectance, and so forth convey similar meanings and suggest comparable qualities.

Flach's engaging study of the relationship between strength and stress employs the term "resilience" to identify the key quality needed for successful living, particularly at crisis times in the life, times Flach calls "bifurcation points."[1] Resilience, the capacity to reintegrate and redirect life during and after bifurcation points, requires the ability to redefine, refine, and reorganize experience and perceptions. This process, according to Flach, is the essence of creativity. A major difficulty with modern schooling, he contends, is that technology limits the diversity of input that is required for the creative act.

In this age of technology and specialization, some of us lack sufficient exposure to a wide variety of input; this is particularly true for professionals. . . . We are hampered even more by the abandonment of required subjects that once constituted the core curriculum in most liberal arts colleges. . . . While it is true that television has broadened our contact with a wide variety of issues and experiences . . . we must keep in mind that such exposure is *largely vicarious. It is not the real thing and cannot substitute for reality.* (Italics mine.)[2]

Students today are less resilient than they were in a pretechnological society. Admittedly, my pronouncements here are conjectural and impressionistic, but I believe they can be supported with research in the realm of experiential education to which we will make more detailed reference later. Children in pretechnological societies who experience material privation stand in marked contrast to children in the United States and Western nations by their resilience. My personal experience with college students participating in short-term cross-cultural study tours in Second and Third World countries continues to startle me with the limited capacity of middle-class American students to adapt to situations of modest privation. Long-term exposure to cross-cultural contexts provides a better opportunity for student adjustment. I have seen children in Egypt and Turkey and the Middle East demonstrate singular resilience as they seek daily to survive. Under comparable circumstances, the typical U.S. child, nurtured within the technological womb would probably expire.

Athletic imagery and military metaphors commend themselves for framing educational situations and designing learning experiences. I do not, of course, wish to commend the associations these terms convey in actual social practice today. I decry the barbarity of war (and ironically as the military has become more technological, war has become more barbaric), and I deplore both the narcissism and commercialism of much of contemporary sports. I wish to draw upon these two activities, and draw principally from their historic associations, for the ennobling agonic element that permeated them.

Athletic imagery as the Greek term connotes (and it was the genius of the Greeks to define and create it) involved two inescapable, coexisting and mutually enriching elements: competition and excellence. The elements are expressed in the respective Greek terms agon and areté. Agon for the Greeks, although related to play, was not the same as ludi for the Romans. Gardiner's treatise makes the contrast clear:

These Roman Games, however were very different from the athletic festivals of the Greeks. The difference is implied in the very word "ludi." The Greek meetings are never described as games but as contests (agones). Whether dramatic, musical, equestrian, or athletic, they are competitions, primarily between free citizens; and they exist primarily for the competitors. The Roman games are ludi, amusements, entertainments and the performers are slaves or hirelings; they exist for the spectators.[3]

Pfitzner concurs with Gardiner in identifying the contrasting styles of the Greek and Roman approaches to athletics. Pfitzner, however, contends that the agon concept extended not only individually but collectively to all of Greek civil life, "so that the entire civic life of a Greek became, as it were an Agon in which to exert himself and excel over others."[4]

One of the prevailing problems in modern education involves the insidious claim that education is entertainment. Such a concept would be foreign to the ancient mind and contrary to common sense. Education may, and perhaps should be enjoyable—enjoyable in the sense that it is the natural function of the mind to learn as it is the function of the stomach to digest, and in performing both processes properly, enjoyment occurs. But entertainment is noneducative, and, unarguably, amusement is (as the word's etymology indicates: no thought) the antithesis of thought and learning. The Roman world with its decadence and eventual demise communicates the idea all too forcibly. Education as a spectator activity performed by showmen for the amusement of students is the most perverse travesty one can consider. True education involves a noble and enriching engagement in which students strive to master, first themselves and then material, not for vain glorification, but for the virtue inherent in the task.

Sir Richard Livingstone's exegesis and exposition of the term in the context of Greek society provide a penetrating analysis of its significance in that society and offers an inviting basis on which to build education today. In two of his works, *Greek Ideals and Modern Life*, and his aptly titled, *Education for a World Adrift*, areté constitutes the core concept for understanding the genius and accomplishment of the ancient Greek society. Areté is a primitive, perennially significant term emerging within Greek life as the vision of greatness and the quest for excellence became articulated. It is not simply a technical term employed by philosophers in their dialectics; it predates them, being pregnant with both philosophical and pedagogical meaning.

Without an adequate understanding of this fundamental term and without a recognition of the weightiness of the burden and the grandeur of the vision involved, education reduces itself to mere technical proficiency in performance, and if this is all that results, it is indeed a tragic loss. Agonic education insists upon a clear-eyed pursuit of excellence, toward virtue, toward areté. The struggle metaphors, which permeate the Greek approach to education, can provide fruitful imagery to shape contemporary education. We need to dialogue with this Greek past in order to understand the creative genius which they bequeathed to us. Vlachos maintains that in the Greek sense of the word, agon, "Athens was in a perpetual state of agony," because the Greeks pursued personal and social acclaim and recognition.[5]

Creativity is a loosely regulated term spanning the unfocused spectrum from dilettantism and dabbling to undeniable and unrepeatable genius. Without resorting to the excessive technical trappings given to genius by researchers like Sir Francis Galton and Lewis Terman, we can maintain, nevertheless, that creativity involves uniqueness, imagination, and value. At the simplest level, creativity may be any individual's moment of fulfillment, a specific point in one's experience when something of the quintessential self has manifested itself in a way that is indisputably valuable. At the most-profound level, creativity is the unrepeatable discovery or creation of superb excellence by genius. But creativity without value is a misnomer. Creative criminality is a contradiction in terms, but in our society which indulges extravagant claims and is fond of "cooling out the mark" (Erving Goffman's phrase), oxymorons are the stock in trade of publicists. Creativity typically does not occur apart from agony. The classic paradigm of creativity beginning with preparation, germinating during incubation, advancing to illumination, and culminating in verification regrettably neglects to state explicitly the role of agony. Intensive agonic struggle must occur somewhere or, like birth, creativity will be stillborn.

Among struggling artists, especially those who have eventually received notoriety and public acclaim, the agonic aspect of their suffering has been highlighted. English painter Samuel Palmer lived a life of pain and privation. William Cowper, noted eighteenth-century English poet, was an anguished individual who seldom seemed to be free from the persistent torment that contributed to his creativity and his confinement.[6] Poets, painters, traditionally the creative, but also scientists and thinkers, all who have aspired, have experienced trauma and agony and even grief. In fact, grief (which is the mourning of loss) may be a precondition for creativity. Creativity and agony are kinsmen. "The greater the grief, the greater the creative energy to which it gives rise," says Paul Tournier, Swiss psychologist.[7] True education requires agony and grief. Technology is antiagony! Technology is designed to eradicate struggle and privation, loss and grief. But life requires deprivation, and education cannot be, in any meaningful sense, a series of gleeful, effortless expeditions into fantasy lands.

Any commentary on the role of agony in life is incomplete without reference to the writings of Victor Frankl and particularly *Man's Search for Meaning*. A recent survey asking people to identify the book that had the greatest influence on their lives produced a list of ten books which included Frankl's work. In this autobiographical account of life in Auschwitz, Frankl describes his conditions and the role of privation in creating meaning. He was one of the few who survived. I am not suggesting that education should include anything so severe as the prison-camp experience, but survivors of such places, as Terrence Des Pres has told us, have unique stories to tell and lessons for us to learn.[8] The greatest truth Frankl had ever discovered, he discovered amid the misery and mutilation of that internment camp. Here's how he tells it:

A thought transfixed me: for the first time in my life I saw the truth as it is set into song by so many poets, proclaimed as the final wisdom by so many thinkers. The truth—that love is the ultimate and the highest goal to which man can aspire. Then I grasped the meaning of the greatest secret that human poetry and human thought and belief have to impart: The salvation of man is through love and in love.[9]

If we could have students in our schools glimpse but the beginnings of this startling truth, we would have accomplished more than we are presently doing with all of our sophisticated technology. Perhaps (I say perhaps) privation is the *sine qua non*, the necessary prerequisite for creativity and for ultimate self-renewal. Mary Council in the *Journal of Creative Behavior* assures us that the path to creativity

is seen as arduous and onerous. Yet, creating inspiration is a milestone for magic, mystery and miracles. Those who do not seek this path are perhaps confined to the maelstrom of superficial existence. . . . It is the obligation of each of us to generate and emote an ambiance [*sic*] for creating inspiration. For if we as a species do not inspire, it would seem we are destined to expire.[10]

Although education is inescapably social in nature, it is fundamentally personal and individual. In a world that little tolerates solitude and often sees aloneness as a symptom of psychological disorder, we would do well to remember that each of us needs space to grow, the kind of space that Parker Palmer describes as space "in which audience to truth is practiced."[11] The active weeks of engagement with the environment in wilderness encounter programs will not yield long-range results without the three-day solo experiences in which space and silence come together. The shrillness of this cacophonous age destroys space and certainly erects barriers to solitude. I recall with fondness elementary school days when teachers gave us "free time," not to talk or read necessarily (but we could if we wished), not to be active, but to create our own space, to listen to the inner voice, or to dialogue with silence. That was before technology intruded. In our society, it is all but impossible to escape the ubiquity of social sound. It assaults us everywhere we go, and schools, which should be the places of leisured silence at times, become echo chambers for the world's verbosity.

Therapist-poet Edward Tick contends that creativity can only be spawned in solitude: "It is indeed creative solitude that is the necessary condition."[12] During solitude, we are least alone; chronic, unchosen loneliness is a dreaded state, but freely embraced solitude is the only climate for cultivating creativity's exotic flower. But solitude is not to be mistaken for morbid self-preoccupation; it is not time for narcissistic indulgence. Retreat into the "interior" can only be helpful when students seek within themselves resources which they have developed in the interaction with the real world. Agonic activity, during which personal testing occurs and strength accrues, generates a store of psychic, emotional, and spiritual supplies upon which people can draw for creative responses to life's difficulties and obstinateness. Just as young children require the uninterrupted periods of "daydreaming" when cortical neurology is enriched, and when runners "spin out" and meditators "tune in," all of us can profit from the placid periods when the mind and soul renew themselves and face the future, fortified with the successes of the past, and creatively pursuing new paths to the future. Csikszentmihalyi cites significant research that demonstrates the critical need for solitude and prolonged attention to tasks. The tyrannical "peer group" of today that often monopolizes students' time detracts significantly from the creative potential and from productivity itself. Although social interaction is important, superficial, unprofitable, and sustained peer-group dominance retards creativity and irreparably damages cognitive and creative growth.[13]

Minimal requirements for life must be maintained. Sufficient food, clothing, and shelter ensure survival. Fulfillment of basic psychological needs (love, worth, joy, etc.) keep our emotional equilibrium intact. But excess may be dangerous. More of a good thing is not necessarily a good thing. The problem of obesity among our population testifies to that truism. There must be periods of privation as well as periods of plenty. In education, excess is as deleterious as insufficiency. We are too quick to load a student's day with demands. We fret when there is unscheduled time, and we see every unused moment as a vacuum that must be filled. Testimonies that come from the creative and wise among us attribute both the creativity and the wisdom to lack as well as to abundance; to loss as well as to availability. But this is an extremely difficult lesson to teach, for everyone in our technocracy raises his voice against it.

Tournier contends that there is a critical link between deprivation and creativity, and he cites the record of numbers of orphans who have risen to positions of eminence and influence beyond what probability would have been predicted.[14] Authors and artists of significance almost without exception identify the critical loss or trauma that took the form of artistic expression. The loss not uncommonly sublimates itself into the work of art and as D. H. Lawrence declares: "One sheds one's sickness in books, repeats and presents again one's emotions to be master of them." David Aberbach concludes that "creativity in the wake of loss is treated as a means . . . [to] struggle to express and to master his grief and, in doing so, find meaning in continued life."[15]

I am not proposing that schoolchildren be subjected mercilessly to loss simply to foster potential creativity, nor am I naive enough to believe that all loss or suffering will result in benefit. For some people, loss is crippling and something from which they may never recover. But for many others, the opportunity for strategic aloneness, for strategic deprivation—the uncluttering of the environment when space is cleared away for growth, when the technological toys are removed—allows their creative capacities to be called into play. Our caloric curriculums are bloated with undigested bits and pieces of everything, a great deal unpalatable, tending to generate more heat than light. Time apart for each student without the slavish ties to other people and certainly not to technology may be the simple but effective antidote to much of the madness that is so pervasive.

Hans Selye's concept of *eustress* is helpful here. The legitimate demands placed upon us which lead neither to neuroticism or another's notice allow for expression of our inner selves that is most satisfying. The fragmentation of life today has been labeled and lamented by all reflective people. Dare the curriculum contribute to this disease? Why allow a society out of control to inflict its illness upon schoolchildren? Despite the rhetoric of "wholeness," fragmentation prevails. Agonic effort, which will produce eustress that moves the student beyond himself into a critical engagement with true life, coupled with alternating, reflective silences in which periods of inner cohesion can occur, can facilitate integration of self and connection with life.

Nostalgia aside, I recall my childhood days in a war-weary society when industry made munitions and armaments and had little to spare for amusements and distractions. In our neighborhood, pastimes were occasions for creative play. Children were required to construct their own play worlds or have none. Games and activities emerged from collective enterprise and from personal resourcefulness. There was no technological genie of the lamp granting wishes, nor experts available to advise us how to order our days. I do not wish to return to those times; I am too much a child of this present age. But if history can provide learning for the present, the one lesson there for our profit is that too little is probably better than too much. Too little prods us to creative resolution; too much makes us lethargic and complacent.

Chapter 11

Agon and Athletic Imagery

The agon motif is a felicitous term derived from athletics and adaptable to education. For the ancient Greeks, "[t]he agon was simply the outward expression of the characteristic Greek outlook upon life and upon the whole human scene."[1] Jeremiads abound today lamenting the loss of striving for excellence. Books about business and education proliferate from polemic pens indicting this generation for its indifference to standards of excellence.[2] But the loss of the pursuit of excellence is a critical manifestation of a general lack of a wholesome, competitive spirit in society. The homogenization of the culture repudiates differences and distinctions. Richard Weaver addressed this issue more than a generation ago when he noted that "the most portentous general event of our time is the steady obliteration of those distinctions which create society."[3]

A society without legitimate, functional distinctions cannot endure, and distortion of these distinctions will eventuate in perversions of our educational programs. People are not all alike. Although democracy demands that equal opportunities to succeed be afforded all citizens, not all will succeed in similar ways, and in terms of the values that create and maintain the society, some people are more capable of achieving them than other people.

Distinctions will inevitably result when legitimate competition is allowed. Of course, I am not subscribing to a system of ruthless, cutthroat competition where might makes right. Implicit in all this is the element of excellence, and we need to reclaim an educational system that makes excellence its creed; when this is restored to its preeminent place, we will have returned to Plato's concept of the just society ruled over by wise leaders. The agon motif is the cornerstone on which the educational edifice must be built. Huizinga's observation still provides the classic crystallization of the idea:

> From the life of the child right up to the highest achievement of civilization one of the strongest incentives to perfection, both individual and social, is the desire to be praised and honored for one's excellence. In praising another each praises himself. We want the satisfaction of having done something well. Doing something well means doing it better than others. In order to excel one must prove one's excellence; in order to merit recognition, merit must be manifest. Competition serves to give proof of superiority.[4]

Loy and Hesketh have provided a four-stage model of the agon motif.[5] Stage one involves recognition of the quest for excellence and designing a disciplined, training program in preparation to become the best. Stage two requires opportunities for testing oneself against oneself, and against peer competitors. Stage three involves the demonstration of superiority over those peers by appropriate competition in agonal tests. Stage four is the culmination of the agonal enterprise in the manifestation of excellence by victory in competition, and in recognition and celebration by agonal peers. The similarity between the model and the actual structures developed for the Olympic games is apparent.

Social stratification "is a primary process underlying agonal systems." Differences and distinctions are not only unavoidable, they are desirable. The criticism that typically surfaces when this kind of program is suggested is that it is nonegalitarian and will lead to abuses and unfair advantages. Such a criticism is not without merit. Sadly, human nature has all too readily demonstrated its penchant for excess and inequity. The corrective to such an outcome requires that the system be built upon a moral base. Axiological issues are paramount. Ruthless, unprincipled exploitation is never the goal of the game nor the basis on which any system should be established. The society must accept and abide by the ethical imperatives, and contestants have a noble obligation to adhere to them. Rewards are distributed as achievement approximates excellence, but excellence (areté), although individually attained, derives from social commitments. Moral qualities combined with competitive valor are reflected in the concept of *kalos k' agathos*: an individual who is both good and noble; both virtuous and valorous. Gardiner sums the virtues of this competitor in *aidos*: "the feeling of respect for what is due to the gods, to one's fellow men, to oneself."[6]

Discipline shares kinship with pedagogy. The English word connotes "self-mastery," and the Greek word which translates as "discipline" comes from the root that yields our word "mathematics." We speak of academic specialty areas as disciplines. The word weaves its way like a skein through the fabric of education.

Athletics take place within arenas, in places of contest and struggle, where effort, achievement, and success are rewarded. Arenas are not places for indifference or indulgence. Pleasure results from accomplishment and is considered virtuous only as a consequence of preparation and privation. Each level of performance demands its distinct discipline and its areté. School-age children cannot be expected to exhibit the same degree of mastery as mature adults, but there is, nevertheless, a degree of mastery that can be demanded. Indifference to appropriate discipline, or acceptance of inferior styles restricts development. Competition has always been a critical element in athletics, and the Greek ideal includes participation at appropriate levels. At the Olympic games, on the table that displayed the prizes the figure of agon (competition) was represented.[7] Roman games (and undoubtedly Greek games during the period of Greece's decline) were little more than gruesome, violent spectacles provided for an effete society which chose the effortless, enervating, passive activity of viewing (sadly, not unlike much of what we see in society today). At their best, Greek games were noble contests where individuals were recognized and rewarded, but only as their participation was encouraged and sanctioned by society, and only as their performance contributed to the glory of the polis and honored the gods.

Education needs to recapture the twin virtues of personal conquest and civic welfare, the axes on which life rotates. By conquest, I do not mean, of course, the wanton pursuit of personal vainglory and material goods. Conquest does not imply domination over others, nor control for control's sake. "Competition" is a Latin-derived term akin to "competent" and means to "seek with or seek together." Competition as reflected in agonic education is unlike the notions that commercialized sports connote. Competition creates a context for the quest (again the notion of seeking is involved) for excellence. Without a standard against which to gauge one's activity, there is no assurance that progress is being made or excellence is being achieved.

The variety of athletic events and the skills and disciplines involved provide images for education. Running or racing may be the premiere metaphor. In addition to the strength-enhancing qualities which the act of running provides and the positive addictive qualities it promotes (which in themselves would commend it for inclusion in the curriculum), as an image to inform the educational process, it is exquisite. The curriculum is a course to be traveled, a road to be taken, terrain to be traversed. It involves a starting and an ending point, physical and mental discipline, and renewal of energy to be exerted in the task. One simply cannot run without expending effort. Speed may be of value in rather limited areas of skill manipulation, but endurance is by far the superior virtue in accomplishing the task.

Education is a long-time (lifetime?) enterprise. It is the marathon, not the sprint, that should shape our thinking as we lay out the educational course. Breaking down long-term goals into achievable and manageable short-term tasks is desirable, but, mistakenly, reducing education to a simple series of short-term tasks distorts the purpose. Television with its short-term attention span, dictated by the need for programmed commercials, has shaped perceptions for at least two generations of American students. Students do not pay attention for very long. Scott Peck lists attention among the critical prerequisites for growth.[8] Computers, similarly, with accelerated processing and time distortion, have made havoc of natural time cycles.[9] Technology, fiendishly, creates temporal aberrations; to last the long haul, students must learn to endure. Success in schools and life are linked to both the willingness to endure and the capacity for persistence and stick-to-itness. And that is the commodity conspicuously lacking today, and, of course, the commodity least encouraged today in modern society. Expedience, instantaneousness, and the fast-food mentality have elevated immediacy to the status of prime virtue. It seems that no one wants to stay with the task for very long.

The society that laments limited relationships, aborted commitments, and the lack of hard-fought, future aspirations creates and encourages the conditions for these very situations. Children raised before a television screen, by which they are not only amused but continuously visually stimulated (albeit, passively) seek only the titillating; and this caprice is translated into education as entertainment. A recent newspaper interview with a veteran, retiring teacher identified this as the major complaint of teachers—that students demanded to be entertained. My own experience confirms this perception. During the three decades of my professional educational involvement, the trickle of student indifference and desire for novelty has cascaded into a torrent of apathy and a demand for entertainment. Neil Postman characterizes the contrast as between Athenians and Visigoths. Athenians, regardless of their vocational pursuits, admire grace and virtue in pursuit and cultivate a sense of and appreciation for the quality that can only be the result of a long-term commitment; whereas Visigoths are cliché people, reveling in the immediate, desiring only present gratification and personal pleasure. In that sense, Visigoths are hedonic and idiotic (using the Greek definitions of the terms).[10]

These observations are not original, although often unacknowledged, and anyone who accepts their claims runs the risk of being labeled anachronistic and reactionary. Students need to run the race of education. They need to be reminded, by reiteration, that education serves other functions than current reality and present relevancy. The image must be impressed upon them. Successful marathoners are people of disciplined life-styles who practice daily and diligently, and who have learned to subordinate present, petty cravings to future, critical goals. James Shapiro, author of *Ultramarathon*, described the longest race of his life, a race that involved a twenty-four-hour endurance run at the Crystal Palace Sports Centre in London. He had been selected as one of the elite corps of marathoners to participate in this grueling test of endurance. The object was simple: run for twenty-four hours around a track. The one who covered the greatest distance would, of course, be declared the winner; but anyone who completed the agonizing, complete-day duration would be a winner.

Seventeen runners started, and a distance of 130 miles was considered a reasonable goal for the runners. Shapiro narrates his personal agon and relates his thoughts and feelings, his elation and his fears, and above all, the struggles he endured to complete the twenty-four-hour assignment. Read his words as he recalls the last phase of the race, of the challenge he confronted when the temptation to give up goaded him:

Straight pain on the thighs. There is no verbal equivalent for this, and my mind, often so happy to chew on verbal models of the world has nothing to say. Running now is trying to swim far below the ocean surface. The pain is crushing. The world becomes a flow of gravity that pierces any attempt to sit up. No release, no relief, no easing of limbs will come now from attempting to run. Better now to give up and let the creeping current of a walk carry me a few yards further. It has occurred to me before the race that it would be reasonable to run 23 hours and just sit out the last hour. I consider it now. What more can I do? Is it worth pushing in such a wretched state for the sake of a mile or so? But the race is about distance covered and it is done however one looks doing it.[11]

And as Shapiro strains toward the very end, he records his thoughts about the last minute:

One minute to go. This is happiness, if I stop to think about it but now I just feel it. Mad as a hatter, I go around curves past the yelling faces. Someone runs toward me with an orange traffic cone, the final marker of my voyage. . . . I utter some

strangled half-broken sobs and then at last, the long-sought release comes. . . .
There are hugs, pictures, handshakes, congratulations all around. Word comes
that I have covered 138 miles, 1,228 yards. . . . I am profoundly grateful. I am
content at last.[12]

Perhaps some will consider this too masochistic, the imagery too
brazenly stoical. Perhaps it is. But maybe we have done and continue to
do an injustice to students by "de-stressing" education and life. Perhaps,
conversely, by "de-agonizing" education, we pervert the process that
provides them with strength. Of course, there is a cost. This kind of
education will undoubtedly leave scars and take its toll, but dare we
capitulate to a cosmetic culture that makes appearances everything? The
internal, autonomous being is of greatest value.

The ancient, Olympic games celebrated the victors of the agons. A
variety of competitive athletic events were staged and success depended
upon skill and discipline, Dilettantes dared not enter, but rewards for the
victorious given in public recognition of devotion and discipline were
incentives enough for the privation the participants endured. But the
agon-incentive predates the Olympics and is woven into the fabric of
Greek life. Burckhardt's characterization of Greece as fundamentally
agonic and attributing, as he did, its genius to this motivation have captured
the dynamic of a society which even today elicits our commendation and
admiration for its successes and nobility.[13]

Within the gymnasium, agonic education (paideia) was focused and
formed. The term "gymnasium" continues to identify the type of schooling
in European countries that represents the superior form of education. It
reflects the quintessential culture, the epitome of the purposes of schooling
combining a harmonious arrangement of experiences established upon a
holistic awareness of human complexity with integration of body, mind,
and spirit, with individual development within a social cultural (polis-
paideia) context. The gymnasium as the physical center of agonic activity
serves also as a potent symbol of the collective agonic elements inherent
in the education of the youth of Greece, and what I would propose as a
model for the education of today's youth. Pfitzner's rich study of the agon
motif provides a comprehensive survey of the metaphoric and symbolic
value of the Greek terms involved in athletic imagery, and he clearly
identifies the gymnasium as the focal point for the agonic paideia:

The Greek gymnasium is of interest not only so far as it formed a center where
the agonistic ideals of Greek life were inculcated and fostered, but also because
the education which it offered largely contributed to the popularization and

extension of athletic imagery. . . . Education in the gymnasium was based on the principle that everything was to be reached through training and exercise, through the maximum development of the individual with his innate latent powers.[14]

Gymnastic education was not restricted to bodily exercise. Plato and Socrates never approved of exclusive emphasis on the physical although they understood that the mental could not reach its potential unless a healthy body contributed to the mind's full functioning. Socrates describes this education: "Then what will this education be like? It seems difficult to discover a better one than that which our forefathers adopted, gymnastics for the body and 'music' for the soul."[15]

Music, it must be stated, included all of the lofty intellectual, aesthetic, and religious exercises that were represented by the muses. Both "music" and "muscles" needed, however, to be linked together by morality. The term paideia has no meaning if not a moral meaning. Classical humanism, as the flowering and modern manifestation of Greek culture, based its education upon a clear and persistent morality. Training perhaps may continue in the sense of technical proficiency, but education as the cultivation of the defining human qualities dare not be allowed to become simply a slogan for someone's personal agenda, such as the sophists who notoriously parlayed this technical training into a profitable pursuit. Morality, as Marrou reminds us, made education the handmaiden of an absolute ideal. A. N. Whitehead's vision of excellence and education as a moral enterprise accords with Socrates's ideal. An education that served an agonic culture, that continually strove for excellence, and that encouraged its citizens to emulate the godly virtues required a cultural consensus, a commonly held and reverently received core of beliefs. The Greek world was held together by this uncompromised center, and when those beliefs were jeopardized, disintegration followed. Marrou, even in his day, which was closer than our own to the Greek ideal, lamented the loss of this grand vision and consensual vitality:

In a classical culture, all men have in common a wealth of things they can all admire and emulate; the same rules; the same metaphors, images, words—the same language. Is there anyone acquainted with modern culture who can think of all this without feeling a certain nostalgia?[16]

Neither Plato nor Socrates, nor philosophers in their tradition, unduly elevated competition. Competition was not the same as conquest, although Plato saw the principal benefit of competition as enhancing military prowess. The agon of athletic competition was not intended as a license for unbridled violence and inhumane excesses. Sadly, in Greek culture, as subsequently in Rome, and tragically in today's untempered times, sport was controlled by a professional elite which exploited it for power and profit. Agon was the attractive quality of the amateur, and "amateur" implies engagement for the love of the activity. Professionalization of sports, and control of amateur athletics by professionals have perverted the original intention of such games. Robert Hutchins, wisely during his tenure at the University of Chicago, restored sensibility to the role of athletics with the institution of a comprehensive, intramural program and by deemphasizing intercollegiate competition. The Ivy League ideal (although not always followed faithfully) remains one of the last bastions of the noble agon in academia. Although a diatribe against the commercialization, professionalization and bastardization of American sports is not the intention of this writing, I cannot resist pointing out the sad anomaly that higher education has become the willing handmaiden (harlot?) of this prostitution of athletics. It is difficult to employ such imagery today without the unsavory associations of greed, cruelty, and aggrandizement clinging to it.

Agonal education must of necessity include an element of stoicism but a stoicism ennobled, like that of Marcus Aurelius with a spiritual purpose. The difference between the savage and the sage is not so much in their struggles but in the reflection the latter brings to the experience and the wisdom he acquires; whereas the former "nourishes a blind life within the brain." Endurance through the unendurable, bearing with the unbearable, and continuing to struggle when energy seems expended mark the true agonistic experience. The athletic imagery alerts us to all this. Life itself is a contest, a struggle, an agon, and there is no escaping it unless one opts for a stillborn life of apathy, insanity, or suicide. Kazantzakis's writings are replete with agonal imagery, and his philosophy of life, his religious quest, his *raison d'etre*, centers on the classic struggle to overcome the gravitational pull of flesh, and yield to the transcendence of spiritual elevation. If in this secularized age, one permits the possibility of deity, then it is God who summons us to this struggle.

The pancration expresses the collective competitions that test the mettle of the best prepared. All areas of athletic endeavor are brought into play, and weakness will soon reveal itself. However, each specialized sport provides its own unique agonal test. Running involves speed and endurance. Wrestling relies on strength and skill. Boxing requires dexterity and agility. Other events such as discus throwing, javelin, and so forth highlight other specialized requirements in competition. The Greeks referred to all these combative events as agons. Present society seems to be, except at the purest amateur level, attracted to boxing and wrestling for the violence that has come to characterize them. Present preference, as indicated by attendance and financial reward, is for so-called team sports— baseball, basketball, football—all of which more or less reduce each player to a specialized, discrete part of a sport's system. Admittedly, there must be a successful group effort if the team is to be competitive, but the contest loses the individual, agonal element except as individuals are singled out from the team for their personal prowess; but even here, the personal prowess is impossible without the effort of teammates. In professional football, for example, the quarterback has emerged as the prima donna. But the quarterback cannot participate unless he is part of the team. His efforts have no meaning without his companions. True agonal games test one man against another, or test a man against a mark.

The popularity of athletics today commends the imagery to contemporary students; one with which they can identify. A difficulty, however, in full appreciation of the image for education is the lack of access for many students to the rigors of training, and the disciplinary requirements as well as the time constraints imposed upon contestants. The media glamorize conquest and victory, but make little reference to the preparation periods. Television, particularly, portrays the life of a successful athlete as an effortless accomplishment. Commercial endorsements catapult athletes into public attention, and the notion of an overnight sensation is too easily associated with superstar appeal. Without the prerequisite training and trials, which are typically ignored by the media, athletes accomplish little.

Employment of words like arena, racecourse, stadium, marathon, and their concomitant verbal associations in both describing the educational endeavor and prescribing the curricular processes may enhance the perception of and appreciation for learning as an active, disciplinary activity. Restructuring of education along lines suggested by these images may restore seriousness to schools and a sense of significance to students.

Chapter 12

Agon and Military Metaphors

Military terms unfortunately have been narrowly associated with aggression and imperialistic imposition; and hence, have been eschewed in describing educational programs. Rigid, totalitarian systems, akin to military academies, are not the happy choices of educators in structuring school systems. Nor am I proposing this military model for schools. I have no desire to see schools conform to some martial model of severe regimentation, especially where technology is taught as the ultimate end of the curriculum. Scenes from *The Great Santini* should not serve as the basis for schools. Neither do I propose to adopt Hyman Rickover's Sputnik-inspired system of uniforms for students, technology-based curriculum, and national military-industrial-complex program. Athens, not Sparta, continues to be the model of antiquity on which we build educational reform. But this does not mean we cannot appropriate suitable and serviceable imagery, such as military metaphors, to inform our educational programs. Selective, strategic adoption of military terms consistent with the agon motif need not impose upon us a militaristic pedagogy based upon fear and coercion.

Early origins of the agon motif are to be found in warrior societies, for within these societies "war activity offered the most prestigious avenue for displaying prowess."[1] Haplology, a specialized, interdisciplinary branch of study (subsumed within agonomics) deals with "man's combative nature and endeavors." Hoplites were heavily armored soldiers within the Greek society, comparable to modern infantrymen, who fought hand-to-hand combat. The idealized concept of medieval knighthood can be traced to the Greeks with the addition, however, of the somewhat romanticized notions of defending one's personal honor and providing justice. The medieval "paladin," comparable to the Greek concept of "pallikari," embodies these chivalrous elements of virtue, valor, and nobility in contention for a just and noble cause.

Modern military technology, as recently as World War II but most intrusively in the post-Sputnik era has deglamorized combat with the disappearance of both the moral element and the focus on the individual, engaging in one-on-one, hand-to-hand combat. Today's depersonalized militarism emphasizing megakills and technological advantage reduces the fighter or soldier to a cipher. Military metaphors are only useful if warfare is viewed as a moral enterprise in which conflict results from the consensual acknowledgment of a violation of human rights—rights so fundamental and inviolate that warfare is the only recourse for the survival of those values. The uncompromising commitment to such values is reflected in the ephebic oath to which Athenian youth publicly subscribed:

I will never disgrace these sacred arms nor desert my companions in rank but will fight for the temples and public property, alone and with others. I will leave my fatherland, not less but greater and better, than I received it. . . . I will honor the religion of my fatherland.[2]

Associations with the military invariably invite comparisons with ancient Sparta, for that ancient city-state continues to stand as the symbol of the society driven by and committed to military supremacy and physical prowess. Although we reject, uncompromisingly, its savagery, we can extract salient themes which afford a sanguine imagery. We need not be reminded that Athens survived as the cultural tour de force in Western civilization by its military prowess. The cultural legacy Athens bequeathed and the torch of tradition, which has survived extinction from generation to generation, would have been a part of the cultural incineration had it not been able to protect its way of life by military means.

If there is a persistent criticism of modern youth, more than their apathy or refusal to abide by convention and custom, it is that modern youth is undisciplined in its conduct and unmindful of goals beyond the utilitarian, the immediate, and the gratifying. Civilian life can afford the luxuries of periodic indifference to social structure and constraints; military life never can. The military creed is one of duty—commitment to the prescribed program, unerring allegiance to the course of action, and dedication to unflagging pursuit and execution of the plan. Success demands excellence, and excellence can only be bought with the price of exacting discipline.

In athletics, discipline contributes to victory in games; in warfare, discipline is a matter of life and death. The agon curriculum imposes discipline upon students; it will not tolerate breaches in conduct that detract from the pursuit of excellence. A degree of healthy regimentation is necessary. Denial of immediate gratification for more substantial, future-oriented goals brings with it enrichment of self and awareness of others.

Life is filled with unavoidable conflict. When teachers avoid or eliminate conflict for students, they are guilty of committing educational crimes. Conflict resolution should be included as a critical ingredient in the curriculum. Opposing points of view, different perspectives on issues, clashes over courses of action to take, appreciation of and appeals to different value systems—all inevitably occur in life, and must be reflected in school. Students need to learn to wrestle with issues, engage in disagreement over options, battle for beliefs, and defend against any unwarranted and illegitimate encroachments on territory. Education must include an abrasive element; there must be a gritty side to learning. Debate itself is a warlike endeavor as the Greek word (*makologomai*: word battles) indicates.

Such imagery within education evokes an emphasis upon strategy (the Greek word for soldier is *strategos*), for planning and executing educational designs. Cognitive strategies rank high among the adopted, pedagogical priorities in the present educational agenda of schools. Providing students with an understanding of the need to agonize and struggle through to the problem's solution enlarges their capacity for personal strength. Persistence in the face of obstacles, and creative consideration of strategic options enhance self-esteem. Seligman's study of learned helplessness among students highlights the important role endurance and patience play in seeking solutions.[3] One of the most-common complaints by teachers relates to the lack of student persistence. Students do not pursue goals to completion. Aborting or abandoning goals is much too common. Any military movement will fail if there is no commitment to completing the task, irrespective of the obstacles encountered. Spartan education for all its shortsightedness and misplaced emphasis upon physical prowess, demonstrated, nevertheless, that success can only be achieved when personal courage is cultivated and becomes a salient virtue in pursuit of goals.

Warfare is a collective enterprise in which personal pursuits are subordinated to or brought into harmony with the social good. A singular soldier is a contradiction. Even the gallant knight of medieval lore was devoted to a cause, was motivated by a code of chivalry, was part of an

order, and was committed to a lord. The agon motif manifested in warfare
grew out of athletic competition. Warfare was conducted by the same rules
that circumscribed sporting events. Although personal fame (an expression of areté) was initially valued and cultivated, the communal goal
eventually achieved paramount place in conquest. Public recognition and
conferment of awards were incentives to valor, and fame was the legacy
of the hero. Heroism was the ultimate, military expression of areté, for
the hero was accorded a godlike status, as the term implies. Honor was
the concomitant of heroism, and, according to Xenophon, honor was the
object of agonal effort "and herein precisely lies the difference between a
man and other animals, in this outstretching after honor."[4] I must confess
that the contemporary image of warfare in this technologized era of
impersonal megakill does mute the military metaphor somewhat and
detracts from its appeal in application to education. But as they are linked
with athletic imagery and partake of the agonal element, military metaphors,
nevertheless, commend themselves as serviceable rubrics for conceptual-
izing educational processes.

Is it too simplistic or sentimental to imagine the student as knight errant?
Is gallantry too outmoded a notion around which to build pedagogic
practice? Contemporary education scoffingly relegates such notions to its
self-constructed trash bins of trivia. Regrettably, romantic ideals are not
perceived as congruent with the hard-facts reality of a world tainted by
discrimination, AIDS, unemployment, ecological blight, and the myriad
social disorders and diseases that are wreaking havoc on civilization. But
that is precisely the point! We lost our innocence when we ill-advisedly
opened the Pandora's box that liberated the, heretofore, incarcerated
legions that have now made it harder for us to achieve paradise. It was the
very awareness of such a potential catastrophe that kept the lid on our
savage impulses.

Chivalric codes of conduct, romanticized to be sure, created civilization.
Heroism coupled with honor are the lasting legacies of the true military,
and we would be wise to revive the tandem virtues today. Modern
professional sports (and now, lamentably, amateur athletics) divorces the
two, and to have either alone is to promote savagery or suicide. Modern
warfare is equally improvident, and the star status given to the "top-gun"
aviators who chalk up missions for which they are accorded celebrity
status is akin to that of the lineman in professional football who is credited
with the most sacks of a quarterback. There is little need to search for the
source of the problems of modern youth whose identities are acquired by
vicarious association with petulant and high-priced athletes and entertainers (two groups within society whose visibility and rewards are inversely

related to their value!). Society is enamored of entertainment above all else, and television is the handmaiden of entertainment. Television is designed more to amuse than inform, and apart from rare, discriminating programs by Public Television (and a few cable systems), television is a generic, entertainment medium—a medium which increasingly caters to base tastes. Any medium driven by the principle of maximization of profits must ultimately pander to the crudest appetites society will allow, and in this era of extreme permissivism, society has relinquished all limits and restraints.

Several years ago, along with a number of college faculty, I was invited by a local television station to dialogue with a number of media notables including the president and a vice-president of the news department of a major television network. When my turn came to interrogate the panel, I prefaced my question by saying that I would never trust any television news program that depended upon commercial advertising. If you are seeking the largest viewing audience to satisfy commercial sponsors (typically huckstering such products as antacids, laxatives, depilatories, and the like), you must tailor your news toward sensationalism and topics of popular appeal. All of the panel except one member dismissed my observation out of hand and insisted that they, themselves, were guided most scrupulously by the canons of journalism and integrity. The one dissenter praised my observation and reflectively questioned the legitimacy of commercially sponsored news. Interestingly, that lone respondent subsequently moved to Public Television and has become a visible presence producing and hosting a number of that network's quality programs.

We need new views, not new news. Approaches and perspectives that colorfully, poetically depict and paint with spontaneity and informed whimsy, radical though they be, can infuse life into moribund forms. Metaphors from music and designs from dance, artistic analogies and agonic imagery—these are the starting points for educational reform. We have listened far too long to the strident voices from industry, from business, from within the management model and the production paradigms, from the much-too-tightly constructed mechanical worlds of science, from technicians whose only skill is salesmanship. The dull, weary direction in which behaviorism has taken schools during the last several decades has damaged both minds and motives; we need to dance from now on. Computer models only process. Input, output, bytes—an unimaginatively pedestrian catalogue of commands. Pseudoterms like "artificial intelligence" and "memory" purport to legitimate a suspect enterprise. The dictum: overwhelm with exotic means when the ends are of dubious value. What has happened to magic and mystery? To enchantment and ecstasy?

To splendor and serendipity? Words we use are not incidental. Images are created by vocabulary. Electrical circuitry, conductors, and processors are terms that rob education of its vibrancy. Let's restore the richness of the imagery of the muses that created education; let's refuse the rhetoric of the marketplace that has reduced schools to places where students learn skills only to serve a gadget-mad world.

Chapter 13

Experiential Education

Experiential education provides an approach to learning that emphasizes student contacts with situations and environments outside the boundaries of traditional schooling. Education has in the last decades become increasingly institutionalized, overly structuralized, and bureaucratized. Modern school buildings and school programs conspire to keep students within the confines of artificial environments and away from the realities of everyday life. The utilization of sophisticated technology, and necessary access to power sources to run the technology has, of course, institutionalized much of American life. Medical services are provided in complex medical facilities that rely upon a vast array of technologies for diagnosis and treatment of disorders. Businesses with their dependence upon elaborate communication and data-processing networks require huge organizations and buildings. Schools, as well, both pre- and postsecondary, have developed "edifice complexes," and sprawling, often aesthetically unappealing, structures, not uncommonly isolated from the everyday demands of life have sprouted all over the educational landscape. Institutionalization has potentially damaging effects. Contacts with natural environments are necessary to sustain lives that are healthy and lived responsibly. Lack of critical contacts, as sensory deprivation studies have demonstrated, distort views of and involvements with reality.

Experiential education has received renewed consideration in the decades since the 1960s. Experiential learning, however, is not a new concept. It has always been on the agendas of insightful educators. Historically, the tradition of experiential education can be traced to the

active learning of the ancient Greeks. However, modern education
spawned by the ideas of eighteenth-century Europe and particularly in
the writings of Rousseau, Pestalozzi, and Froebel eventually witnessed
the recognition of the element of activity in learning. In *Émile*, notably,
Rousseau would have his student learn from nature and by active engagement with the "necessity" that nature decreed. John Dewey and the
progressives continued and refined this tradition and "learning by doing"
became a shibboleth of the progressive education movement. In *Schools
of Tomorrow*, Dewey and his daughter describe a variety of experiential
learning programs ignited by the torch of progressive education, and they
document the effectiveness of these programs in providing students with
innovative programs.[1]

One does not need to endorse everything John Dewey has said or adopt
his progressivism to see the value of much of what he said and the
programs he has instituted. The concept of "experience" is critical in
Dewey's approach to education within the natural or managed environment
in which the student functions. Dewey's dictum that education is basically
the "reconstruction of experience" implies a selection factor in promoting
certain experiences as desirable and rejecting others as undesirable,
limiting growth and interfering with maturity; for it is, after all, full growth
and maturity toward which Dewey's (and Francis Parker's) education
leads. But experience is both a critical beginning and an ongoing element
of education for Dewey. And so he advises teachers to be attuned to this:

A primary responsibility of educators is that they not only be aware of the general
principle of the shaping of actual experiences by environing conditions, but that
they also recognize in the concrete what surroundings are conducive to having
experiences that lead to growth. Above all, they should know how to utilize the
surroundings, physical and social, that exist so as to extract from them all that
they have to contribute to building up experiences that are worth while.[2]

Dewey wisely recognized the need for educators to be attuned to the
impulses of the learner, but he is not, as he has often been unfairly accused,
in favor of whimsical indulgence of learners; nor does he suggest that
experiences as such are, ipso facto, educative; nor are all experiences
equally educative. Choosing, planning, preparing, structuring, evaluating
are all elements in experiential education. A perverted Rousseauian
"return to nature" or a naive acceptance of the "noble savage," concepts
which assume that the instinctive response of humans to their immediate
environments will develop character and maturity are in error. Neither a
misguided permissivism nor a spontaneous encounter with the environ-

ment will elicit appropriate responses in intelligent students endowed with
the mediation of thought, feeling, and value choices. Hence, Dewey's
education requires insightful awareness of and pedagogical insistence
upon experiences developmentally appropriate and growth-directed that
are meaningfully and deliberately ordered within a curricular design.

One of the fundamental critiques of traditional education by experiential-
oriented educators is that "the institutionalizing process of schools is not
conducive to maturation and self-direction."[3] Numerous voices have been
raised in clear opposition to the excessive institutionalization of American
life, and schools have been targeted by many as the woeful victims of this
perhaps unintended conspiracy. Experiential education calls for a renewed
awareness of the role of the natural environment in shaping life and
establishing a healthy lifestyle, and decries the detachment of students
from direct contacts with the environment in learning.

David Kolb prescribes a four-phase sequence of experiential learning,
beginning with concrete experience, proceeding to reflective observations
and conceptualizations of abstractions, and culminating in experimentation
and application.[4] All learning has its roots in some direct, environmentally
relevant situation that prompts cognitive engagement and eventually,
leads, through experimentation and testing, to real life application.
Students begin with the tangible and tactual and end with practical
application. Abstractions and rationality are the necessary mediating
cognitive functions that unite the other two.

Although not identical with experiential education, the outward-bound
movement has a clear "conceptual affinity" with it.[5] Outward Bound and
companion experiential programs, such as Wilderness Encounter, have
been endorsed by educators for their effectiveness in motivating previously
disenchanted and high-risk students. Outward Bound has achieved both
high visibility for its successes and adoption as an alternative education
program for at-risk students. Experiential education should not, however,
be viewed simply as an alternative education mode, but should be considered as an option among the many available that have unique contributions
to make. Additionally, they can serve to inform more-traditional institutional
programs and provide a basis for salubrious modifications.

Outward Bound had its origins in the efforts of the German educator
Dr. Kurt Hahn in the early 1940s. His initial effort in Wales with seamen
during a four-week program, focusing on community-service work, rock
climbing, and related activities, produced encouraging results and generated
both personal growth among the seamen and a sense of commitment to
community. Outward-bound programs have proliferated and are enjoying
popularity throughout the world.

The philosophical basis of Outward Bound has been described as

adventure-based experiential education programs for people 14 years of age and
older. The term experiential defines a "doing" approach to teaching and learning,
and thus first hand encounters with the world, i.e., concrete activities are the
foundation upon which an experiential endeavor is based.[6]

Outward Bound as a structured, educational program embodies the
fundamental elements that have permeated agonic education since the Greek
conceptualization. That is not to say that agonic education and Outward
Bound are identical; but Outward Bound as a prescribed program with
stated goals and structured experiences comes close to reintroducing the
struggle that traditional education, especially technologically enslaved
education, has omitted. Adventure, risk, struggle, goal setting, cooperative
effort, solo experiences, and contact with the environment are all components
of outward-bound programs, and these elements are clearly agonic.
The programs seek to have students encounter themselves by encountering
the concrete reality of the world, unmediated by elaborate technology. The
vision is to have students, particularly high-risk students who have,
heretofore, been unsuccessful in school, engage in intensive reality testing
and acquire immediate feedback for their efforts. Ultimately, self-concept
and self-understanding are explored. The persona is "peeled away," the
socially styled self is unmasked, and self-confrontation occurs. But it is
not simply a stripping away of the acquired masks or faces held up only
to public view; it is not intended to be an uncovering but a discovery of
potential and eventual true identity. Legitimate and earned self-esteem is
the target toward which the activities aim. Students are given opportunity
to take charge, to be in control of their lives in, admittedly, limited and
supportive contexts, but they are, nevertheless, given an opportunity that
most of them never previously had. They confront themselves, their
weaknesses and strengths, their deficiencies and resources, and are held
accountable for their actions. They must struggle not only "to get," but
struggle "to be." Being is not a socially imposed persona or passively
acquired identification. Being is the emergence of the true self through
contact with unmediated, concrete reality. The course is intended to set
them toward discovering their source of strength, and it is the strength
upon which true identity can be built.

Traditional institutionalized education is monumentally deficient in this
critical area and shares this deficiency with society generally. Psychologist
Sidney Jourard examined the dispiriting, enervating influence of stultifying social images and cried out for programs that would cultivate true

identity which has depth and substance. An excerpt from a journal of a participant in the Outward Bound program reveals the changes that can result from honest encounter of this kind.

I think my view of myself has changed a great deal in this last month. I feel like a person whereas before I thought of myself as a piece of shit, and everything I did was rotten. I also feel that I'm just as good as the next guy. . . . on the last trail we did when I got to the bottom, I felt so good about myself that I thought I was going to cry and that was the first time in my entire 15 years that I have felt good about myself or about what I did.[7]

The principle that permeates the outward-bound movement is one of self-expansion through challenge. Reflection apart from rugged reality is inadequate. Excessive cerebration promotes interior lives that often are unable to discern between their idiosyncratic world and the realm of reality. Introspection is a powerful cognitive tool that helps us to assess our person and our progress. I am not advocating a blind, brutish approach to life, one that abandons reason or reflection. I am suggesting, however, that there must be testing against the concreteness of sense reality so that we do not cultivate a morbid and unhealthy inner life that avoids engagement with outer life. John Dewey's words bear reiteration when he said that students need to be given opportunities to test themselves against the real world of things and people so that they could learn to choose appropriate behaviors for living and reject the inappropriate.

Closed-mindedness, according to Milton Rokeach, is an attitude toward life which is not present-time centered.[8] Education which does not treat today as a meaningful moment in life distorts purpose and limits learning. I concur with the perennialist school which admits the immaturity of the learners, and recognizes that learning can never be exclusively relevant to the immediate situation. Education is necessarily and appropriately preparation for maturity. But that does not mean that today should not receive attention. The future-not-yet-lived or the past-never-to-be-relived should not dominate the educational experiences of the present. We will need to live in the future when it arrives, and we cannot escape what the past continues to provide for us; but it is the cutting edge of the present that must engage education. Dewey's reconstruction of experience as the core of education captures, in part, the important notion. Selection from the past, serviceable for the future, but always significant at the present time should circumscribe our curricular design. The intensity of the "now" (which may be threatening) makes us want to live in the "then."

Challenge requires risk and adversity. Technology abhors adversity.

Technology's task is to smooth out the roads, reduce the stress, eliminate toil, and, in the process, undermine the very source of strength that makes people creatively capable. Adversity alone reveals our resources, manifests our deficiencies, and alerts us to the need to develop more effective ways to live. The outward-bound movement is built upon the creation of adversity and cultivation of strength to overcome it.

A college English instructor, dissatisfied with her traditional approach to the prosaic topics in her freshman composition classes, sought a way to have students explore the phenomenological world about them as they were engaged in thinking and writing. She wanted to zero in on the attitude behind the choices students made, and she wanted to bring awareness of the agonic processes with which they needed to engage themselves. She sought in the outward-bound model a basis for assignments in which students would move toward self-discovery, extend their personal perspectives, and realize the need to make choices that would move them beyond their comfort zone. She sought for them the "mystical conversion experience" that was so much the part of the testimonies of those who had profited from Outward Bound. She saw the outward-bound spirit as embracing a complex of meanings and conditions, but fundamental

among these meanings are the belief in the value of creating adversity in order to overcome it, the belief that important things happen to people under stresses and challenges different from those met in everyday life, a belief that there are some things that cannot be taught although they can be learned. And most important, there is the belief in teaching an attitude that will help people survive rather than teaching survival itself.[9]

Education needs to consist of a series of personalized experiences during which students carve a sense of cosmos from chaos. Chance and risk are chaotic. The unpredictable is mildly frightening; the uncontrollable is terrorizing. But students need to learn to order their lives. Children as they grow must realize that eventually they will be responsible for what becomes of them, and, ultimately, they will only become what they choose to become. The appeal of existentialism (and not all of existentialism is appealing) is the centrality of choice, the need for responsible decision making and action. Curriculums in schools that are too precise, too calculated, too controlled, which allow no whimsy and serendipity, and exclude student choice may be comfortable, but they create misfit conformists, and bored intolerants.

Adversity and chaos for young children, of course within limits, are the very ingredients that go into a savory, robust life. These are not new notions. Testimonies from survivors of ordeals, unimagined and incomprehensible, hit upon this critical note. This comes, not from masochists who pathologically seek adversity for its perverse pleasure, but from ordinary people who, without their consent, have been placed in intolerable situations and not only survive but excel. They come out of their furnace of affliction, from their adversity, from their agonies to tell us that it was there they found something incalculable, something that could never be taught but could be, and was, learned.

Victor Frankl like a phantom from the brooding mists of Auschwitz tells us. Elie Wiesel confirms it. Alexander Solzenhitzyn and his survival kin tell us. All of the voices that Terrence Des Pres lets speak unite in a chorus of affirmation.[10]

The survivors are the exemplars, the rare exceptional people, who have been subjected to the agon that they would never have chosen. And there are with them a host of others, not subjected to such extremity perhaps, who celebrate survivorhood. Some have needed to escape crippling lives of dependency, or have needed to establish identity or affirm integrity, about whom we read only in isolated vignettes in some limited-circulation magazine, or who have appeared for a celebrity's instant on some program.

There are the clinical cases that psychiatrists and medical people write about. The seemingly helpless addict or alcoholic or depressive who, when submitted to a regime of agonic effort—running, weight lifting, or some other strenuous challenge—became whole again, survived and succeeded. George Sheehan's compelling story of his own middle-age mastery when he took up running, took it up before it became a craze, before there were many marathons, before the roadways became crowded with joggers. The challenges of white-water-rafting, of skydiving, and, the recent, more vaudevillian attraction of bungee jumping, challenge participants to test themselves and see what they're made of. We need to be tested in existential, experiential life. Not in the womb of technological safety and risklessness, but in the sometimes frightening and capricious world of the uncontrollable, where true maturity occurs.

The surveys, studies, and experimental research performed in conjunction with outward-bound programs consistently support the value of the programs and empirically substantiate the impressions that participants report. Study upon study with hard-to-handle kids, at-risk students, and low self-esteem youth and adults repeatedly demonstrate that the survival experiences, adversity and risk, challenge and struggle which comprise the experiences of the program, contributed to increased confidence, positive self-esteem and changed lives.

Using pre- and posttest measures on psychometric research instruments, parental evaluations, and information from school records, Sakofs found that students participating in the outward-bound programs acquired a stronger sense of self, displayed increased confidence, were more comfortable in social situations, better able to communicate, had a more positive outlook on the future, and felt they could make a difference in effecting positive social change. The students became more optimistic, and their scores on hopelessness and self-depreciation lowered. Eighty-five percent of the parents of these students indicated that they saw significant worthwhile changes in their children and the same percentage supported the inclusion of such programs as part of regular school curriculums.[11]

A program in Australia for low-achieving high-school males reported similar results and concluded that the program coupled with parental involvement contributed to increase in academic achievement and positive self-concept.[12]

Using the "Self Report Survey Form" developed by G. G. Jernstedt of Dartmouth specifically to assess participants in Outward Bound, a Greenwich, Connecticut program involving seventy-five minority high-school students in The Career Beginnings Project evaluated the progress of the participants in an 1987 Outward Bound program. The survey form involved these six areas: self-depreciation, sociability, achievement motivation, social consciousness, hopelessness, and self-confidence. The data obtained by pre- and postadministrations were analyzed using a repeated measures, analysis of variance procedure. On all but the achievement-motivation variable (although improved in the predicted direction, it did not reach statistical significance), the group showed statistically significant change. The researchers concluded, "This study was primarily designed to answer one question: did the Outward Bound experience significantly enhance the self-reported psychological functioning of Career Beginnings students? The data support an affirmative response to that question."[13]

Even short-term experiences in experiential education seem to have positive effects on students' self-concepts and confidence. A ten-day experience spread out over three weekends resulted in elevated scores in the areas of improved identity and locus of control. The improvement in scores was modest and did not occur for all of the variables subsumed within self-concept (Tennessee Self-Concept Scale) and locus of control (Rotter Scale). The researcher hypothesized that the limitation of time adversely affected the results.[14]

This short-term study reveals the important role that time plays in producing positive changes in the areas of identity and responsibility. Superficial agonic experiences may prove to have an inoculation effect on participants, and may render students unreceptive to further effort activities. Studies need to be undertaken to identify the minimum time framework in which changes may take place. Three-week outward-bound programs tend to be minimally necessary for activities to have a positive effect and for serious modification of self-perceptions to occur. Weekends may not provide sufficient time, and for obdurate participants, especially those predisposed to view the experience negatively (perhaps because they are forced to be involved), longer periods may be necessary.

My personal observation based on conducting cross-cultural study programs for college students suggests that three-week programs abroad are effective only for a few. A three-week experience in another culture not uncommonly produces a superficial acquaintance with the culture and exaggerates the perceived distasteful elements of the culture (typically interpreted as lack of American amenities and contact with the extremely unfamiliar in the culture). However, an experience of two semesters with students studying in African settings (Kenya) who were embedded completely in the culture produced dramatically different results. Without exception, the students developed empathy with the people and a genuine love for the country, and they did this in difficult circumstances.

An emerging country, short on advanced technology and long on simple basic necessities, provided a good agonic context for them to test themselves and grow; and they did. But they couldn't have succeeded in a few short weeks. Perhaps forty-five to sixty days is minimally necessary for students to shed their antipathy toward unfamiliar surroundings and experiences, and to "relax into" the challenge. Nevertheless, more data are necessary from time trials to determine the optimum immersion experience needed to produce significant changes. Of course, there may have been differences that developed but did not register on the quantitative measures. Qualitative changes are not always (and usually, never immediately) transformed into quantitatively validated results.

Bertolami conducted a quasi-experimental study of self-discovery in a twenty-six-day, high-risk wilderness program for young adult males and females, supplemented by descriptive data obtained through self-evaluations and journal entries. The activities in the wilderness-encounter program included rock climbing, rappelling, mountain rescue, backpacking, kayaking, orienting, and a three-day solo experience. Results based on comparison with a control group showed significant increase in self-esteem for both male and female participants. Additionally, the students felt more in control of their lives while still recognizing realistic limits, and they evidenced greater self-awareness leading to higher feelings of self-worth. Bertolami concluded that similar to a rites-of-passage transi-

tion, the wilderness-encounter program allowed students to test themselves against the real world of nature to reveal true capabilities and limits.
Reality testing of this kind, as one student put it, "draws honesty out of
you . . . you can't sit there and lie to yourself when you're sitting with
everything that's so bare and open to you."[15]

Confluent education gained popularity during the searching decades of
the 1960s and 1970s when disenchantment with excessive behavioral
management and the Skinnerian programmed worlds prompted educators
to revitalize the role of the affective domain. Preoccupation with conditioning approaches to learning, which often placed the learner in a passive,
respondent role, stripped purpose and meaning from learning. The radical
behaviorists relegated purpose to the category of vestigial, evolutionary
artifacts which, although important at specific developmental periods of
the species, no longer served a useful function as "autonomous man" had
been demystified.

Peter Bien, scholar and translator of some of Kazantzakis's works
identifies the motivation of the student revolt against the tyranny of
technique during the 1970s:

In the largest sense, what the students seem to be against was the entire value
system of our present, technological civilization . . . the realm of the external and
stultifying. What they seemed to be for was an entirely different value system
which we could call, perhaps, aesthetic, or noumenal or maybe even religious.
But perhaps the best word would be mystic.[16]

By mystic, Bien means, I believe, something akin to the concepts
inherent in confluent education which focuses upon holism and harmony
with nature. Confluence connotes many streams flowing together to produce
a cascading, refreshing, and productive oceanic source of creativity and
energy. Rigid reliance upon data derived exclusively from one single
domain of learning denies the holistic nature of truth, and education is
correspondingly reduced to an apprenticeship to that domain's technique.
Feelings, emotions, intuitions, as well as thoughts and behaviors, have a
legitimate place in education. Experiential education, especially in
wilderness settings freed from the fetters of routinized, artificial bureaucracies, is conducive to holistic education and agonic activity. Within the
wilderness, apart from the corrosive "acids of modernity," distant from
the strident, strait-jacket dictates of the media, separate from the maddening conformity of "group-think" and "group-act," opportunity exists for
rediscovery of strength within the person; this is what Piaget calls significant learning, the learning about oneself.

One of the most effective ways to become aware of basic realities—natural feelings and instincts, primary needs . . . is to experience directly the world that man did not make . . . by making the world out-of-doors the classroom—the natural world of streams, canyons, wind, sun, fire, trees, mountains, hills, water, and rocks. This is a manifestation of holism, of experiencing self-in-environment, of being in contact with one's own inner nature and with the outer world of nature.[17]

There is something shockingly primitive about such a proposal, and it provokes defense reactions from a social system that is so technologically top heavy that it bristles at the prospect of students not being immediately immersed into education that teaches them how to use man-made things. I repeat, this is not a call for a naive Rousseauian retreat from the quite-necessary instruction in technical skills and minimal proficiencies; but it is a cry for reconsideration of the unquestioned capitulation to the ravenous appetite of modern technology. We must style ourselves as "loving resistance fighters," as Neil Postman maintains,[18] and insist upon an irreducible active element of experience in education. Where else in the tamed culture of today will students be taught the survival skills they will need to build a life worth living? How else will reservoirs of strength be developed unless there is a reality touchstone, a flinty rock of realism, that will bear up under the oppressive burden of a society irrevocably committed to technology, and to a technopoly which cannot possibly provide what it promises. The "stresses of civilized living" (when civilization is equated with technological advantage) are taking their daily toll, and problems, fundamentally emotional and inner, plague this neurotic generation. Violence on streets and in schools, despair in homes and in homerooms, addictions and boredom and a multitude of maladies find no solution through technology. But perhaps in the wilderness, there may be help.

Nadler documents the value of a demonstration project that combined the principles of confluent education and outward-bound programs in accentuating affective learning. With programs of this type, the experiences in wilderness settings eliminated "social commodities" that "block the awareness of the natural environment" and "the simplicity allows students to touch their environment and then respond to it in the way that is necessitated."[19]

Although the positive effects of outward-bound programs have been consistently demonstrated and documented, by combining them with a confluent education curriculum (with its focus on educating the whole person and calling attention to feelings and attitudes and meaning), the programs provided a more-powerful learning experience. Statistical analyses provided empirical substantiation for the heightened inner awareness of self and the perceived value of the social relations dimension. Physical challenges of risk and adversity, yoked with self-sensitivity and inner awareness, based upon clear cognitively directed goals (quite obviously within a nurturing, educative context) yielded learnings of personal and enduring value that seem to transcend conventional pedagogy.[20]

As Kolb points out, the term "self-esteem" became the educational buzzword during the 1980s and continues to be considered, justifiably, the critical element in student learning during the 1990s. Kolb, along with others, recognized intuitively the value of adventure programs in which students are able to test themselves and respond to legitimate challenges. Numerous research studies are cited in his article to support the change toward improved self-esteem as a result of adventure challenges upon low self-esteem students.

Kolb undertook a study to determine the impact of a mandatory, experiential educational program on moderate self-esteem students. The ten-week program was designed for high-school juniors and seniors who are student leaders in an independent preparatory school. The program consisted of the typical wilderness-encounter activities. In order to provide recognizable and rigorous scientifically valid data, he developed a Solomon Four Group Design using pretest-posttest and posttest-only methods with a treatment and a control group. Eighty-seven subjects were administered the "Piers Harris Children's Self Concept Scale," an instrument consisting of eighty items, which provides a total score and six cluster scores measuring specific areas of self-concept. Multivariate analysis of variance was performed, and generally resulted in findings of significant differences for all variables. He concluded that "the results indicated significant positive change in treatment groups after participation. . . . The overall self-esteem of the participants increased as did the personal perception of physical self and popularity."[21]

Even in the seemingly remote and meditative world of the traditional liberal arts curriculum with its leisurely pursuit of the life of the mind, experiential education can play a valuable role. John Smith, a college professor and advocate for the liberal arts in collegiate programs, makes the case for merging the two worlds—the academic and the applied, the cerebral and tactual. He says that "these seeming distinctions understandably grew alongside the growth of educational bureaucracies, and such distinctions refer more to turf than to truth, to expediency and not educational good sense."[22]

The modern economic order in its madness for more has not always brought the better. Refinement of foods has, in the processing, stripped away the essential nutrients, and now we must supplement our diets to restore artificially what would have remained naturally. Similarly our education has stripped away the natural experiential component, the fiber of educational life. Now education seeks to compensate for this loss of the natural educational, experiential order, with increased technology. Transportation has reduced the size of our world and mechanization of travel has its obvious benefits, but overreliance on transportation technology has produced a generation with a disproportionate percentage of the population overweight, lazy, and unfit. Society must now mount an all-out assault on this appalling state of physical unwellness and provide a host of remedial programs to restore what would have been naturally beneficial if we had not tinkered in the first place. So students are transported by buses that increase expenses and taxes which could be used for other social causes. And the natural process of walking, which could contribute to fitness and physical accomplishment (not to mention opportunities for socialization), gives way to reliance upon machines.[23]

Without difficulty, one could point to many sources of dysfunction within society generated by deference to technology. Many human experiences, naturally occurring and profitably available, have been eroded or eliminated and now a generation later we lament our folly, but are unable or unwilling to reverse the enervating trend. Indeed, we allow experts to con us into further folly, and interests groups with self-serving agendas and shortsighted vision conjure up one crazy scheme after another until education has become a fragmented series of accommodations to the most vocal and occasionally vindictive elements within society. Reform movements proliferate but not uncommonly reform is sanctioned by the currently accepted buzzword, by some self-serving group, and students are made the victims of "curriculum-scam" and another set of goals for schools and experiences for students dominate the discussion. No sooner has one reform movement been activated than another novelty asserts itself, and the evanescent status quo created but yesterday is challenged by the latest "in thing." Mercurial moods within schools are seldom content with anything that takes time or builds character. "Sweep away" is the game of the experts. Anything that has roots needs to be "uprooted" and replaced with the most-fashionable technique according to the conventional wisdom, but this is not wisdom, nor are they who say it wise. It is the ultimate arrogance and may be the final folly.

Why do we give such credence to suicidal schemes in education, and why do we elevate to celebrity status those who propose them? When the dust settles after the curriculum-cyclone revolutions sweep through the educa-

tional landscape, we have nothing but a wasteland inhabited by hollow
men. Conservative wisdom, which is not too eager to discard the lessons
of the past, endorses educational novelties and neologisms cautiously and
insists that we weigh the proposals and programs and consider the consequences. Traditional societies that know nature and live in harmony with
it can teach us something that technology cannot. Civilizations created
over time, selectively enriching themselves by the considered scrutiny of
new cultural contenders and the judicious choosing by substance not
shibboleths, should be our guides as we frame our educational ideologies
and as we establish our curricular priorities. We need to rethink our
ideological assumptions and abandon our rash reliance upon the latest
thing, always assuming it is the best. The tradition of John Henry Newman
who provided a stable foundation for the idea of the university would not
be a bad place to start:

But the compulsive spirit of innovation, the lust for change and the new which . . .
Newman fought in . . . the educational realm was a chief effect of the intoxications
of scientism and it has continued to increase in effect in many other areas of
modern life. . . . the field of education feels the need to produce bogus innovation
in order to show that it emulates the scientific paradigm.[24]

Chapter 14

A Modest Proposal:
An Agonic Curriculum

Van Cleve Morris, in his book *Existentialism in Education*, sought to prescribe a practical pedagogy for his educational philosophy.[1] He began with the Socratic paradigm, but chose as the working model which best approximated his ideal, A. S. Neil's Summerhill.[2] Now, I would not begin there (although some aspects of Neil's school are appealing) for there are some fundamental differences between existentialism and agonic education. Choice, freedom, and definition of self are points of compatibility. Responsibility for deciding educational choices commends itself as does the call to authenticity—seeking and adopting values that are one's own. And the nature of education as encounter and the dialogic imperative are equally attractive elements. Translated into experiential, agonic education, existentialism shares a camaraderie with my educational program. The area where there is dissonance, however, is in the lack of a prescriptive agenda in Neil's program. What is worthwhile in education is what the student views as worthwhile is Summerhill's approach, but I see this as recklessly superficial. I would order a normative educational agenda that includes perennial imperatives and which admits the existence of absolutes. I would not start with the small "self" of personal being. I must begin with transcendent truth and ultimate reality.

Nevertheless, the pedagogy of agonic education is of more concern in this proposal. What should be done, and how should it be done? A systematic, ordered, and sequenced set of experiences for students within school settings can be proposed and implemented, notwithstanding the societal constraints and controversy. Clearly, experiential education programs such as Outward Bound provide models to be used, with critique and modification, to be sure, for an agonic curriculum; but agonic education is not simply another name for the existing programs. Although all of the practical curricular developments will bear a resemblance to the progressive education programs, and an undeniable debt is owed to the progressive education movement, some fundamental distinctions exist among the programs and their philosophical foundations.[3]

Williamson's experiential curriculum using activity-based and community-involvement elements does occur within the traditional, public-school framework with modest modifications to scheduling, class and unit modules, and teacher deployment. In fact, the model that Williamson proposes is clearly based on Dewey's problem-solving steps, ranging from problem identification to testing of solutions.[4] He developed an eight-week unit of environmental education joining traditional classroom study and natural, *in situ*, study of the environment. The latter element allows for what I term the agonic element to occur.

In Plato's *Republic*, we find a paradigm for an educational system tailored to create the philosopher-king and to channel citizens into appropriate, profitable lifetime activity. It is selective and stratified and perhaps elitist by today's standards, but it is, nevertheless, a useful paradigm and does include agonic elements along with traditional-learning activities. Jerome Bruner's "Spiral Curriculum" and Edgar Dale's "Cone of Experience" both provide a sequenced program based upon a hierarchy of experiences—some of lesser value and others of greater value; some that are specific and discrete, others that are embedded and continuous. Designated learnings occur at specified ages or steps that serve the learner only at that particular time; others persist, in various forms, through the lifetime of learning. I will identify what are to me important agonic elements, and I will suggest the ways in which they can be included and implemented in the school program. Changes in existing structures may be required at times, and alternative environments will be needed as well. But it is possible to initiate such a program without a radical revision of present curriculums or accepted approaches, but I acknowledge that there may have to be a shift in perceptions, values, and priorities if such a proposal is to be adopted.

COMMUNITY INVOLVEMENT

Plato included social service at every step in his *Republic*. He could not envision paideia apart from the "polis." Students and school must be firmly embedded in the social system, in the network of ongoing activities—not so much a social reconstructionist call to change, as to social responsibility and challenge. From the very start of their school programs, students should be required to participate in social-work experiences. Adoption of highways for betterment and beautification by business and social organizations has become popular throughout the country as posters along these routes testify. Schoolchildren, as part of the regular curriculum, should engage in work projects under the direction and supervision of the school. These activities are not to be viewed only as ecological concerns for student involvement but legitimate work experience which requires physical effort as part of each week's program according to each student's physical capabilities. It provides a time for direct involvement with the real environment and gives immediate feedback confirming that present accomplishment has occurred.

Experiential education is not, however, to be limited to environmental education programs. Although education in outdoor settings is essential, such programs should not be confused with the care-for-the-environment activities, which are largely ecological commitments toward enhancing biospheric life. A number of programs do combine the agonic effort and the ecological-awareness factors. An eleven-member European nation project entitled "Environment and School Initiative" seems to embrace both elements. The curriculum for this initiative includes personal involvement and emotional commitment of students and reflective action to improve the environment. The program is both "community-based and action-oriented."[5] Endeavors of this nature certainly justify inclusion in the agonic curriculum.

The state of Maryland recently adopted a curricular provision for a specified amount of hours of mandatory community service to be performed by all students in sixth through twelfth grades. I heartily applaud the proposal but only wish it would begin at kindergarten and continue through college. Civic identity and community involvement through such programs of agonic activity sensitize students to the interconnectedness of communities and restore the commitment and caring that should constitute community feeling. Consumerism has replaced community in this technocratic society, and children have been told that they are there to receive, to consume; not there to give, to produce. Ironically, participation in a recently mandated community service program as part of high school graduation requirements for students in Bethlehem, Pennsylvania, is being challenged in court by high school students and parents. One senior was quoted as saying: "Why should I work for free? No way." If such a comment is typical of the reactions of most school students, it may then be symptomatic of a social malady more pervasive and more serious than

I assumed. Let's hope that these kinds of reactions to such proposals by misguided sentimentalists who view childhood as a stressless period of irresponsible indulgence will be held in check.

But such programs must not be frills or add-ons. They must be integral elements of an agonic nature. They must involve real work and real effort, and they must consume time and energy. Within the school itself, contributions to the physical surroundings should be included. Students can develop self-esteem, pride in their schools, and gain responsibility, and this may even reduce the need for expenditures of tax dollars which could be more profitably channeled into other school needs. The school could also serve as a center for outward social activity in which students could become involved. I recall the "paper troopers" during World War II who collected and brought newspaper to school (long before the recycling efforts became fashionable) as part of the "war effort." Saving stamps and bond programs that required discipline in use of funds and the forgoing of immediate gratification through investment in the future were beneficial to society and students alike. In junior high school, I was part of a small group of budding entrepreneurs, under the direction of a business education teacher, who formed a school store that stocked a host of useful items for students. Stock shares were issued and the capital invested in merchandise. The program was so successful that the "corporation" declared dividends of 300 percent at the year's end.

Assignment of tasks and deployment of students would be according to student ability and teacher's appraisal of maximum student benefit. Scheduling would be part of the curricular responsibilities, and may be in conjunction with existing classroom experience, or programs could be revised to include it. But it must be curricular and effortful.

AGONIC CHALLENGE

Curriculums should be sufficiently diversified and individualized to provide each student with challenges in all curricular domains, challenges which students are capable of meeting and completing. Clearly, physical challenges are essential. Students need opportunities, through diligence and discipline, to test themselves against the real world of material and physical reality. Physical education programs traditionally have been responsible for these types of challenges, but such experiences must not be limited to the purview of the physical education specialists. In conjunction with classroom teachers and school personnel, so called "gym" activities should be based on prior student assessment and needs identification. Although profit will certainly accrue in fitness (well being, weight control, etc.), the agonic challenge that makes the student undertake a regimen of training that moves toward specified physical goals can contribute to the self-esteem and sense of personality so lacking today. Without resorting to the obsessive interests in certain physical activities such as marathon running, weight training, and the like, which soon dominate one's sense of self and sweep away all other engagements, obligatory scheduling of physically demanding, developmental activities provides unmistakable and assessable contacts with the environment.

Schedules of activities which students are expected to undertake during the year should be developed, and time frames appropriately designed to accomplish the goals. Regular monitoring and reflection on the experience through journal writing and verbal interaction with peers and instructors must be an integral element in all programs.

SOLITUDE

Time spent alone is time well spent. To be alone is not the same thing as being lonely. Solitary activity can be as enriching and is as vitally necessary as collective activity. Intrusive technology abhors unscheduled time and militates against the solace that comes from reflective solitude. A true ascetic is not an unhappy misanthrope who loathes communion and companionship. The ascetic is (as the word implies) an athlete who wrestles within himself to resolve conflicts, find new sources of strength, enlarge personal horizons, and pursue new vistas. Portable audio and video technologies with alarming ubiquity pervade our social space. It is virtually impossible in the modern world to find places that are free from their obtrusive presence. Unsolicited verbal and visual stimulation assaults us on all sides. Billboards with their "big brother" pronouncements proliferate, and the imagery, typically seductive or silly, lures the undiscriminating.

Students need to learn reflective inquiry that contributes to critical cognition. Schools need to provide sanctuaries of solitude into which a reasoned retreat can be made and where sanity can be restored—oases in schools, natural environments with soft, human-textured interiors, uncontaminated with technology's virus, accommodatingly kindred to the inner life. Not lotus lands offering narcotic indulgence but palestras for battling in the sphere of the spirit and souls—where agonists can take on their torture, work out the inner world of being, and see the spirit take fleshly forms and learn to transmute flesh into spirit.

It is becoming difficult to find places where people can retreat from technology's intrusiveness. Schools should set aside designated, strategically designed "solitude zones" where students can be unencumbered by artificial constraints and in which they are forced to confront themselves as vital beings—not as technological artifacts. And solitude is a necessary condition for creativity. To insist upon the priority of creativity in the curriculum and then provide schools and programs in which solitude is dismissed is to engage in an ironic pedagogy which can never deliver to students what it professes as supremely important.

CONFLICT RESOLUTION

Life is an unavoidable series of conflicts. In part, energy finds its source in friction, and academic energy can be unleashed in conflict situations. Social systems, even of the most fraternal nature, are not free of conflict, and complex systems which increasingly characterize the world in which we live are notoriously filled with friction. Obstacles emerge for everyone. The most gratuitous and felicitous setting will inevitably bring about its share of impediments to personal and collective progress. Barriers block us, opposition emerges to confront us, and resistance arises to deter us from our goals. Yet technology tries to teach the opposite lesson, that nothing need impede our progress.

The agonic curriculum should include conflict situations, physical, psychological, and social. Students will be taught resolution skills, including identification of the source of conflict, the elements involved in the conflict, the strategies for resolving conflict, and the strength that accrues from the process, including generalization and application of the strategies to other situations. Initially in elementary grades, situations may involve conflict over individual versus class goals, and the allocation of limited resources within the school. The negotiation-and-compromise process must involve struggle toward consensus in determining the benefits that will be gained and the sacrifices that must be accepted. Routine weekly sessions involving the classroom's resources could constitute the basis for meaningful activity. Subsequently, through secondary schools, the larger social context may be called into play as maturing students are confronted with the dramatic realities of living in a society of scarce resources. Skilled teacher-guides will initiate students into these activities and lead them, reflectively, through the resolution process.

Avoidance of conflict, which may be necessary in certain situations where the cost-gain ratio is not critical, is a less-appealing option than strategic, didactic use of conflict situations. As students struggle through to resolution, they acquire, not only a specific set of useable skills, but they gain a disciplined perspective and mature understanding of a physical and social world in which they must live, but a world which will not automatically or readily respond to their needs and desires.

CROSS-CULTURAL EXPERIENCES

Few things provide greater agon challenges than moving out of the comfort zone of the typical American educational milieu into an unfamiliar culture. Travel to distant lands is not necessary for a different cultural experience. The diversity of groupings within the United States provides accessible laboratory settings for students to struggle with strangeness and surprise. Schools tend to become cultural "comfort zones" in which the unvarying normative patterns, too familiarly, sedate students, and they "flow" instead of "grow." And this is true of all subcultures—urban, rural, and points in between. Even inner-city students may respond unthinkingly to the prevailing patterns about them and forgo the struggle involved in challenging the system.

Outward Bound programs provide a new physiogeographical context in which students can test themselves. Dramatically unlike their school settings, which are replete with amenities, these wilderness environments are characterized by scarcity and require struggle to survive. But new cultures may provide social struggle-situations in which success requires both accommodation and adaptation to different norms. Periodic immersion in such unfamiliar settings can aid students to struggle toward growth. I would be particularly fond of short-term programs and, for selected students, summer and extended-tour time. Elementary-school students would need a limited, carefully planned exposure, and after the elementary years, increasingly longer and more varied, as well as more intensive, programs. High-school students should be required to live in homes or community residences and work through the cultural conflicts and confusion that result from inexperience and inaccurate perceptions. Living with people who are different from themselves and learning their patterns of behavior will provoke awareness of nonstereotypic thinking and problem solving. Idiosyncratic approaches to life's problems are modified and new networks are developed. All of these struggle situations are potentially growth-enhancing.

Postlude

Serious book writing is agonic activity. It belongs to the category of "creative agonies" and Kazantzakis's analogy to a pregnant woman with morning sickness nourishing the life within her is apropos. The conception of an idea and the struggle to bring it to birth, to fruition, is an unrelenting process of merciless (and perhaps masochistic) persistence against distractions, doubts, and diversions. The blank sheets of paper that demand inscription compel the writer to select and reject, to inscribe and revise, to explicate and erase, and to vacillate between the twin temptations of superficiality in style and treatment and the confessedly alluring option, at times, to call it quits. Even the presence of a word processor does not lighten the load or mitigate the burden. It helps with the mechanics, but for that matter an amanuensis could be hired to help there. The substance of the manuscript and, if one is sensitive to literacy, its style require mental and emotional effort. The task of writing is as demanding, albeit different, than any physical feat we undertake if we undertake it seriously. Perhaps the most agonizing feature of book writing, in addition to content importance and accuracy, involves the numerous choices that need to be made, the options that are open. The mental agony in making decisions of various kinds can give a writer a headache, and the emotional, ego-involved agony can give a writer a heartache. So what I have proposed for students in schools, I (along with others) have submitted to, myself.

I suppose a case could be made for the relationship between the value of an enterprise (such as book writing) and the effort that went into it. Was the writing of a pretechnological age superior to the writing of the present?

Did writers produce something more worthwhile when they relied solely upon pen and paper? Did typing reduce the agonic element in prose writing and has the word processor with its formatting possibilities destroyed the agonic element that writing always required? Did the agonic nature of writing and the creative necessity imposed upon writers by lack of materials select out the more-committed (and possibly more talented) writers who have thereby produced the more-enduring works? Has the ready availability of technology made writers of us all, but made authors of none (authority and author share an etymological kinship)? People with little worthwhile to say, through mechanical and electronic aids, can put something on paper and have it marketed (media marketing itself is able to produce best sellers!). Is there inherent in the unnatural process of writing (as opposed to the more-natural form of communication—speaking) a dynamic that energizes and channels creativity? Is there a neuromuscular linkage that is unlocked through the agony of writing? After all, all societies have oral communication but fewer have written languages. Has the process of reducing oral speech to written language activated an area of cognitive creativity in certain groups of persons that has translated into a communal and cultural phenomenon? And if so, will the computer's programmed ease militate against the transmission to new generations? Will the word processor with its capacity for stylizing, and even syntaxing, close off forever the source of cultural vitality that was awakened with writing?

As an activity in the curriculum, writing, undoubtedly, is critical, and I would advocate its inclusion, in the early grades—a tactile, kinesthetic process where pen and pencil are again used, and computers initially, at least, avoided. Both Ernest Hemingway and James Joyce wrote standing up. The agonic act of writing in such a manner may serve to eliminate the daunted, and, thereby, reserve the writing arena for the truly devoted.

My fundamental purpose at this point, however, is to illustrate the agonic ordeal by reference to writing. If this had been an athletic encounter or a legal debate or some drama, observation alone would be the means of documenting the agon. But words on paper are inert and can only commend themselves through the imagery they employed. The narrative may involve or depict an agon, but the production of the writing is also an agon. Fiction with its emotionality may communicate the agon more explicitly. Scholarly writing, by virtue of style and sometimes substance, is less amenable to direct emotionality. Nevertheless, writing of merit is a labor (agon) of love as well as an activity of the intellect. And all who compete and complete (when the temptations to abandon are, at times, assailably strong) in the writing arena are better for having done so. And for those among us, particularly the young, who assume that the task will get easier with age, the truth is it gets harder. Age never ameliorates the agony. It accentuates it. The words of writer Joyce Carol Oates, who has written much, much more than I and certainly with greater success, say it so well: "One is frequently asked whether the process becomes easier, with the passage of time, and the reply is obvious—*Nothing gets easier with the passage of time, not even the passing of time.*[1]

Notes

INTRODUCTION

1. Robert N. Bellah et al., *The Good Society* (New York: Vintage Books, 1992), 44. See also, *Habits of the Heart* (New York: Harper and Row, 1985). The fundamental theme of the inquiry that generated the substance of this book is the relationship between character and culture, between individual freedom and social commitment.

2. Malcolm I. Thomas, *The Luddites* (Hamden, CT: Archon Books, 1970), 11–12. The term apparently employed in 1811 referred to threatening letters to employers from disgruntled employees bearing the signature "Ned Ludd." An alternative explanation derives it from an "ignorant youth named Ludl who took a hammer and smashed the stocking-frame his father used." Historians have now "accepted it as the generic term for machines-breakers whatever their time and place in history."

3. Stanley Jaki, *Brain, Mind and Computers* (New York: Herder and Herder, 1969), 9.

4. Sir Richard Livingstone, *Education for a World Adrift* (London: Cambridge University Press, 1943), 42.

5. M. Scott Peck, *The Road Less Traveled* (New York: Touchstone Books, 1978), 133.

CHAPTER 1

1. Laurence Shames, *The Hunger for More: Searching for Values in an Age of Greed* (New York: BDD Promotional Book Company, 1990). Although Shames contends his work is based on optimism, there is an ominous cloud that hovers over the work. He contends that the 1980s were an anomaly and such a period will never be repeated. See especially, chap. 2, "Normal Is What You're Used To."

2. Marshall Berman provides a provocative discussion of modernism. See, Berman, *All That Is Solid Melts Into Air: The Experience of Modernity* (New York: Viking, 1988).

3. For an engaging treatment of the topic, see Jeremy Rifkin, *Time Wars: The Primary Conflict in Human History* (New York: Henry Holt and Company, 1987).

4. Neil Postman, *Amusing Ourselves to Death* (New York: Penguin Books, 1985).

5. There is a rich source of inquiry into the role of technology in the works of Jacques Ellul. See, for example, Jacques Ellul, *The Technological Society* (New York: Vintage Books, 1964); *The Technological Bluff* (Grand Rapids, MI: W. B. Eerdmans, 1990); and *The Technological System* (New York: Continuum, 1980). For a more charitable view of technology, see Witold Rybczynski, *Taming the Tiger: The Struggle to Control Technology* (New York: Penguin Books, 1985).

6. Theodore Roszak, *The Cult of Information: The Folklore of Computers and the True Art of Thinking* (New York: Pantheon Books, 1986).

7. Peter G. Beidler, "A Turn Down the Harbor," *Experiential Education and the Schools*, 2nd ed., ed. by Richard J. Kraft and James Kielsmeier (Boulder, CO: Association for Experimental Education, 1986), 118–119.

8. Dan Conrad and Diane Hedin, "National Assessment of Experiential Education: Summary and Implications," ibid., 229.

9. Max Weber, "Bureaucracy," in *From Max Weber*, ed. and trans. by Hans H. Gerth and C. Wright Mills (New York: Oxford University Press, 1964).

10. Lionel Tiger, *The Manufacture of Evil* (New York: Harper and Row, 1987), 286–287.

11. Alice Miller, *The Untouched Key: Tracing Childhood Trauma in Creativity and Destructiveness* (New York: Anchor Books, 1990), 43.

12. John and Evelyn Dewey, *Schools of Tomorrow* (New York: Dutton, 1915), 102.

13. Frederick Nietzsche, *Beyond Good and Evil*, quoted in Philip Reiff, *The Triumph of the Therapeutic* (Chicago: University of Chicago Press, 1987), 14 note.

14. "In High Tech Dorms, A Call for Power," *New York Times*, 12 April 1991, A1. For a similar commentary on the issue directed specifically to college personnel, see "As Students Cram Rooms with Electronic Gadgetry," *Chronicle of Higher Education* vol. 38 (September 1991), A1, A42.

15. Haim Ginott, *Teacher and Child* (New York: Macmillan, 1972), 137.

16. Berman, *All That Is Solid Melts Into Air*, 26.

CHAPTER 2

1. Nikos Kazantzakis, *Report to Greco*, trans. by P. A. Bien (New York: Touchstone Books, 1965), 481.

2. Ian Hunter, *Malcolm Muggeridge: A Life* (Nashville, TN: Thomas Nelson, 1980), 58.

3. John Nef, *A Search for Civilization* (Chicago: Henry Regnery Co., 1962).

4. Alasdair MacIntyre, *After Virtue* (Notre Dame, IN: University of Notre Dame Press, 1981), 245.

5. Quoted in Nef, *A Search for Civilization*, 2.

6. See, for example, Robert E. Proctor, *Education's Great Amnesia* (Bloomington: Indiana University Press, 1988).

7. Stanislav Andreski, *Social Sciences as Sorcery* (New York: St. Martin's Press, 1972), 26–27. Chap. 2, "The Witch Doctor's Dilemma," deals with the relationship between the proliferation of specialists and the decline of quality.

8. David Ehrenfield, *The Arrogance of Humanism* (New York: Oxford University Press, 1978), 21.

CHAPTER 3

1. Hans Selye, *The Stress of Life* (New York: McGraw-Hill, 1976). For a study of the impact of eustress on physical well-being, see the interesting research reported in Jeffrey Edwards and Cary Cooper, "The Impacts of Positive Psychological States on Physical Health: A Review and Theoretical Framework," *Social Science and Medicine*, vol. 27 (1988), 1447–1459.

2. See, for example, such usage in F. F. Strayer and J. Strayer, "An Ethological Analysis of Social Agonism and Dominance Relations Among Preschool Children," *Child Development* 47 (1976), 980–989.

3. Werner Jaeger, *Paideia: The Ideals of Greek Culture*, 3 vols. (New York: Oxford University Press, 1943). Stephen Byrum provides what I believe is an inaccurate distinction between agon and paideia in his discussion of administrative-leadership styles. Using his definition, agon denotes an aggressive, destructive style; whereas, I contend that agon should be viewed historically as a positive virtue, and critically, as a helpful quality. See Stephen Byrum, "The Hamstringing of Moral Education: Athletic Metaphors and Educational Administration" (Washington, D.C.: ERIC Document ED266081, 1985).

4. Cited in Mihaly Csikszentmihalyi, *Flow: The Psychology of Optimal Experience* (New York: Harper and Row, 1990), 72.

5. Johan Huizinga, *Homo Ludens: A Study of the Play Element in Culture* (New York: Harper and Row, 1970). Among other writers who view agon as a favorable feature, see, H. J. Rose, "The Greek Agones," *Aberystwyth Studies* 3 (1922); and Victor C. Pfitzner, *Paul and the Agon Motif* (Leiden, Netherlands: E. J. Brill, 1967).

6. Irene Ringwood, "Agonistic Features of Local Greek Festivals Chiefly From Inscriptional Evidence" (Ph.D. diss., Columbia University, 1927).

7. Jacob Burckhardt, *History of Greek Culture*, trans. by Palmer Hilty (London: Constable, 1963), 117.

8. Anthony E. Raubitschek, "The Agonistic Spirit in Greek Culture," *The Ancient World*, vol. 7 (1983), 7.

9. James Ellsworth, "Agon: Studies in the Use of a Word" (Ph.D. diss., University of California, Berkeley, 1971), 24.

10. Ibid., 13, 127, passim.

11. Miguel De Unamuno, *The Agony of Christianity* (New York: F. Ungar Pub., 1960).

12. W. Jaeger, *Paideia*, 15.

13. Sir Richard Livingstone, *Greek Ideals and Modern Life*, 71, quoted in, E. B. Castle, *Ancient Education and Today* (Baltimore: Penguin Books, 1961), 101.

14. Richard Weaver, *Ideas Have Consequences* (Chicago: University of Chicago Press, 1948), 44.

CHAPTER 4

1. Anthony E. Raubitschek, "The Agonistic Spirit in Greek Culture," *The Ancient World*, vol. 7 (1983), 7.

2. Werner Jaeger, *Paideia: The Ideals of Greek Culture* 3 vols. (New York: Oxford University Press, 1943).

3. John Nef, *A Search for Civilization* (Chicago: Henry Regnery, 1962), 12–14.

4. Parker Palmer, *To Know as We are Known: A Spirituality of Education* (San Francisco: Harper and Row, 1983), 1–9.

5. Ibid., 7. "Our desire to control has put deadly power in some very unsteady hands."

6. Leon Festinger, *A Theory of Cognitive Dissonance* (Stanford, CA: Stanford University Press, 1962).

7. Jean Piaget and Bärbel Inhelder, *The Psychology of the Child* (New York: Basic Books, 1969).

8. L. S. Vygotsky, *Mind in Society*, ed. by M. Cole et al. (Cambridge, MA: Harvard University Press, 1978).

9. H. I. Marrou, *History of Education in Antiquity* (New York: Mentor Books, 1956), 300.

10. Raymond Callahan, *Education and the Cult of Efficiency* (Chicago: University of Chicago Press, 1962). For a more recent, albeit brief, book on the topic, see H. Thomas James, *The New Cult of Efficiency and Education* (Pittsburgh: University of Pittsburgh Press, 1969).

11. For a discussion of "boredom," see Wayne C. Booth, *The Vocation of a Teacher* (Chicago: University of Chicago Press, 1988). Booth attributes the first use of the word "bore" to an Englishman, the Earl of Carlisle, in 1768. And Lord Byron placed society into two tribes: the bores and the bored, 282–283.

12. For a discussion, see "Chronobiology: The Clock that Makes Us Run" in Jeremy Rifkin, *Time Wars: The Primary Conflict in Human History* (New York: Henry Holt and Company, 1987), 29–47.

13. The term "manage" apparently is derived originally from Latin "to handle" and from Italian *maneggiare*, "to train horses." And so managers put us through our paces!

14. William Glasser, *Positive Addiction* (New York: Harper and Row, 1976). The term is presented as a creative, strength-enhancing alternative to "negative addiction."

15. Norman E. Gardiner, *Athletics of the Ancient World* (Oxford: Oxford University Press, 1930), 117.

16. Ibid., 119.

17. Johan Huizinga, *Homo Ludens: A Study of the Play Element in Culture* (New York: Harper and Row, 1970), 30–31.

18. Ibid., 48.

19. "Paideia" refers to "child rearing" and the education provided to children. "Paidia" refers to play, sport, game, or pastime. For the etymology and definition of the terms, see H. G. Liddell and Robert Scott, *Greek-English Lexicon*, 8th ed. (New York: American Book Co., 1882), 1107. For an amplified discussion of the "play concept" and the corresponding Greek terms, see, Roger Caillois, "Unity of Play: Diversity of Games," *Diogenes*, vol. 19 (July 1957), 92–121. Caillois provides six criteria for play activities which, I believe, permit agonic games to be called playful. See, 120.

20. Norman E. Gardiner, *Athletics of the Ancient World*, 49. "The athletic festival was to the Romans nothing more than a show. The populace . . . had long been brutalized by gladiatorial shows and craved an excitement."

21. Donald Kyle, *Athletics in Ancient Athens* (Leiden, Netherlands: E. J. Brill, 1987), 155.

22. Eugene Peterson, *Run with the Horses* (Downers Grove, IL: InterVarsity Press, 1983), 11.

23. Neil Postman, *Technopoly: The Surrender of Culture to Technology* (New York: Knopf, 1992), chap. 3.

24. C. S. Lewis and other writers have commented sagely on this fascination with novelty and immediacy to the neglect of the time-tested truths. See, Lewis, *God in the Dock*, ed. by Walter Hooper (Grand Rapids, MI: W. B. Eerdmans, 1970), 202.

25. Jacques Ellul calls this "technical automatism" in *The Technological Society* (New York: Vintage Books, 1964), 79–94.

26. A. N. Whitehead quoted in E. B. Castle, *Ancient Education and Today* (Baltimore: Penguin Books, 1961), 195–196. Both G. K. Chesterton and C. S. Lewis have commented on this. See Michael D. Aeschliman, *The Restitution of Man* (Grand Rapids, MI: W. B. Eerdmans, 1983), 84, notes 24 and 26.

CHAPTER 5

1. See Stanley L. Jaki, *Brain, Mind and Computers* (New York: Herder and Herder, 1969) for an insightful analysis from a "philosopher-historian of science" point of view.

2. Ellul differentiates between "technique" and "technology." For his discussion see Jacques Ellul, *The Technological Society*, especially Introduction and chap. 1, "Techniques," and *Perspectives on Our Age* (New York: Seabury Press, 1981), 33.

3. Lionel Tiger, *The Manufacture of Evil* (New York: Harper and Row, 1987), 159.

4. Ibid., 166.

5. Jaki's discussion of "scientism" is helpful. See Stanley Jaki, *The Road of Science and the Ways to God* (Chicago: University of Chicago Press, 1978). Also, Michael D. Aeschliman provides a provocative discussion of scientism in, *The Restitution of Man* (Grand Rapids, MI: W. B. Eerdmans, 1983), especially chap. 3, "Scientism: The Current Debate."

6. Ellul, *The Technological Society*, 349.

7. Bernard Bell, *Beyond Agnosticism* (London: George Allen and Unwin, 1930), 48.

8. Peter Bien, "Metaphysics, Myth and Politics," *Excellence in University Teaching*, ed. by Thomas H. Buxton (Columbia: University of South Carolina Press, 1975), 170.

9. Dudley Plunkett, *Secular and Spiritual Values: Grounds for Hope in Education* (New York: Routledge, 1990), 63.

10. During the 1970s, *Jonathan Livingston Seagull* emerged as the most-popular reading for college students, displacing B. F. Skinner's *Beyond Freedom and Dignity*. Richard Bach, *Jonathan Livingston Seagull* (New York: Macmillan, 1970).

11. Huston Smith, *Beyond the Postmodern Mind* (New York: Crossroads Publisher, 1982), 114.

12. Ibid., 76.

13. Victor Frankl, *Man's Search for Meaning* (New York: Pocket Books, 1963), 59.

14. Aeschliman, *The Restitution of Man*, 68.

15. Parker Palmer, *To Know as We Are Known: A Spirituality of Education* (San Francisco: Harper and Row, 1983), 113. See also M. Scott Peck's "role of grace" in *The Road Less Traveled* (New York: Touchstone Books, 1978), 297–312.

16. Ibid.

17. Richard Weaver, *Ideas Have Consequences* (Chicago: University of Chicago Press, 1948), 3.

18. Ibid., 4.

19. Thomas Szasz, *The Myth of Mental Illness* (New York: Harper and Row, 1974).

20. Weaver, *Ideas Have Consequences*, 26.

21. Neil Postman, "The Educationist as Painkiller," *Conscientious Objections* (New York: Vintage Books, 1988), 87–89.

22. John Wilkinson in Jacques Ellul, *The Technological Society*, xvi.

23. Ibid., vii.

24. Palmer, *To Know as We are Known*, 39.

25. See, Stanley L. Jaki, *Angels, Apes and Men* (Peru, IL: Sherwood, Sugden and Company, 1990), especially chap. 1, "Fallen Angel."

26. Weaver, *Ideas Have Consequences*, 4.

27. C. S. Lewis in Michael D. Aeschliman, *The Restitution of Man*, 9.

28. George Leonard, *Education and Ecstasy: The Great School Reform Hoax* (New York: Delta Books, 1968), 16.

29. For discussions of the concept, see, Elliott Eisner, *The Educational Imagination* 2d ed. (New York: Macmillan, 1985); and *The Enlightened Eye* (New York: Macmillan, 1992).

30. Kolb provides an insightful distinction between "comprehension" and "apprehension." See David Kolb, *Experiential Learning* (Englewood Cliffs, NJ: Prentice-Hall, 1984), 104.

31. See Peter Berger and Thomas Luckmann, *The Social Construction of Reality* (New York: Doubleday, 1966).

32. Huston Smith, *Forgotten Truth* (New York: Harper and Row, 1976). See chap. 5, "The Place of Science."

33. Who is not, by this time, familiar with the controversy between the "two cultures" ignited by the scientistic spirit and the technological threat to civilization? Carl Rogers, Abraham Maslow, Arthur Combs, and B. F. Skinner have been among the notables who kept the discussion alive.

34. B. F. Skinner, *Beyond Freedom and Dignity* (New York: Bantam/Vintage Books, 1971), particularly chap. 9, "What is Man?"

35. Victor Frankl, *The Unheard Cry for Meaning* (New York: Simon and Schuster, 1978), 35–36.

36. Martin Seligman, *Helplessness: On Depression, Development and Death* (San Francisco: W. H. Freeman and Company, 1975). See especially chap. 2, "Controllability."

37. *Harrisburg Evening News*, Harrisburg, PA (June 16, 1991).

38. Jacques Ellul, *The Technological Bluff* (Grand Rapids, MI: W. B. Eerdmans, 1990), 174–175.

39. Frankl, *Man's Search for Meaning*, 58–59.

40. Jacques Ellul, *The Technological Bluff*, 186–187.

41. Christopher Lasch, *The Culture of Narcissism* (New York: Warner Books, 1979), 28.

42. Frankl, *Man's Search for Meaning*, 63–64.

43. Plunkett, *Secular and Spiritual Values: Grounds for Hope in Education*, 85. "A commitment to the spiritual, I want to argue, implies a radical break with the status quo of scientific rationalism."

44. John Nef, *A Search for Civilization* (Chicago: Henry Regnery, 1962), 46.

45. Jaki, *The Road of Science and the Ways to God*, 295–296.

46. Ibid., 229.

47. Peter Berger, *A Rumor of Angels* (Garden City, NY: Doubleday, 1970), 62–75.

48. Johan Huizinga, *Homo Ludens: A Study of the Play Element in Culture* (New York: Harper and Row, 1970), 9.

49. Neil Postman, *The Disappearance of Childhood* (New York: Delacorte Press, 1982).

50. Rousseau's classic study is, of course, *Émile*, and John Dewey's most-lucid writing on the topic is *Schools of Tomorrow*, written with his daughter, Evelyn. Dewey declares in this work his indebtedness to Rousseau. William Boyd's works on Rousseau continue to be among the best. See J. J. Rousseau, *Émile: Selections*, trans. and ed. by W. Boyd (New York: Teachers College Press, 1962).

51. Frankl, *Man's Search for Meaning*, 115.

52. Seligman's stirring chapter on "Death" addresses the notion of hope and the consequences of loss of hope. See Martin Seligman, *Helplessness: On Depression, Development and Death*, chap. 8.

53. Stanislav Andreski, *Social Sciences as Sorcery* (New York: St. Martin's Press, 1972).

54. Sir Richard Livingstone, *Education for a World Adrift* (London: Cambridge University Press, 1943), 42.

55. William Wordsworth, "Prelude," *Selected Poems*, ed. by H. M. Margoliouth (London: Collins, 1959), 131.

56. Jacques Ellul, *Perspectives on Our Age* (New York: Seabury Press, 1981). This is Ellul's personal summing up, and although he accepts a legitimate role for technology, he fervently contends for strict limits on expansion with the burden of proof being placed upon technology.

57. William Glasser discusses the need for happiness and laughter as sources of strength in *The Identity Society* (New York: Harper and Row, 1972), 62–63.

58. Andreski, 88.

CHAPTER 6

1. David Riesman, *The Lonely Crowd* (New York: Doubleday, 1953).

2. Emile Durkheim, *Suicide: A Study in Sociology* (Glencoe, IL: Free Press, 1951).

3. For a study of urban schools and the variables related to healthy school climates, see Wayne Hoy, *Open Schools, Healthy Schools* (Newbury Park, CA: Sage Publications, 1991).

4. Quoted by Lawrence Cremin, *The Transformation of the School* (New York: Vintage Books, 1964), 110–115.

5. See Lionel Tiger, *The Manufacture of Evil* (New York: Harper and Row, 1987), 143–164, for a discussion of testing.

6. Victor Frankl, *Man's Search for Meaning* (New York: Pocket Books, 1963), 5–6.

7. Joseph Weizenbaum, *Computer Power and Human Reason: From Judgment to Calculation* (San Francisco: W. H. Freeman, 1976).

8. Stanley L. Jaki, *Brain, Mind and Computers* (New York: Herder and Herder, 1969).

9. Ellul's corpus of writing on this topic continues to be the most-comprehensive and well-articulated hortative. However, Roszak's trenchant tome is equally persuasive. See Theodore Roszak, *The Cult of Information: The Folklore of Computers and the True Art of Thinking* (New York: Pantheon Books, 1986).

10. Marshall McLuhan in *Understanding Media: The Extensions of Man* (New York: Signet Books, 1964), quoted by Berman, *All That is Solid Melts Into Air*, 26.

11. "The Trouble with Computers," *World Press Review* (December 1990), 38–40.

12. Edward Kuhlman, "Frankenstein: Computer Literate?" *Harrisburg Evening News*, Harrisburg, PA (October 20, 1985).

13. Arthur Zajonc, "Computer Pedagogy: Questions Concerning the New Educational Technology," in Douglas Sloan, ed., *The Computer in Education: A Critical Perspective* (New York: Teachers College Press, 1985), 38.

14. Douglas Sloan, "On Raising Critical Questions About the Computer in Education," ibid., 5.

15. Douglas H. Clements and Bonnie Natasi, "Effects of Computer Environments on Socio-Emotional Development," *Computers in the School* (New York: Hawthorne Press, 1984), 12, 26.

16. William I. Thompson, *Imaginary Landscape* (New York: St. Martin's Press, 1990), 117.

17. Ibid., 117.

18. Robert J. Sardello, "The Technological Threat to Education," in Douglas Sloan, ed., *The Computer in Education: A Critical Perspective* (New York: Teachers College Press, 1985), 93.

19. Ibid., 98.

20. Lewis Yablonsky, *Robopaths: People as Machines* (Baltimore: Penguin Books, 1972), 6.

21. Sherry Turkle, *The Second Self: Computers and the Human Spirit* (New York: Simon and Schuster, 1984), 58–63.

22. Ibid., 99.

23. Roszak, 62.

24. John Searle, "Minds, Brains and Programs," in Douglas Hofstadter, ed., *The Mind's I* (New York: Basic Books, 1981), 353–372.

25. Jaki, *Brain, Mind and Computers*, 12–13.

26. E. B. Castle, *Ancient Education and Today* (Baltimore: Penguin Books, 1961), 101–105.

CHAPTER 7

1. David Williams and Steven Patrick, "Therapy for the Age of Narcissism," *Studies in Formative Spirituality*, vol. 5, no. 1 (February 1984), 95.

2. Ibid., 96.

3. Ibid., 99.

4. Christopher Lasch, *The Culture of Narcissism* (New York: Warner Books, 1979), 25–26.

5. Archibald McLeish, *Riders on the Earth* (Boston: Houghton Mifflin, 1978), 37.

6. "Focus on Teachers," *Education Week*, October 28, 1992, 6.

7. Williams and Patrick, 102.

CHAPTER 8

1. Plato, *The Republic*, trans. by Francis Cornford (New York: Oxford University Press, 1945), 190–191.

2. Richard Weaver, *Ideas Have Consequences* (Chicago: University of Chicago Press, 1948), especially "The Introduction," 1–17.

3. Mihaly Csikszentmihalyi, *Flow: The Psychology of Optimal Experience* (New York: Harper and Row, 1990), 143–163. See also Csikszentmihalyi, *Beyond Boredom and Anxiety* (San Francisco: Jossey-Bass Publishers, 1975), 11–36.

4. Mihaly Csikszentmihalyi, *Beyond Boredom and Anxiety*, 26.

5. Ibid., 30.

6. John and Evelyn Dewey, *Schools of Tomorrow* (New York: Dutton, 1915), chap. 4 on "freedom and discipline." Dewey's most-philosophical discussion of the concept in the context of education is in *Democracy and Education* (New York: Macmillan, 1916), 146–162. For an equally provocative discussion of this same issue, see A. N. Whitehead, "The Rhythmic Claims of Freedom and Discipline," in *The Aims of Education and Other Essays* (New York: Macmillan, 1959), 45–65.

7. Csikszentmihalyi, *Flow*, 36.

8. Arthur Foshay, "The Peak/Spiritual Experience as an Object of Curriculum Analysis," Joint Meeting of the Social Science Education Consortium, West Germany, June 1984.

9. William Glasser, *Positive Addiction* (New York: Harper and Row, 1976), 41–43.

10. James E. Shapiro, *Ultramarathon* (New York: Bantam Books, 1980), particularly chap. 3, "With a Measure of Stubborn Perversity."

11. Csikszentmihalyi, *Flow*, 48–70.

12. The sentiments of the humanistic writers are best expressed in the works of Carl Rogers, Abraham Maslow, and Sidney Jourard. See, Carl Rogers, *Freedom to Learn* (Columbus, OH: Charles Merrill, 1969); A. H. Maslow, *Toward a Psychology of Being* (New York: Van Nostrand Reinhold, 1968); Sidney Jourard, *The Transparent Self* (New York: Van Nostrand Co., 1971).

13. Huston Smith, "Beyond the Modern Western Mind Set" in Douglas Sloan, ed., *Toward the Recovery of Wholeness* (New York: Teachers College Press, 1984), 63–83; and see *Forgotten Truth*, especially chap. 5, "Place of Science."

14. Stanislav Andreski, *Social Sciences as Sorcery* (New York: St. Martin's Press, 1972), especially the chapter on cryptomethodology.

15. Jerome Bruner, *The Process of Education* (Cambridge: Harvard University Press, 1960). See chapter on intuitive thinking.

16. "Truth's Intrepid Ambassador," *Christianity Today*, November 19, 1990, 33–34.

17. The salient sentence occurs in C. S. Lewis, *The Abolition of Man: Reflections on Education* (New York: Macmillan, 1947), 35. "In a sort of ghastly simplicity we remove the organ and demand the function. We make men without chests and expect of them virtue and enterprise. We laugh at honor and are shocked to find traitors in our midst. We castrate and bid the geldings be fruitful."

18. Page Smith, *Killing the Spirit* (New York: Viking, 1990).

19. George Leonard, *Education and Ecstasy: The Great School Reform Hoax* (New York: Delta Books, 1968). See chap. 1, "What is Education?"

CHAPTER 9

1. For a discussion of Durrell's approach, see Alan W. Friedman, *Lawrence Durrell and The Alexandria Quartet* (Norman: University of Oklahoma Press, 1970).

2. Elliott Eisner, *The Enlightened Eye: Qualitative Inquiry and the Enhancement of Educational Practice* (New York: Macmillan, 1991), 3.

3. Stanislav Andreski, *Social Sciences as Sorcery* (New York: St. Martin's Press, 1972), 61 and chap. 6, "The Smoke Screen of Jargon."

4. H. A. Harris, *Greek Athletes and Athletics* (Bloomington: Indiana University Press, 1966), 66.

5. Victor Frankl, *The Unheard Cry for Meaning* (New York: Simon and Schuster, 1978), 72, 122.

6. Stanley J. Clark, "Hemingway and the Agon Motif" (Ph.D. diss., California State University, June 1971), 40.

7. Ibid., 47.

8. Ernest Hemingway, *The Old Man and the Sea* (New York: Scribners, 1952).

9. Clark, 155.

10. Quoted in Clark, 75.

11. Clark, 168.

12. Norman O. Brown, *Love's Body* (New York: Vintage Books, 1966), 19, quoted in Clark, 174.

13. Miguel De Unamuno, *The Agony of Christianity* (New York: F. Ungar Pub., 1960).

14. Michael H. Brown, "Transpersonal Psychology: Facilitating Transformation in Outdoor Experiential Education," *Journal of Experiential Education* 12, no. 3 (September 1989), 48–49.

15. Ernest Cassier, quoted in Elliott Eisner, *The Enlightened Eye*, 121.

16. William Glasser initially addressed this issue in *Schools Without Failure* (New York: Harper and Row, 1969), especially chap. 1 and 7. His recent work has developed it further and more fully. See, William Glasser, *The Quality School*, 2d and expanded edition (New York: Harper, 1992).

17. Geoffrey Bull, *God Holds the Key* (London: Pickering and Inglis, 1959), 114.

18. Wayne Booth, *The Vocation of a Teacher* (Chicago: University of Chicago Press, 1988), 24–26.

19. The drama metaphor has been developed most admirably by Erving Goffman. See, for example, *The Presentation of Self in Everyday Life* (New York: Doubleday Anchor Books, 1959), particularly the "Introduction."

20. Martin Seligman, *Helplessness: On Depression, Development and Death* (San Francisco: W. H. Freeman, 1975), 138–139.

21. Nikos Kazantzakis, *Zorba the Greek*, trans. by Carl Wildman (New York: Simon and Schuster, 1952), 16; and also *Report to Greco*, trans. by P. A. Bien (New York: Touchstone Books, 1965), 467.

22. Kazantzakis, 70–71.

23. George Leonard, *Education and Ecstasy: The Great School Reform Hoax* (New York: Delta Books, 1968), 5.

24. George Leonard, *The Silent Pulse: A Search for Perfect Rhythm* (New York: Arkana, 1991), 2.

25. Ibid., 97–98.

26. The psychomotor domain has been developed by Harrow. See, for the elements of this domain, Tom Kubiszyn and Gary Borich, *Educational Testing and Measurement* (Glenview, IL: Scott Foresman, 1990), 60.

27. Flach's psychiatric study on this topic is illuminating. See Frederic Flach, *Resilience: Discovering a New Strength at Times of Stress* (New York: Fawcett Columbine, 1989).

28. Robert Bersson, "Against Feeling: Aesthetic Experience in Technocratic Society," *Art Education* 35, no. 4 (July 1982), 36.

29. W. I. Thompson, *Imaginary Landscape* (New York: St. Martin's Press, 1990), 117.

30. Huston Smith, *Forgotten Truth* (New York: Harper and Row, 1976), chap. 5.

31. Bersson, 37.

32. Ibid., 39.

CHAPTER 10

1. Frederick Flach, *Resilience: Discovering a New Strength at Times of Stress* (New York: Fawcett Columbine, 1989). See especially his discussion of "bifurcation points."

2. Ibid., 170.

3. Norman E. Gardiner, *Athletics of the Ancient World* (Oxford: Oxford University Press, 1930), 119.

4. Victor C. Pfitzner, *Paul and the Agon Motif* (Leiden, Netherlands: E. J. Brill, 1967), 17.

5. Nicholas P. Vlachos, *Hellas and Hellenism* (Boston: Ginn and Company, 1936), 140.

6. For literate writings that illustrate this agonic element in artists' lives, see works by Sir David Cecil, especially, David Cecil, *The Stricken Deer: or, the Life of Cowper* (London: Constable, 1943); and *Visionary and Dreamer: Two Poetic Painters* (Princeton: Princeton University Press, 1970).

7. Paul Tournier, *Creative Suffering* (San Francisco: Harper and Row, 1983), 58.

8. Terrence Des Pres, *The Survivors* (New York: Oxford University Press, 1980).

9. Victor Frankl, *Man's Search for Meaning* (New York: Pocket Books, 1963), 55–59.

10. Mary Council, "Creating Inspiration," *Journal of Creative Behavior* 22, no. 2 (1989), 131.

11. Parker Palmer, *To Know as We are Known: A Spirituality of Education* (San Francisco: Harper and Row, 1983), 69.

12. Edward Tick, "Creativity and Loneliness," *Psychotherapy-Patient* 4, no. 1 (1987), 136.

13. On this subject of solitude and creativity see Mihaly Csikszentmihalyi, *Flow: The Psychology of Optimal Experience* (New York: Harper and Row, 1990), 272, 273, note 171. Nikos Kazantzakis confesses also to the need for solitude to create. He calls it "a passionate love for solitude and silence." *Report to Greco*, trans. by P. A. Bien (New York: Touchstone Books, 1965), 383.

14. Tournier, chap. 1.

15. Quoted in David Aberbach, "Creativity and the Survivor: The Struggle for Mastery," *The International Review of Psychoanalysis* vol. 16, no. 3 (1989), 274. For a more comprehensive treatment of the topic, see David Aberbach, *Surviving Trauma: Loss, Literature and Psychoanalysis* (New Haven: Yale University Press, 1989).

CHAPTER 11

1. Stanley J. Clark, "Hemingway and the Agon Motif" (Ph.D. diss., California State University, June 1971), 6.

2. The call for excellence is expressed in such popular-selling books as Thomas Peters, *A Passion for Excellence* (New York: Random House, 1985); and in Bloom's more-academically oriented and surprising best seller, *Closing of the American Mind*. See Allan Bloom, *Closing of the American Mind* (New York: Touchstone Books, 1987).

3. Richard Weaver, *Ideas Have Consequences* (Chicago: University of Chicago Press, 1948), 35.

4. Johan Huizinga, *Homo Ludens: A Study of the Play Element in Culture* (New York: Harper and Row, 1970), 63.

5. John W. Loy and Graham L. Hesketh, "The Agon Motif: A Prolegomenon for the Study of Agonetic Behavior," *Contribution of Sociology to the Study of Sport*, ed. by Kalevi Olin (Jyväskylä, Finland: University of Jyväskylä, 1984), 35–36.

6. Norman E. Gardiner, *Athletics of the Ancient World* (Oxford: Oxford University Press, 1930), 70.

7. Clark, 10.

8. Peck provides an extremely insightful analysis of the role of "attention." See, M. Scott Peck, *The Road Less Traveled* (New York: Touchstone Books, 1978), 120–131.

9. Rifkin's discussion of the impact of computers on perception of time is informative. See Jeremy Rifkin, *Time Wars: The Primary Conflict in Human History* (New York: Henry Holt and Company, 1987), 13–28.

10. Neil Postman, "My Graduation Speech," *Conscientious Objections* (New York: Vintage Books, 1988), 185–190.

11. James E. Shapiro, *Ultramarathon* (New York: Bantam Books, 1980), 27.

12. Ibid., 32.

13. Jacob Burckhardt, *History of Greek Culture*, trans. by Palmer Hilty (London: Constable, 1963).

14. Pfitzner, 21.

15. Cited in Marrou, 305.

16. Ibid., 305.

CHAPTER 12

1. John W. Loy and Graham L. Hesketh, "The Agon Motif: A Prolegomenon for the Study of Agonetic Behavior," *Contribution of Sociology to the Study of Sport*, ed. by Kalevi Olin (Jyväskylä, Finland: University of Jyväskylä, 1984), 43.

2. E. B. Castle, *Ancient Education and Today* (Baltimore: Penguin Books, 1961), 48.

3. Martin Seligman, *Helplessness: On Depression, Development and Death* (San Francisco: W. H. Freeman, 1975), 157–159.

4. Cited in W. Robert Morford and Stanley J. Clark, "The Agon Motif," *Exercise and Sport Science Review*, 4 (1976), 163–193.

CHAPTER 13

1. In John and Evelyn Dewey, *Schools of Tomorrow* (New York: Dutton, 1915). John Dewey and his daughter Evelyn describe programs they observed around the country during the implementation of progressive education principles in schools. This is the book that brought the phrase "learn by doing" to public attention. See also John

Dewey, "What Is Freedom?" in *John Dewey on Education*, ed. by Reginald Archambault (New York: Modern Library, 1964), 81–88.

  2. John Dewey, *Experience and Education* (New York: Macmillan, 1938), 35.

  3. Adolph Crew, "A Rationale for Experiential Education," *Contemporary Education*, vol. 58 (Spring 1987), 147.

  4. David Kolb, *Experiential Learning: Experience as the Source of Learning and Development* (Englewood Cliffs, NJ: Prentice-Hall, 1987). See also David Kolb's empirical study with private-school students which affirmed the critical link between agonic challenges and increased self-esteem. "Self-Esteem Change and Mandatory Experiential Education," *Journal of Experiential Education*, vol. 11, no. 3 (Fall 1988), 31–37.

  5. Crew, 147.

  6. Mitchell S. Sakofs, et al., *The Cooperstown Outward Bound Summer Program: An Informal Look at The Program's Impact on the Lives of Students*, Report to the Edna McConnell Clark Foundation (Greenwich, CT: Outward Bound, September 1988), 5–6.

  7. Cheryl Bertolami, "Effects of Wilderness Program on Self-Esteem and Locus of Control Orientation of Young Adults," Sixth Annual Conference on the Application of Curriculum Research. University of Victoria, Victoria, B.C. (November 1981).

  8. Milton Rokeach, *The Open and Closed Mind* (New York: Basic Books, 1960), 63–64.

  9. Linda Weiner, "The Composition Class: Outward Bound," Fall Conference of the College English Association of Ohio, Akron, OH (October 1984).

  10. The writings of Victor Frankl, Alexander Solzhenitzyn, Elie Wiesel, and the book about "survivors" by Terrence Des Pres deal, in vivid and magnificent style, with this issue. Wiesel says that his writings are intended to be the words of a "witness," words intended to "touch the bottom of madness." As a survivor of the Nazi holocaust, he felt constrained, indeed, "duty-bound to give meaning to my survival, to justify every moment of my life. I knew the story had to be told." Elie Wiesel, *From the Kingdom of Memory* (New York: Summit Books, 1990), 13–14.

  11. Mitchell Sakofs, 17.

  12. Herbert Marsh, The Outward Bound Bridging Course for Low-Achieving High School Males: Effect on Academic Achievement and Multidimensional Self Concept (Washington, DC: ERIC Document ED280887, April 1986), 7. See also, Herbert Marsh, Multidimensional Self Concepts: The Effects of Participation in an Outward Bound Program (Washington, DC: ERIC Document 251271, 1984).

  13. Stephen Bacon, *The Career Beginnings Outward Bound Component: An Empirical Evaluation* (Greenwich, CT: Outward Bound, 1987), 20.

  14. Harold Gillis, "The Effects of a Camping Construction Experience on the Self Concept, Locus of Control and Academic Achievement of High School Students" (M.A. thesis, Middle Tennessee State University, August 1981).

  15. Bertolami, 10.

  16. Peter Bien, "Metaphysics, Myth and Politics," *Excellence in University Teaching*, ed. by Thomas H. Buxton (Columbia: University of South Carolina Press, 1975), 170.

  17. John Huie, quoted in Reldan Nadler, "Outward Bound and Confluent Education: A Demonstration Project Accentuating Affective Learning" (M.S. thesis, University of California, Santa Barbara, August 1980), 31.

  18. This is Neil Postman's felicitous phrase, and the sentiment has inspired his polemics against arrogant technology and more-arrogant technocrats. He lists ten qualities of people who are "resistance fighters." Among them are those who are freed from

the magical power of numbers, those who refuse to allow social science to pre-empt the language of thought and common sense, those who are suspicious of the idea of progress, and those who take the narratives of the great religions seriously. See Neil Postman, *Technopoly: The Surrender of Culture to Technology* (New York: Knopf, 1992), chap. 11, 181–199.

19. Reldan Nadler, 83–84.

20. Ibid.

21. David Kolb, 36.

22. John K. Smith, "Experiential Learning and the Liberal Arts," Annual Conference of the New York Cooperative Experiential Education Association, Albany, NY (1986), 2.

23. A news account reported that students in certain school districts in northern California were forced to use horses for transportation to schools because of budget cuts. The students expressed pleasure at this mode of transport which was less expensive, and which provided opportunity for observations of the countryside and for renewed contact with friends and the environment.

24. Michael D. Aeschliman, *The Restitution of Man* (Grand Rapids, MI: W. B. Eerdmans, 1983), 35–36.

CHAPTER 14

1. Van Cleve Morris, *Existentialism in Education* (New York: Harper and Row, 1966), chap. 6.

2. A. S. Neil, *Summerhill* (New York: Hart Publishing Co., 1960).

3. Reldan Nadler, "Outward Bound and Confluent Education: A Demonstration Project Accentuating Affective Learning." M.S. thesis, University of California, Santa Barbara, August 1980, 69.

4. See, John Dewey, *How We Think* (Lexington, MA: Heath, 1960).

5. Ian Robottom, "Technocratic Environmental Education: A Critique and Some Alternatives," *The Journal of Experiential Education* vol. 14, no. 1 (May 1991), 20–26.

POSTLUDE

1. Joyce Carol Oates, "Notes on Failure," in *The Pushcart Press Prize, VII: Best of the Small Presses*, ed. by Bill Henderson (Wainscott, NY: The Pushcart Press, 1983), 195.

Bibliography

Aberbach, David. "Creativity and the Survivor: The Struggle for Mastery." *The International Review of Psychoanalysis* 16 (1989): 273–286.

———. *Surviving Trauma: Loss, Literature and Psychoanalysis*. New Haven: Yale University Press, 1989.

Aeschliman, Michael D. *The Restitution of Man*. Grand Rapids, MI: W. B. Eerdmans, 1983.

Andreski, Stanislav. *Social Sciences as Sorcery*. New York: St. Martin's Press, 1972.

Archambault, Reginald, ed. *John Dewey on Education*. New York: Modern Library, 1964.

"As Students Cram Rooms with Electronic Gadgetry, Colleges Scramble to Meet the Demand for Power." *Chronicle of Higher Education*, 38 (September 25, 1991): A1, A42.

Bach, Richard. *Jonathan Livingston Seagull*. New York: Macmillan, 1970.

Bacon, Stephen. *The Career Beginnings Outward Bound Component: An Empirical Evaluation*. Outward Bound USA, Greenwich, CT (November 1987): 1–21.

Beidler, Peter G. "A Turn Down the Harbor." *Experiential Education and the Schools*. 2nd ed. Edited by Richard J. Kraft and James Kielsmeier. Boulder, CO: Association for Experiential Education, 1986.

Bell, Bernard. *Beyond Agnosticism*. London: George Allen and Unwin, 1930.

Bellah, Robert N., et al. *The Good Society*. New York: Vintage Books, 1992.

———. *Habits of the Heart: Individualism and Commitment in American Life*. New York: Harper and Row, 1985.

Berger, Peter. *A Rumor of Angels*. Garden City, NY: Doubleday, 1970.

———, and Thomas Luckmann. *The Social Construction of Reality*. New York: Doubleday, 1966.

Berman, Marshall. *All That is Solid Melts Into Air: The Experience of Modernity*. New York: Viking, 1988.

Bersson, Robert. "Against Feeling: Aesthetic Experience in Technocratic Society." *Art Education* 34 (July 1982): 34–39.

Bertolami, Cheryl. "Effects of Wilderness Program on Self-Esteem and Locus of Control Orientation of Young Adults." Sixth Annual Conference on the Application of Curriculum Research. University of Victoria, Victoria, B. C., November 1981.

Bien, Peter. "Metaphysics, Myth and Politics." In *Excellence in University Teaching.* Edited by Thomas H. Buxton. Columbia: University of South Carolina Press, 1975.

Bloom, Alan. *Closing of the American Mind.* New York: Touchstone Books, 1987.

Booth, Wayne C. *The Vocation of a Teacher.* Chicago: University of Chicago Press, 1988.

Brown, Michael H. "Transpersonal Psychology: Facilitating Transformation in Outdoor Experiential Education." *Journal of Experiential Education* 12 (September 1989): 47–56.

Brown, Norman O. *Love's Body.* New York: Vintage Books, 1966.

Bruner, Jerome. *The Process of Education.* Cambridge: Harvard University Press, 1960.

Bull, Geoffrey. *God Holds the Key.* London: Pickering and Inglis, 1959.

Burckhardt, Jacob. *History of Greek Culture.* Translated by Palmer Hilty. London: Constable, 1963.

Byrum, C. Stephen. "The Hamstringing of Moral Education: Athletic Metaphors and Educational Administration." Washington, DC: ERIC Document ED266081, 1985.

Callahan, Raymond. *Education and the Cult of Efficiency.* Chicago: University of Chicago Press, 1962.

Caillois, Roger. "Unity of Play: Diversity of Games." *Diogenes* 19 (July 1957): 92–121.

Castle, E. B. *Ancient Education and Today.* Baltimore: Penguin Books, 1961.

Cecil, Sir David. *The Stricken Deer: or, The Life of Cowper.* London: Constable, 1943.

———. *Visionary and Dreamer: Two Poetic Painters.* Princeton: Princeton University Press, 1970.

Clark, Stanley J. "Hemingway and the Agon Motif." Ph.D. diss., California State University, 1971.

Clements, Douglas, and Bonnie Natasi. "Effects of Computer Environments on Socio-Emotional Development." In *Computers in the School.* New York: Hawthorne Press, 1984.

Conrad, Dan, and Diane Hedin. "National Assessment of Experiential Education: Summary and Implications." *Experiential Education and The Schools.* 2nd ed. Edited by Richard J. Kraft and James Kielsmeier. Boulder, CO: Association for Experiential Education, 1986.

Council, Mary. "Creating Inspiration." *Journal of Creative Behavior* 22 (1989): 123–131.

Cremin, Lawrence. *The Transformation of the School.* New York: Vintage Books, 1964.

Crew, Adolph. "A Rationale for Experiential Education." *Contemporary Education* 58 (Spring 1987): 145–147.

Csikszentmihalyi, Mihaly. *Beyond Boredom and Anxiety.* San Francisco: Jossey-Bass Publishers, 1975.

———. *Flow: The Psychology of Optimal Experience.* New York: Harper and Row, 1990.

De Unamuno, Miguel. *The Agony of Christianity.* New York: F. Ungar Pub., 1960.

Des Pres, Terrence. *The Survivors.* New York: Oxford University Press, 1980.

Dewey, John. *Democracy and Education.* New York: Macmillan, 1916.

———. *Experience and Education.* New York: Macmillan, 1938.

———. *How We Think.* Lexington, MA: Heath, 1960.

———. "What Is Freedom?' In *John Dewey on Education: Selected Writings*. Ed. by Reginald D. Archambault. New York: Random House, 1964.

———, and Evelyn Dewey. *Schools of Tomorrow*. New York: Dutton, 1915.

Durkheim, Emile. *Suicide: A Study in Sociology*. Glencoe, IL: Free Press, 1951.

Edwards, Jeffrey, and Cary Cooper. "The Impacts of Positive Psychological States on Physical Health: A Review and Theoretical Framework." *Social Science and Medicine* 27 (1988): 1447–1459.

Ehrenfield, David. *The Arrogance of Humanism*. New York: Oxford University Press, 1978.

Eisner, Elliott. *The Educational Imagination*. 2d ed. New York: Macmillan, 1985.

———. *The Enlightened Eye*. New York: Macmillan, 1992.

Ellsworth, James. "Agon: Studies in the Use of a Word." Ph.D. diss., University of California, Berkeley, 1971.

Ellul, Jacques. *Perspectives on Our Age*. New York: Seabury Press, 1981.

———. *The Technological Bluff*. Grand Rapids, MI: W. B. Eerdmans, 1990.

———. *The Technological Society*. New York: Vintage Books, 1964.

———. *The Technological System*. New York: Continuum, 1980.

Festinger, Leon. *A Theory of Cognitive Dissonance*. Stanford, CA: Stanford University Press, 1962.

Flach, Frederic. *Resilience: Discovering a New Strength at Times of Stress*. New York: Fawcett Columbine, 1989.

"Focus on Teachers." *Education Week* (October 28, 1992): 6.

Foshay, Arthur. "The Peak/Spiritual Experience as an Object of Curriculum Analysis." Paper presented at the Joint Meeting of the Social Science Education Consortium, Bavaria, West Germany, June 18–22, 1984.

Frankl, Victor. *Man's Search for Meaning*. New York: Pocket Books, 1963.

———. *The Unheard Cry for Meaning*. New York: Simon and Schuster, 1978.

Friedman, Alan W. *Lawrence Durrell and The Alexandria Quartet*. Norman: University of Oklahoma Press, 1970.

Gardiner, Norman. *Athletics of the Ancient World*. Oxford: Oxford University Press, 1930.

Gillis, Harold. "The Effects of a Camping Construction Experience on the Self Concept, Locus of Control and Academic Achievement of High School Students." M.A. thesis, Middle Tennessee State University, 1981.

Ginott, Haim. *Teacher and Child*. New York: Macmillan, 1972.

Glasser, William. *Positive Addiction*. New York: Harper and Row, 1976.

———. *The Quality School*. 2d and expanded ed. New York: Harper, 1992.

———. *Schools Without Failure*. New York: Harper and Row, 1969.

———. *The Identity Society*. New York: Harper and Row, 1972.

Goffman, Erving. *The Presentation of Self in Everyday Life*. New York: Doubleday Anchor Books, 1959.

Harris, H. A. *Greek Athletes and Athletics*. Bloomington: Indiana University Press, 1966.

Hemingway, Ernest. *The Old Man and the Sea*. New York: Scribners, 1952.

Hoy, Wayne. *Open Schools, Healthy Schools*. Newbury Park, CA: Sage Publications, 1991.

Hofstadter, Douglas, ed. *The Mind's I*. New York: Basic Books, 1981.

Huie, J. "Confluent Education and Outward Bound." Unpublished manuscript, 1976.

Huizinga, Johan. *Homo Ludens: A Study of the Play Element in Culture*. New York: Harper and Row, 1970.

Hunter, Ian. *Malcolm Muggeridge: A Life.* Nashville, TN: Thomas Nelson, 1980.

"In High Tech Dorms, A Call for Power." *New York Times*, 12 April 1991, A1.

Jaeger, Werner. *Paideia: The Ideals of Greek Culture.* 3 vols. New York: Oxford University Press, 1943.

Jaki, Stanley. *Angels, Apes and Men.* Peru, IL: Sherwood, Sugden and Company, 1990.

————. *Brain, Mind and Computers.* New York: Herder and Herder, 1969.

————. *The Road of Science and the Ways to God.* Chicago: University of Chicago Press, 1978.

James, H. Thomas. *The New Cult of Efficiency and Education.* Pittsburgh: University of Pittsburgh Press, 1969.

Jourard, Sidney. *The Transparent Self.* New York: Van Nostrand Co., 1971.

Kazantzakis, Nikos. *Report to Greco.* Translated by P. A. Bien. New York: Touchstone Books, 1965.

————. *Zorba The Greek.* Translated by Carl Wildman. New York: Simon and Schuster, 1952.

Kolb, David. *Experiential Learning: Experience as the Source of Learning and Development.* Englewood Cliffs, NJ: Prentice-Hall, 1984.

————. "Self-Esteem Change and Mandatory Experiential Education." *Journal of Experiential Education* 11 (Fall 1988): 31–37.

Kraft, Ricard J., and James Kielsmeier, eds. *Experiential Education and the Schools.* 2d ed. Boulder, CO: Association for Experimental Education, 1986.

Kubiszyn, Tom, and Gary Borich. *Educational Testing and Measurement.* Glenview, IL: Scott Foresman, 1990.

Kuhlman, Edward. "Frankenstein: Computer Literate?" *Harrisburg Evening News*, October 20, 1985.

Kyle, Donald. *Athletics in Ancient Athens.* Leiden, Netherlands: E. J. Brill, 1987.

Lasch, Christopher. *The Culture of Narcissism.* New York: Warner Books, 1979.

Leonard, George. *Education and Ecstasy: The Great School Reform Hoax.* New York: Delta Books, 1969.

————. *The Silent Pulse: A Search for the Perfect Rhythm.* New York: Arkana, 1991.

Lewis, C. S. *The Abolition of Man: Reflections on Education.* New York: Macmillan, 1947.

————. *God in the Dock.* Edited by Walter Hooper. Grand Rapids, MI: W. B. Eerdmans, 1970.

Liddell, H. G., and Robert Scott. *Greek-English Lexicon.* 8th ed. New York: American Book Co., 1882.

Livingstone, Sir Richard. *Education for a World Adrift.* London: Cambridge University Press, 1943.

————. *Greek Ideals and Modern Life.* Oxford: Clarendon Press, 1935.

Loy, John W., and Graham L. Hesketh. "The Agon Motif: A Prolegomenon for the Study of Agonetic Behavior." *Contribution of Sociology to the Study of Sport.* Edited by Kalevi Olin. Jyväskylä, Finland: University of Jyväskylä, 1984.

MacIntyre, Alasdair. *After Virtue.* Notre Dame, IN: University of Notre Dame Press, 1981.

Marrou, H. I. *History of Education in Antiquity.* New York: Mentor Books, 1956.

Marsh, Herbert. "The Outward Bound Bridging Course for Low-Achieving High School Males: Effect of Academic Achievement and Multidimensional Self Concepts." Washington, DC: ERIC Document ED280887, April 25, 1986.

Maslow, A. H. *Toward a Psychology of Being.* New York: Van Nostrand Reinhold, 1968.

McLeish, Archibald. *Riders on the Earth*. Boston: Houghton Mifflin, 1978.

McLuhan, Marshall. *Understanding Media: The Extensions of Man*. New York: Signet Books, 1964.

Miller, Alice. *The Untouched Key: Tracing Childhood Trauma in Creativity and Destructiveness*. New York: Anchor Books, 1990.

Morford, W. Robert, and Stanley J. Clark. "The Agon Motif." *Exercise and Sport Science Review* 4 (1976): 163–193.

Morris, Van Cleve. *Existentialism in Education*. New York: Harper and Row, 1966.

Nadler, Reldan. "Outward Bound and Confluent Education: A Demonstration Project Accentuating Affective Learning." M.S. thesis, University of California, Santa Barbara, 1980.

Nef, John. *A Search for Civilization*. Chicago: Henry Regnery Co., 1962.

Neil, A. S. *Summerhill*. New York: Hart Publishing Co., 1960.

Nietzsche, Frederick. *Beyond Good and Evil: Prelude to a Philosophy of the Future*. Baltimore: Penguin Books, 1973.

Oates, Joyce Carol. "Notes on Failure." In *The Pushcart Prize VII: Best of the Small Presses*. Edited by Bill Henderson. Wainscott, NY: The Pushcart Press, 1983.

Palmer, Parker. *To Know as We are Known: A Spirituality of Education*. San Francisco: Harper and Row, 1983.

Peck, M. Scott. *The Road Less Traveled*. New York: Touchstone Books, 1978.

Peters, Thomas. *A Passion for Excellence*. New York: Random House, 1985.

Peterson, Eugene. *Run with the Horses*. Downers Grove, IL: InterVarsity Press, 1983.

Pfitzner, Victor C. *Paul and the Agon Motif*. Leiden, Netherlands: E. J. Brill, 1967.

Piaget, Jean, and Bärbel Inhelder. *The Psychology of the Child*. New York: Basic Books, 1969.

Plato. *The Republic*. Translated by Francis Cornford. New York: Oxford University Press, 1945.

Plunkett, Dudley. *Secular and Spiritual Values: Grounds for Hope in Education*. New York: Routledge, 1990.

Postman, Neil. *Amusing Ourselves to Death*. New York: Penguin Books, 1985.

———. *Conscientious Objections*. New York: Vintage Books, 1988.

———. *The Disappearance of Childhood*. New York: Delacorte Press, 1982.

———. *Technopoly: The Surrender of Culture to Technology*. New York: Knopf, 1992.

Proctor, Robert E. *Education's Great Amnesia*. Bloomington: Indiana University Press, 1988.

Raubitschek, Anthony E. "The Agonistic Spirit in Greek Culture." *The Ancient World* 7 (1983): 3–7.

Reiff, Philip. *The Triumph of the Therapeutic*. Chicago: University of Chicago Press, 1987.

Riesman, David. *The Lonely Crowd*. New York: Doubleday, 1953.

Rifkin, Jeremy. *Time Wars: The Primary Conflict in Human History*. New York: Henry Holt and Company, 1987.

Ringwood, Irene. "Agonistic Features of Local Greek Festivals Chiefly From Inscriptional Evidence." Ph.D. diss., Columbia University, 1927.

Robottom, Ian. "Technocratic Environmental Education: A Critique and Some Alternatives." *The Journal of Experiential Education* 14 (May 1991): 20–26.

Rogers, Carl. *Freedom to Learn*. Columbus, OH: Charles Merrill, 1969.

Rokeach, Milton. *The Open and Closed Mind*. New York: Basic Books, 1960.

Rose, H. J. "The Greek Agones." *Aberystwyth Studies* 3 (1922): 1–26.

Roszak, Theodore. *The Cult of Information: The Folklore of Computers and the True Art of Thinking*. New York: Pantheon Books, 1986.

Rousseau, J. J. *Émile: Selections*. Translated and edited by William Boyd. New York: Teachers College Press, 1962.

Rybczynski, Witold. *Taming the Tiger: The Struggle to Control Technology*. New York: Penguin Books, 1985.

Sakofs, Mitchell S., et al. *The Cooperstown Outward Bound Summer Program: An Informal Look at the Program's Impact on the Lives of Students*. Report to the Edna McConnell Clark Foundation, Greenwich, CT, September, 1988. Greenwich, CT: Outward Bound Inc.

Sardello, Robert J. "The Technological Threat to Education." In *The Computer in Education: A Critical Perspective*. Edited by Douglas Sloan. New York: Teachers College Press, 1985.

Searle, John. "Minds, Brains and Programs." In *The Mind's I*. Edited by Douglas Hofstadter. New York: Basic Books, 1981.

Seligman, Martin. *Helplessness: On Depression, Development and Death*. San Francisco: W. H. Freeman and Company, 1975.

Selye, Hans. *The Stress of Life*. New York: McGraw-Hill, 1976.

Shames, Laurence. *The Hunger for More: Searching for Values in an Age of Greed*. New York: BDD Promotional Book Company, 1990.

Shapiro, James E. *Ultramarathon*. New York: Bantam Books, 1980.

Skinner, B. F. *Beyond Freedom and Dignity*. New York: Bantam/Vintage Books, 1971.

Sloan, Douglas, ed. *The Computer in Education: A Critical Perspective*. New York: Teachers College Press, 1985.

———, ed. *Toward the Recovery of Wholeness*. New York: Teachers College Press, 1984.

Smith, Huston. *Beyond the Postmodern Mind*. New York: Crossroads Publisher, 1982.

———. *Forgotten Truth*. New York: Harper and Row, 1976.

Smith, John K. "Experiential Learning and the Liberal Arts." Paper presented at the Annual Conference of the New York Cooperative Experiential Education Association, Albany, NY, 1986.

Smith, Page. *Killing the Spirit*. New York: Viking, 1990.

Strayer, F. F., and J. Strayer. "An Ethological Analysis of Social Agonism and Dominance Relations Among Preschool Children." *Child Development* 47 (1976): 980–989.

Szasz, Thomas. *The Myth of Mental Illness*. New York: Harper and Row, 1974.

Thomas, Malcolm I. *The Luddites*. Hamden, CT: Archon Books, 1970.

Thompson, William I. *Imaginary Landscape*. New York: St. Martin's Press, 1990.

Tick, Edward. "Creativity and Loneliness." *Psychotherapy-Patient* 4 (1987): 131–137.

Tiger, Lionel. *The Manufacture of Evil*. New York: Harper and Row, 1987.

Tournier, Paul. *Creative Suffering*. San Francisco: Harper and Row, 1983.

"The Trouble with Computers." *World Press Review* (December 1990): 38–40.

"Truth's Intrepid Ambassador." *Christianity Today* (November 19, 1990): 33–34.

Turkle, Sherry. *The Second Self: Computers and the Human Spirit*. New York: Simon and Schuster, 1984.

Vlachos, Nicholas P. *Hellas and Hellenism*. Boston: Ginn and Company, 1936.

Vygotsky, L. S. *Mind in Society*. Edited by M. Cole, et al. Cambridge: Harvard University Press, 1978.

Weaver, Richard. *Ideas Have Consequences*. Chicago: University of Chicago Press, 1948.

Weber, Max. "Bureaucracy." In *From Max Weber*. Edited and translated by Hans H. Gerth and C. Wright Mills. New York: Oxford University Press, 1964.

Weiner, Linda. "The Composition Class: Outward Bound." Paper presented at the Fall Conference of the College English Association of Ohio, Akron, Ohio, October 19–20, 1984.

Weizenbaum, Joseph. *Computer Power and Human Reason: From Judgment to Calculation*. San Francisco: W. H. Freeman, 1976.

Whitehead, A. N. *The Aims of Education and Other Essays*. New York: Macmillan, 1959.

Wiesel, Elie. *From the Kingdom of Memory*. New York: Summit Books, 1990.

Williams, David, and Steven Patrick. "Therapy for the Age of Narcissism." *Studies in Formative Spirituality* 5 (February 1984): 95–103.

Wordsworth, William. "Prelude." In *Selected Poems*. Edited by H. M. Margoliouth. London: Collins, 1959.

Yablonsky, Lewis. *Robopaths: People as Machines*. Baltimore: Penguin Books, 1972.

Zajonc, Arthur. "Computer Pedagogy: Questions Concerning the New Educational Technology." In *The Computer in Education: A Critical Perspective*. Edited by Douglas Sloan. New York: Teachers College Press, 1985.

Index

Festinger, Leon, 37
First Amendment, 67, 92
Flach, Frederic, 124, 127
Flow, 98, 103-4; and boredom, 106;
    and self, 112
Frankenstein, 11, 81
Frankl, Victor, 53, 61, 62, 66, 68, 71,
    95, 99, 111, 130, 131, 157
Freud, Sigmund, 61, 95
Freudian(ism), 15, 78, 99
Froebel, Frederich, 118, 152
Futuristic, 20, 25, 64, 85
Futurologist, 25-26

Galton, Sir Francis, 130
Games, 70, 133; made-up, 105
Gardiner, Norman, 40, 41, 42, 128, 136
Gender lifestyles, 16
Generation, 5-7, 10, 24, 42, 43, 65, 40
    143, 149, 160; and change, 26
Genetic engineering, 90
Genius engineering, 90
Gershwin, George, 116
Glasser, William, 74, 103-4, 106, 128
Global village, 5
Godel's theorem, 91
Goffman, Erving, 36, 119, 130
The Good Society, 1. *See also* Bellah,
    Robert
Grace, 53, 54, 101, 117, 121, 138, 181
    n. 15
The Great Santini, 145
Greece, 22, 31-32, 114
Greek civilization, 22, 35
Greek culture, 30-32, 37, 41, 141, 142
Greek Ideals and Modern Life, 129. *See
    also* Livingstone, Sir Richard
Greek mind, 22
Greek society, 30, 114, 129, 145
Greek soul, 35
Greek spirit, 35
Grieg, Edvard, 116
Gymnasium, 39, 140
Gymnastics, 122

Habits of the Heart, 1. *See also* Bellah,
    Robert
Hahn, Kurt, 153
Haplology, 145

Harris, H. A., 111
Harvard University, 90
Haverford College, 19
Heisenberg principle of indeterminacy,
    60
Hemingway, Ernest, 113-14, 174
Heroism, 27, 36, 41, 43, 113, 148
Hesketh, Graham, L., 136
Hierarchy of needs, 78
Hitler, Adolph, 73
Holocaust, 20, 73, 111
Homer, 42, 92, 113, 148
Homo calcula, 14
Homo faber, 14
Homo ludens, 14, 41
Homo sapiens, 14
Hope, 71-72
Hoplites, 145
Huizinga, Johan, 30, 41, 70, 136
Humor, 74-75
Hutchins, Robert M., 142

Identity, 52, 57, 77, 78, 82, 102, 104;
    and computers 86-87; and experien-
    tial education, 154-155, 158; and
    self-transcendence, 62; of youth, 148
Imagery, 82, 109-25; athletic, 128;
    dolphins, 118-19, 122; electronic,
    68; expressive, 110; heuristic, 110;
    mediated, 82; perverse, 92
Imagination, 68, 86, 105, 107, 108,
    116, 130, 197
Industrial Revolution, 23
Infrastructure costs, 19
Intelligence tests, 80
Ivy League ideal, 142

Jaeger, Werner, 30, 32, 35, 44
Jaki, Stanley, 2, 49, 52, 58, 60, 66, 69,
    80, 91
Jernstedt, G. G., 158
Jonathan Livingston Seagull, 51
Jourard, Sidney, 106, 154
Journal of Creative Behavior, 131
Joyce, James, 174

Kalos k'agathos, 136
Kazantzakis, Nikos, 21, 27, 114-15,
    117-20, 142, 160, 173

Rokeach, Milton, 155
Rome, 40-42, 128-29, 142
Roszak, Theodore, 11, 13, 80, 87, 88
Rotter Scale, 158
Rousseau, J. J., 38, 59, 70, 88, 124, 152, 161

Sakofs, Mitchell, 158
Samson Agonistes, 3
Sardello, Robert, 49, 84, 85, 86
Sartre, Jean Paul, 49
Scholarly publication and writing, 110, 111, 174
Schools, and motivation, 106; as arenas, 122; ciphering of, 77-93; as edifice complex, 151; design of, 116-17; images of, 88-89; leisure, 39; as pathogenic places, 78; as places of possibilities, 59-60; as studios of dance, 121
Schools of Tomorrow (Dewey), 152
Science, 2, 47, 48, 49, 50, 52, 54, 59-61, 69, 71, 72, 78, 84, 110, 149; happiness, as gift of, 65; mystique of, 64; and spirit, 91
Searle, John, 90
Self, 42, 61, 62, 66, 67, 77, 97, 98, 104, 106, 112, 133, 162, 169; enrichment of, 147; and Kolb's research, 162; and Outward Bound, 158; socially styled, 154; and Summerhill, 165
Self-actualization, 61, 65, 66, 67, 103, 112
Self-esteem, 63, 127, 154, 157, 168, 169; and Outward Bound, 157, 159
"Self Report Survey Form," 158
Self-transcendence, 62, 112
Seligman, Martin, 63, 71, 120, 147
Selye, Hans, 30, 133
Sensate culture, 43
Shames, Laurence, 6
Shapiro, Jim, 139
Sheehan, George, 157
Signals of transcendence, 69-75. *See also* Berger, Peter
Silent pulse, 121
Skinner, B. F., 61-62, 69, 160
Sloan, Douglas, 82

Smith, Huston, 52, 60, 107, 108, 118, 124
Smith, John, 162
Smith, Page, 108
Social-exchange theory, 120
Socrates, 77, 141, 165
Solitude, 131, 132, 169-170
Solzenhitzyn, Alexander, 157
Sophists, 72, 141
Soteriology, 20, 71, 80-81
Spain, 32, 113-114
Sparta, 92, 145, 146, 147
Spinning out, 103, 106, 132
Spiral curriculum, 166
Spirit(ual), 44, 51, 59, 60, 66, 67, 68, 91, 103, 108, 115, 123, 124, 132, 140, 142; Outward Bound, 156; solitude, 169
Sputnik, 14, 24, 119, 145-46
Stanford University, 90
Strategos, 147
Stress, 29, 40, 124, 127, 156
Struggle, 21, 26-27, 29, 31, 35-36, 58, 86; and equilibrium, 36; and God, 142; Kazantzakis' view, 114, 120; and loss, 133; and meaning, 61; noble, 113; and performance, 57; and schools 118; of the seed, 117; and transcendence, 61; transmutation of flesh into spirit, 115
Summerhill, 165
Szasz, Thomas, 55

Technical, 14, 50, 52; expertise, 72; proficiency, 37
Technical automatism, 181 n.25
Technique(s), 1, 5, 10, 14, 23, 26, 62, 73, 99, 111, 163; operationalization of measurement, 80; and performance, 56-57; and struggle, 27
Technocentric education, 125
Technocracy, 49
Technocratic, 4, 106, 124, 125, 167; elite, 25, 72, 97, 125
Technocrats, 3, 20, 70, 71
Technocryptic, 78, 79
Technoligarchy, 1
Technology(ies), 2-3, 5, 7, 9-11, 14, 16-17; agonal element, 40; appeal and

ABOUT THE AUTHOR

EDWARD L. KUHLMAN is Professor of Education at Messiah College in Grantham, Pennsylvania. He is the author of *An Overwhelming Interference* (1985) and *Master Teacher* (1987).

ISBN 0-89789-374-3

9 780897 893749

90000>

EAN

HARDCOVER BAR CODE